THE BEHAVIORAL SCIENCES:
AN INTERPRETATION

THE BEHAVIORAL SCIENCES:
AN INTERPRETATION

JAMES D. THOMPSON, *Vanderbilt University*
DONALD R. VAN HOUTEN, *University of Oregon*

ADDISON-WESLEY PUBLISHING COMPANY
Reading, Massachusetts
Menlo Park, California • London • Don Mills, Ontario

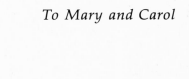

To Mary and Carol

PREFACE

The behavioral sciences, like the older and more established sciences, proceed to new understandings through refinement, through closer scrutiny of smaller aspects of their topics. By subdividing and by focusing attention on more minute aspects, scientists can describe phenomena and processes with greater precision, and therefore can often observe things which had gone unnoticed before.

The sciences dealing especially with human behavior have followed this pattern enthusiastically for several decades, and have thereby gained new knowledge. But because of the proliferation of disciplines and specialties and subspecialties in the behavioral sciences, it has become difficult for the interested layman to gain an appreciation of the larger enterprise. Rather than meeting the behavioral sciences, the layman is introduced to one or another of the disciplines which constitute them.

In the United States, at least, the individual formally introduced to the behavioral sciences usually meets them in a psychology course. Some stop at that point, and some progress more deeply in that single discipline. But others move on to an introduction to sociology. Or political behavior. Or cultural anthropology. For many, then, the behavioral sciences are viewed from the perspective of a single discipline. For those with greater exposure, the cafeteria system of courses leaves it to the individual student to determine how each is related to the others. And the traditional system of examining and grading by course does not encourage the individual to seek to integrate his several exposures.

Some students are fortunate enough to experience an "integrated" course on the social or behavioral sciences, but for this to be truly integrated there must be a team of enthusiastic teachers, and faculty turnover mitigates against this. Often the "interdisciplinary" course turns out to be a sequence of short courses—"multi-," but not "inter-" disciplinary.

The situation is hardly better for the professional behavioral scientist. True, he usually has a rather clear idea of how his specialty relates to the larger discipline of which it is a part. But professional training and opportunities tend to be defined within a discipline, and especially when information is produced faster than it can be absorbed, the professional finds it increasingly difficult to keep an eye on neighboring disciplines. Even if his earlier experience was multidisciplinary, the tendency is to recall other disciplines as they existed then, and to overlook the fact that they are changing, just as his own special area is changing.

This volume seeks to counteract these trends.

We have taken the liberty of roaming through the several disciplines which constitute the behavioral sciences, looking in on various specialties within them, and asking which portion certain specialists are working on. But we have tried always to see each specialty as a portion of something larger. Thus we are offering a guide through the behavioral sciences rather than a first course in principles of any one of them. Indeed, this book does not pretend to substitute for "principles" textbooks in the established disciplines.

Many who pick this volume up will know more—perhaps much more—about one of the disciplines than this volume covers. But we believe that few will be conversant with the several disciplines, and we have written on the assumption, therefore, that the reader has had no background in the behavioral sciences. The professional will recognize that there are limits to our statements, that qualifications and refinements could be added at many points. We sincerely hope that he will agree that, within the limitations of space, we have not seriously distorted his specialty. Equally, we hope that the professional as well as the newly interested layman will gain greater appreciation of the interaction of the disciplines and of their specialties, and will recognize anew the fact that human behavior is not a single-discipline thing.

Since we were not content to select topics according to the traditions of one or more disciplines, how did we do the selecting? We tried to keep a focus on those aspects of human behavior that seem most closely related to the experiences and activities of "normal" men and women. Such behavior, we believe, is oriented toward family and friends, toward school, or toward work. Large segments of the behavioral sciences deal with "abnormal" behavior, such as behavior of prison inmates or psychiatric cases. We have touched on these only incidentally. Other segments of the behavioral sciences focus on behavior (of animals as well as humans) in contrived or laboratory situations. We have not hesitated to incorporate knowledge gained from such research—and it is important for the development of science—but we have not attempted to describe why and how individuals behave in contrived situations.

For the most part we have worked with concepts already well anchored in the behavioral sciences. In a few places, however, we felt that the related materials needed to be tied together with a missing label, and we have not hesitated to supply one in order to exploit the significance of the literature. One such concept is *sphere of action,* which we introduce in Chapter 5.

In other cases, we have refrained from rather specific concepts and have substituted more general ones; an example is the fact that we refer to ethnic categories rather than focusing especially on the Negro. We have deliberately tried to avoid writing about behavior in a single society or cluster of nations. Although most of our references and "browsing recommendations" after each chapter are American or European, the behavioral sciences are seeking universal understanding, not limited to a particular time or place. Hence we have tried to deal with categories general enough to fit all cases.

Specialists will be painfully aware—and we repeatedly remind the reader—that our concepts and statements are simplifications of what the specialist knows. But this is not a volume for those who insist on simplicity. Human behavior is anything but simple, and the net impact of our trip through the behavioral sciences is to emphasize the range of variables involved in day-to-day living.

We have also tried to make the volume orderly, progressing from the less complicated to the more complicated. Hence we introduce early in the volume concepts that we continue to work with and build on as the book unfolds. Those readers already familiar with psychology will find Chapter 1 somewhat repetitive, and those versed in anthropology or sociology will have the same reaction to Chapter 2. In both cases, however, we recommend that the introductory chapters be reviewed so that the reader will know which alternatives we have chosen, and why. The remainder of the book should then make more sense.

Because we have been seeking comprehension rather than comprehensiveness, we have assumed that this volume will be supplemented by other materials, both theoretical and empirical, and we have tried to write it so that it can be supplemented by different kinds of materials for different kinds of readers. For the independent reader, we have suggested in the text, in sentences set off by italics and spaces, follow-up *topics* or important *names* which should guide the reader to library card catalogs for elaborations. And after each chapter we have indicated a sampling of books and articles for further reading. The lists are not exhaustive, but will enable the reader with access to an academic library to make contact with the major bodies of knowledge in the behavioral sciences. We hope that this book, when it is used in formal courses, will be sufficiently flexible to enable instructors to combine it with other materials—especially empirical ones—most appropriate to the discipline or profession the student is preparing for. In any event, we intend the book as a guide to further study.

But what do we mean by "the behavioral sciences?" The term emerged with World War II, perhaps with a clear-cut meaning at the time. But in the 1950s and 1960s, the term became both popular and useful in the search for research funds, and was adopted by varied groups who gave it their own meanings or interpretations. We have tried in this book to work with what we believe to be the central theme, but perhaps we should briefly indicate what we consider that to be. This requires consideration of "behavioral" and a separate discussion of "science."

An original reason for the term "behavioral sciences" was dissatisfaction with the separateness of the several disciplines and even with the sharp division between biological and social sciences. Early documents, such as those describing the Behavioral Science Division of the Ford Foundation and the Center for Advanced Study in the Behavioral

Sciences at Palo Alto, California, usually pointed to psychology, sociology, and anthropology as central to the behavioral sciences, but were quick to point out that perhaps not everything in those disciplines was germane, and that portions of the biological sciences, along with portions of economics and political science, *were* germane. Thus one central theme is the multidisciplinary character of human behavior.

In psychology, however, "behaviorism" was an older term with a very different meaning, and those psychologists of the "behavioral" persuasion sometimes equate "behavioral psychology" with "behavioral science." They usually are not multidisciplinary about it; instead they use the term to mean the study of behavior that can be explained physiologically; that is, without resort to such notions as "mental," "the mind," or "ideas." The tendency of some who hold this view to regard themselves as *the* behavioral scientists has been one of the reasons for confusion about the term.

Behavior psychologists were not alone in emphasizing "hard methods" as the factor which separated the behavioral sciences from the "softer" social sciences. Within political science, for example, the "behavioral school" became identified as the *counting* school: the branch emphasizing numbers and statistics. It has been attached to studies of voting behavior, by individuals or by members of groups who constitute electorates or legislative or judicial bodies.

One of the consequences of adopting a "hard methods" definition of the behavioral sciences is that attention is focused on the behavior of single individuals, or what some call "micro" phenomena. If the only acceptable methods involve observing, recording, counting, and statistically analyzing phenomena, then the focus of attention is on those kinds of phenomena that can easily be observed, recorded, counted, and subjected to statistical manipulations. Better to study 1000 individuals than one society!

We believe this to be an unfortunate trend, and happily not everyone in the behavioral sciences has followed it. As the reader of this volume will soon discover, we are convinced that we can understand the behavior of the individual in normal, everyday situations only by considering the larger contexts, by moving in the "macro" direction. Indeed, we point to many contributions by macro scientists who certainly consider themselves behavioral scientists.

But then, what do we mean by science? Here we are referring to a *strategy for learning.* The scientific strategy is not the only useful strategy for learning, nor is it foolproof, but it has proved to be an extremely economical strategy when directed toward physical and biological phenomena, and we have reason to believe that it holds the same sort of promise for human behavior. As we understand the strategy for science, it calls for (a) explicit reasoning, and (b) rigorous evidence, and the essential feature is that any statement, to be scientific, must be consistent *simultaneously* with that reasoning and evidence.

The economy of this strategy lies in its efficiency in ferreting out error. By insisting that a statement be consistent with two perspectives simultaneously, science is quicker than other strategies in spotting inconsistencies.

The value of science lies *not* in what it proves to be true, but in what it proves to be untrue. Perhaps the behavioral sciences have not progressed to the point at which we know true explanations of behavior, but the behavioral sciences have rendered untenable a number of beliefs which once were quite popular. We believe that the statements in this volume are consistent with accepted theory (explicit reasoning) and with evidence currently accepted by behavioral scientists; beyond that we make no claim to truth.

We could not have written this book were it not for the many builders of the behavioral sciences, some but not all of whom are cited herein. Nor could we have written it without the questions of our students in sociology, and in business and public administration, who challenged us to seek a coherent path through the behavioral sciences. We have had helpful questions and reactions to earlier versions of various chapters by Robert W. Hawkes, David Landy, Leroy Rieselback, Karl Weick, Jay Zawacki, and J. Richard Hackman. Finally, our work was greatly facilitated by the secretarial help of Nancy Turry and Louise C. Patton.

J. D. T.   *September 1969*
D. R. V. H.   *Eugene, Oregon*

CONTENTS

MODELS AND UNDERSTANDING

How are we to approach human behavior? Each discipline studies a portion, leaving to others the analysis of other portions. We must learn to find the larger picture, but how?

To make matters even more difficult, each discipline contains several schools, each with its own concepts which act as lenses, filtering out some things which can be found in the discipline and magnifying others.

We thus have choices among alternative, sometimes competing, concepts or ways of observing human behavior. But we cannot choose simply by popularity, or because we like the way a word or phrase rolls off the tongue. Each concept governs what we see and what we shall be blinded to, and we need to be quite careful in our choices.

There is a further problem, however. Behavioral scientists are not content simply to invent concepts; they try to lace *sets of concepts* together into *logical systems* which seem to *explain* some form of behavior. We speak of these logical systems of concepts as *models*.

To the extent that our concepts are tailored for specific models, our choice of key concepts not only directs and limits what we observe about human behavior but also locks us into a system of thinking and ultimately into a set of explanations. Just as concepts tend to direct our views, models tend to determine our conclusions.

With alternative concepts and models, we need a strategy for sorting. In Part One we take inventory of fundamental concepts, searching within the several disciplines for models which are *not closed* to influences from other disciplines. We can hardly expect to see the larger picture while using models which claim to give complete explanations

1

for fragments of behavior. Thus, if the personality makes a difference in behavior, and if social interaction makes a difference in behavior, we would like to find a model of personality which leaves room for social interaction variables, and a model for social interaction which would allow for the impact of personality. We seek models which can be used across disciplines.

CHAPTER 1

MODELS OF MAN

Without raising the possibly embarrassing question of why you behave as you do, what about the other fellow? How do we account for
the behavior of those we know? Or those in the news?

At one point in history this question would immediately get us
involved in a controversy over the relative importance of heredity and
environment. In some pockets of the contemporary world this may still
be a hotly contested issue, but a modern statement with which almost
all behavioral scientists would agree is that both heredity and environment are important factors in human behavior; the question is not whether both are influential, but how and in what combinations they influence behavior.

The contemporary position was expressed graphically and simply
by psychologist Kurt Lewin in a famous formula:

$$B = f\,(P,\ E).$$

Spelled out, this says that (B) behavior is a (f) function or result of interaction between (P) person and (E) environment. This is not quite
the heredity-versus-environment distinction, because "person" in
this equation is only in part genetically determined. In the modern
view, the person at any point after the first few weeks of life is partly
a product of learning. But the equation does remind us handily that
if we want to understand or explain or predict human behavior at any
point in time, we need to take into consideration the human (both as
genetically developed and as trained) and his environment. This book
will start from Lewin's equation.

If we take the equation seriously, it is obvious that our understanding or prediction will be wrong if we make a mistake either in what we

3

think about a man or about his environment. If both person and environment contribute to the behavior, an error on our part in describing either will result in error in our prediction of behavior. In this chapter, then, we shall consider the major ways of thinking about the person. In Chapter 2 we shall consider his environment.

Models in Abundance

Every day every one of us uses some "model" of man. Or perhaps several models of man. Whether behavioral scientist or layman, we employ some notion about what a man (or woman) "is" and how he "works." Whether we make our models explicit or not, we do form expectations about how others will behave toward us or will respond to something we do. We predict, for instance, that a particular sales pitch will move a prospect to buy, or that a particular line will lead to a date, or that a particular form of discipline will straighten out our erring child. Juries and legislators likewise explain why an act was performed or how publics will respond to specific statutes.

None of us is always right in our predictions, for in some cases we lack sufficient information about the other party. But another important reason why our expectations sometimes prove faulty is that our model of man is incomplete or inappropriate for the conditions. Those who specialize in studying man and his behavior—humanists and behavioral scientists—do not agree on a single model, and it is a safe prediction that by the time you read this, we shall not know which model is the correct one.

Still, systematic and precise efforts to understand man and his behavior have helped us identify the alternative models available, and some of the implications of choosing one or another of them.

THREE BASIC STRATEGIES

There appears to be an endless variety of models for thinking about a man, but on closer examination we find three basic approaches or strategies. The wide variety of specific models, that is, appear to be variations of one of the three basic strategies. Rather than get detailed here about any of the variations, we shall examine the strategy employed in each of the three basic approaches. The detailed variations may be more important for professional behavioral scientists than for those of us who do not plan to conduct research.

Two of the three strategies are well established. One rests on the assumption that/man is governed primarily by conflict. Another approaches/man as a machine. The third is more recent and perhaps less well defined, but we shall label it an open-system approach to man.

Conflict Models of Man

Perhaps the oldest way of thinking about man, at least in Western civilization, is through conflict models. In the most primitive versions of this, man's behavior is determined by the relative strength at a particular time of forces for good and evil. Whether we conceive of these forces in terms of angels and devils, or in the framework of voodoo or witchcraft, the basic strategy is the same. It incorporates opposing forces which somehow contest for control of man. In primitive versions, man is often an innocent bystander, and if his behavior is considered undesirable by others, he is a victim who is possessed by evil forces, or bewitched, or under a spell.

In these very simple forms, the conflict strategy puts most of the explanation for behavior in the environment; man simply is a vehicle through which conflict unfolds. Thus the simple forms are inconsistent with our starting assumption of interplay between person and environment. These simple forms of the conflict strategy also seem inadequate for scientific purposes because generally they rely on some form of magic or supernatural activity to account for the conflicting forces "getting into" man. So we can quickly set these aside as models of man to be used for our understanding, even though some men do believe in such models and we may need to take those beliefs into account in order to understand the behavior of such men.

But there are more complicated and sophisticated versions of the conflict strategy, and these cannot be so easily dismissed. In these more modern versions the conflict is not necessarily between forces of good or evil, but simply between opposing forces, and the explanations of how these forces happen to be present are more plausible to those of us who insist on natural or secular explanations. The pioneer in the development of modern conflict theory undoubtedly was Sigmund Freud. Although there are newer schools of thought—neo-Freudian and non-Freudian—which have modified and extended his work, Freud's general approach serves as the best illustration of the conflict approach in psychology.

> *Conflict models have generally been associated with* clinical psychology. *Major figures in their development include—in addition to Sigmund Freud—Karen Horney, Carl Jung, Karl Menninger.*   <

For Freud, the battle lines of conflict are laid early in life in what he held to be the three basic components of the personality: the *id*, the *ego*, and the *superego*. Freud saw the *id* as the genetically developed component, containing basic urges or cravings or instincts. At birth, in this view, the personality consists entirely of this bundle of *unconscious* urges which demand immediate satisfaction. But at this point the person is entirely dependent, for the *id* does not provide the individual with skills for relating to his environment, for coping with reality. Hence the *ego* gradually develops in the personality to interpret reality and to plan action so as to get as much satisfaction as conditions permit. Where the *id* works on the pleasure principle, the *ego* holds to the reality principle, in Freud's terms. One source of conflict or tension, then, is the conflict between the urges of the *id* for immediate gratification and the *ego*'s needs to defer that gratification until the proper time and place.

But it seems clear that if the *id* is strong and the *ego* crafty and cunning, there would be no morality and society would be impossible. Freud handled this problem by introducing the third component, the *superego*, which develops rather early in life as the child begins to internalize the moral code displayed and taught by his parents. The superego contains, in this system of thinking, both the *conscience* which makes the person feel guilt when he violates the moral code, and an *ego ideal*, or conception of how the individual should behave. The *ego ideal* serves as a source of rewards when the individual in fact lives up to it. Here is another potential for conflict, for the reality-facing *ego* may demand behavior which requires violation of the *conscience* or failure to achieve the *ego ideal.*

Freud offered plausible explanations for the source of conflicting forces in the person: The *id* is acquired genetically, through biological inheritance, while the *ego* develops through experience and training, and the *superego* is implanted during childhood through identification with the parents.

But in addition to suggesting how those basic components come to be present, and that they are buried in the person's "unconscious," Freud added another important aspect, by giving the person a conscious role in determining his own behavior. For the *ego* serves not only to plot paths through reality to obtain gratifications, but also to hold those demands in check when their gratification would violate the *superego.* The ego functions, in Freud's thinking, to control the conflict inherent in the personality, and when the ego is overwhelmed severe anxiety may result.

It was out of his work with patients exhibiting such anxieties that Freud developed his model of man. He was not trying to explain shopping behavior or vacation planning, but instead deep-seated drives and conflicts which sometimes immobilized persons. This is also reflected in Freud's method for helping such persons, *psychoanalysis,* which involved listening to free associations by patients, to their accounts of dreams, memories of childhood, and so on. The technique is to tip the balance in favor of the ego, by dredging up out of the unconscious the conflicts which are causing the anxiety, and thereby letting the ego grapple with them more effectively.

Freud's model, both directly and through the neo-Freudian models, made significant impact on twentieth-century thought in the Western world, not only among professional therapists, but in literary and art forms, and in the explanatory thinking of many people in many walks of life. But these models have also met resistances. The conflict models usually involve elements which we are not able to point to and measure; who has ever seen an *id*? Hence the conflict approach has been set aside by those who insist on quantitative rigor in research. But even if we, as laymen, do not plan to do research and are willing to be less rigorous, the conflict approach does not give us very much leverage if we are dissatisfied with the behavior of those around us. In its simplest versions, where magic or supernatural forces are involved, about all we can do is to invoke counter-magic or arouse the gods or spirits in our favor. Even with the more sophisticated versions, the techniques of dealing with behavior we dislike are so complicated that they should be used only by the highly trained specialist, who has much more time to work with the client than most of us ever have. As parts of the other person's environment, we may be able to increase or decrease the stimulation which arouses anxiety in that individual, but that usually is of very limited help to us. In the Freudian versions, especially, the greatest impact of the environment occurs in the first few years of life, when the superego is formed, and in most of the persons we deal with, we can do nothing about that.

It may very well be true that basic drives and conflicts are not altered by dropping out of college to work in another country, or by changing a course of study, or becoming engaged to a different girl. Still, we have reasons to believe that quite a bit of the student's behavior is significantly influenced by such changes in environments—or in his relations with those environments—and it is difficult to deal with such changes by using the conflict strategy.

Machine Models of Man

If we set a man on a hot stove, we can predict with considerable accuracy that he will get off. Quickly. We would have so much confidence in that prediction that if he continued to sizzle without trying to get off, we would "know" that something was wrong with him: paralysis, intoxication, unconsciousness, or something similar.

Our ability to predict behavior of the hot-stove type is based on use of a machine model. In this simple case, a main requirement is that the machine be a physiological one, equipped with sense organs (receptors, in technical language), conductors (neurons), switching devices (brain and spinal cord), muscles (effectors) attached to levers (bones). This picture of the insides of the machine tells us where to look for the trouble if our man does not behave according to expectations.

For the hot-stove class of problems, we can point clearly to a *stimulus* and to a *response*, and we can account physiologically for the connection between them. But we have not explained the behavior until we suggest a *reason* for it, and those who use the machine models usually point to *physiological drives* (such as hunger, thirst, pain, or sex) or basic *emotions* (such as fear or anger) as forces which arouse or activate man. In the hot-stove case, it is pain which triggers or motivates the response of getting off, and because man can respond to such drives automatically, we speak of reflex behavior.

> *In this section we are dealing with models usually associated with the* behavioral *school of psychology and sometimes referred to as* stimulus-response *or S-R psychology. This was pioneered by such figures as John B. Watson, Ivan P. Pavlov, and C. L. Hull. More recent leaders have been Kenneth W. Spence and B. F. Skinner.* <

The view of man as *simply* a physiological machine responding to genetically implanted drives and environmental stimulation is held by few students of human behavior. Without ignoring the physiological aspects, most behaviorist psychologists also recognize *acquired drives:* those which do not exist at birth but are learned. (Some would prefer the term "needs" or "wants" to the word "drive," in this connection.) Among the acquired drives or needs are those related to interactions with other persons and others related to self-competence or self-satisfaction. Thus machine man can be conceived of as having drives for nourishment and security with respect to his environment, but also as having learned such drives as those for social acceptance, prestige, or self-fulfillment.

The basic logic, then, is that *responses* to *stimuli* are elicited by the expectation of satisfaction or pleasure or some other reward. When the reward is received, the behavior is said to be *reinforced.* Even in this simple form, the machine model of man leads to important research, for it not only raises questions of what responses are associated with what stimuli, but also reveals for us wide variations from one person to another in the strength of drives, in sensitivity to stimuli, or in rapidity and strength of response.

> *The study of variations in response to stimuli is a major facet of the* psychology of individual differences. *In recent years much research attention has focused on* arousal, *or the sensitivity of individuals to varying strengths of stimuli.* <

Even such a simple model as Stimulus-Response-Reinforcement gives us quite a bit of room to experiment and manipulate situations, for we can work either on the stimulus side of behavior or on the reinforcement side of behavior. The significance of the machine model was underscored when Pavlov discovered what is now known as classical conditioning, or substitution of one stimulus for another. Pavlov found that the machine—in this case the dog—could learn to associate one stimulus with another, and thus learn to respond to the substitute. The hungry dog, for example, salivates at the sight of food, and if a bell is rung each time the food appears, the hungry dog earns to associate that sound with the sight of food. Eventually the dog will salivate at the sound of the bell even without the appearance of food. At this point he is responding to a substitute stimulus, and we say he has been *conditioned.*

>   *Focus on the stimulus side of the equation generally characterizes the school of S-R psychology known for* classical conditioning.   <

This kind of research was significant not simply for training animals but because it showed that a basically physiological machine can be activated with symbolic stimuli The child can learn to respond to the word "hot" and move away from the stove rather than having to feel the pain. Much of our training of children relies on the conditioning idea.

But we can focus attention on reinforcement rather than on stimulus substitute. In this case we are less interested in the stimulus which originally triggers behavior than in the reinforcement which fo.lows the appropriate response. The hungry animal in an experimental situation may for one reason or another move a lever which releases food. Or the baby making vocal sounds, apparently at random, may make the one we like to hear and elicit reinforcement from the parent. When either the rat or the baby learns that he may deliberately use the appropriate behavior to win the reinforcement, we speak of *instrumental conditioning.* Now—regardless of the initial stimulus—we say Response is emitted in order to bring about the (reinforcing) Stimulus.

>   *The focus on reinforcement is characteristic of the school in psychology known for* instrumental *conditioning. It most vigorous recent exponent is B. F. Skinner, whose particular version of reinforcement theory is known as* operant *conditioning.*   <

Development of the notions of instrumental conditioning gave the machine model of man a much wider range of application. First, it shifted attention away from physiological connections between stimulus and response, and made it possible for us to consider behavior in relation to *learned* or *acquired drives,* or *motives.* Thus we can consider behavior designed to win the respect or affection of other people as well as behavior stimulated by hunger. Instrumental conditioning also makes it possible to consider that behavior may occur spontaneously or deliberately on the part of the individual doing it and that he may behave instrumentally; that is, he may (by responding in appropriate ways) determine what will happen to him.

Of course when we extend stimulus-response-reinforcement kinds of thinking in these newer directions, we can no longer make the assumption that man is *simply* a physiological machine. But one school of thought believes that the higher-order motives can be broken down into smaller units and ultimately explained biologically. And another school of S-R proponents insist that it makes no difference, really, because with enough research and training, we can control or predict all behavior via instrumental conditioning. These, of course, are approaches which avoid the messy area of understanding man's mental activity. It is precisely that aspect which characterizes the third approach to man.

The Open-System Model of Man

The two strategies we have discussed are so well established and recognized that those who follow either of them can easily identify their position with respect to them. And those who argue for one specific version rather than another can specify precisely how they differ from those attached to another version. Thus a neo-Freudian knows how he differs from the follower of Freud—and also how he differs from other kinds of neo-Freudians. Those who believe in the instrumental-conditioning scheme know precisely how and why they differ from those who hold another reinforcement theory. For each of the two strategies there is a point of reference, and the theorist can locate himself in relation to that point.

But when we move to the Open-System strategy, we are working with an emerging model rather than a highly refined and easily recognized model. The ingredients for this emerging model are being supplied from several sources within psychology, and from adjacent disciplines as well. There is as yet no classic statement of the open-system strategy which is so widely recognized that those in the several streams can locate themselves relative to each other. Our task, then, is to piece together the major threads.

Perhaps the most emphatic feature of the emerging strategy is its *transactional* view of man. Here the focus is shifted from man as a passive agent, *re*-acting to stimuli, to man as an active agent. This view sometimes is referred to as the *pro*-active one, indicating that man may take the initiative. The large role given to man's relation to his environment is one reason we refer to "open-system" man."

A second strand of the emerging strategy is concern with *purposive* behavior. This view assumes that man is capable of having goals or aspirations, and of working toward these. It calls attention to *mental processes,* to such topics in modern psychology as problem-solving, planning, thinking, creativity, and decision-making. Following this path leads us to consider man as acting according to standards of success and of failure, and it places much more emphasis on the *future* dimension of man—of present behavior designed to bring about future rewards. This is generally referred to as *deferred gratification*.

> *These topics are major ones in the psychology of* cognitive processes, *a term which is coming to stand for a much wider array of behavior than just perception, as it once did. Consideration of purpose also appears in studies of* personality. <

The third feature of the emerging strategy is concern for man's *mental content* and how it is acquired. Here it is assumed that mental content can be understood only in terms of its *meaning* for the person, and that for an item to have meaning it must be *perceived* and *interpreted*. Studies of the psychology of perception have established that man perceives selectively; he does not attend to everything in his environment. The psychology of cognition (or knowing) also reveals that perceived items are interpreted in light of other things. Thus what man knows or believes has much to do with what he perceives and how he interprets it.

> *A major impetus for this work was* Gestalt *psychology, which stresses the importance of configurations of things rather than those things in isolation. Pioneers in Gestalt psychology were Max Wertheimer, Wolfgang Kohler, Kurt Koffka, and Kurt Lewin, whose particular formulation of Gestalt psychology is known as* field theory.   <

A final major emphasis of the newer strategy is that man is *social,* often acting in relation to others. His transactions with the environment are often with persons. His purposes often are defined in terms of the behavior of others, such as eliciting their favorable evaluations. His perceptions and cognitions often are shaped by what he learns from others.

> *This is the special field of* social psychology, *which was pioneered by E. A. Ross, a sociologist, and by William McDougall, a psychologist. Both disciplines are actively and sometimes competitively developing social psychology.*   <

The open-system strategy thus views man as purposive, as interdependent with the physical and social environment, and as actively involved in transactions with that environment as he pursues his goals. This requires not only that man develop mental processing capabilities —for thinking, deciding, and so on—but also that he acquire information and beliefs which allow him to "know" the persons and things in his environment and to cope with them.

Clearly this is a different view of man than either of the earlier strategies emphasizes.

SELECTING A STRATEGY

Faced with several different strategies, we must choose. Choice is complicated by the fact that each strategy deals with kinds of human behavior that the others barely touch. Since each is still being developed and modified and extended, it is conceivable that one will ultimately reach out to encompass the topics covered by the others. After all, it is reasonable to start with relatively simple models, adding complexity as we learn more about the phenomena and as we are forced to add complications.

But it is equally conceivable that none of the present strategies will prove adequate and that something we do not now even glimpse will emerge to replace them all. Such possibilities are present in every field of knowledge, but we cannot wait. We need some criteria for selecting among admittedly incomplete and perhaps imperfect strategies. We can suggest several.

(1) *The model chosen should be one designed for the kind of problem we are facing.*   The fact that a model of man affords great predictability for some classes of behavior does not necessarily warrant its use for other classes of behavior.   The machine model seems well suited for hot-stove problems and rote learning, for example, but was not designed for use in remodeling unhappy personalities.

(2) *When two or more models appear capable of handling a problem, the simpler one is preferred.* If we are interested in teaching the child to perform repetitive actions on command, the open-system and conflict strategies probably are more elaborate and complex than we need. On topics of that kind, the machine strategy seems to do very well, and has the obvious advantage of dealing rather precisely with a rather limited kit of observable variables.

(3) *The model chosen should make no more assumptions than absolutely necessary for the level of understanding desired.*   The more assumptions we make, the more we limit the kinds of evidence we can consider; in the extreme, if we assumed everything about man's behavior we would have no room, nor need, for evidence. The general point holds for less extreme cases. If evidence would explain someone's behavior without assuming internal conflict, then a beginning assumption of conflict would only hamper our understanding of his behavior. Assumptions relinquish our freedom, and we should make them only grudgingly.

(4) Since we start from the position that (*B*) behavior is a (*f*) of *both* (*P*) person *and* (*E*) environment, *we want to be sure that the model of person chosen is one that can be fitted into that equation.*   When we are interested in behavior under conditions in which genetically implanted

instincts are aroused, then we need a model of man which is equipped to sense instinct-linked stimulation. If our interests switch to behavior in politically intricate situations—international treaty negotiations, for example—then the model of man chosen should permit our connecting it to that kind of environmental situation.

In short, our problem is not to choose one strategy and forever give up the others, but rather to treat the several strategies as items in a tool kit to be used selectively as the need and opportunity arise.

Now we are prepared to argue that for the kinds of behaving we laymen do, every day, and the kinds of behavior we meet in others on a daily basis, the open-system strategy is more helpful than the others available. The open-system strategy focuses our attention on those aspects of behavior most significant to us in daily living.

Perhaps we can best illustrate that contention by considering how we would construct a man if we had that opportunity. If we could start with a clean slate and build for the future—if we were to raise a child from birth—what ingredients would we want to include? What things, elements, characteristics, or variables would we specify?

The answers to such questions would vary, depending on the kind of world we expected our man to spend his adult lifetime in. If we were trying to build a man for Apache society of the nineteenth century, our list of ingredients might be different from the list we would specify for a twentieth-century Australian, and still different for a twenty-first-century citizen-of-the-world. But if we started in the last third of the twentieth century, expecting our man to live through the first half of the twenty-first century, what would we order?

Surely we would want to start with good genetic stock; the nervous system, brain, anatomy, and biological processes should not pose unusual restrictions or handicaps. But after that, what is important? How specific would we want to be? We probably would want him to be "successful," but in what terms? Should we specify his occupation, his hobbies, the number of children he should have, or that he marry a girl from Roanoke? Chances are that we would like to specify such things as his religious orientation (although some of us might want to leave that blank), but it is unlikely that we would want to determine exact occupation, family size, or wife sources. We realize that life will be somewhat different 50 years hence, and we would not want to tie our man too tightly.

Our culture, or at least that portion of it with which readers of this book are likely to be most familiar, recognizes change as inevitable, and this suggests that we would be wiser to specify that our man have *qualities* which would help him develop and adapt, rather than specifying *results*. Assuming that we want to concentrate on those qualities which will permit him to be flexible, adaptive, and realistic in an unknown future, what sorts of qualities might we work on? There appear to be a minimum of four "dimensions" of man.

DIMENSIONS OF OPEN-SYSTEM MAN

A Goal Dimension

In modern societies parents usually want their children to have ambitions or targets, to work or study toward something, to have aspirations or goals. We shall refer to this as a *goal* dimension of man, and note that although your notion of what might be reasonable or acceptable goals will differ from some others, you will find few members of your society who would not agree that goals are important in man.

A Means Dimension

Without some ways of striving for them, goals are empty. The same parents who encourage their children to have aspirations also usually encourage them to develop skills, know-how, or ability, and hope or insist that these be the means appropriate to goals.

A Realism Dimension

Goals and means give man something to work for and tools for doing so, but which goals are available at a particular time, and which means are appropriate in a particular place remain to be determined. Man's accomplishments depend in part on the conditions existing around him, on the context in which he behaves. And one type of behavior may have very different consequences if the surrounding conditions change. Thus parents usually try to help their children learn to be realistic, to be able to sense and define the environment.

A Normative Dimension

Few of us are satisfied to equip man with goals, means, and realism, without also adding a dimension to guide and regulate his behavior. Equipped with the first three dimensions, man can be dangerous unless his behavior is regulated, and most parents appear to believe that the controls should come from within the person, rather than simply being imposed upon him. Virtually all of us recognize some definitions of honesty, fairness, equity, justice, and similar norms. We will refer to this as a *normative* dimension and suggest that it is found in all societies, although the content of what is considered fair or just differs from place to place and time to time.

We believe that much of your parental behavior, if indeed you are a parent, is designed to shape the content of those four dimensions in your child. But parents or not, all of us must meet and deal with other adults, and we believe that your judgments or estimates of others usually are in terms of these four dimensions (except perhaps those you know *very* well, and either love or hate). And to the extent that you do use such dimensions, we believe that there is support for our contention that the open-system strategy is useful for us laymen.

> *These dimensions of man, and the model from which they stem, are adapted from theoretical work by Talcott Parsons, E. A. Shils, R. F. Bales, and others, and known as a* general theory of action. <

FREEDOM AND IMPERATIVES OF OPEN-SYSTEM STRATEGY

Although we have asserted that open-system man is four-dimensional, we cannot at this point explain or predict his behavior, because we know nothing of his content on those four dimensions. This is in one sense the major weakness of the open-system approach; it is imprecise, lacking in specificity. It is neutral. Yet the very fact that the model does *not* assert specific drives or goals, specific means, and so on, ultimately is in its favor. For the neutrality of the model gives us freedom to consider the entire range of man's *experiences* as "inputs" to him.

Because the model does not prejudge which inputs are important, we are not enticed into limiting our attention to those things we experimenters or parents have put into man through conditioning or reinforcement. Nor are we forced to limit our attention to man's experiences during the first few years of life. We are free, with the open-system model, to search throughout man's experiences for clues to his content. This lets us face the fact that the nineteenth-century Apache was not identical to the twentieth-century Australian, and suggest why: Different men learn different things, either because capacity on the several dimensions is curtailed or because, as open systems, they are exposed to different content sources.

The open system model is also neutral with respect to time. We can recognize that the person in our formula, $B = f(P, E)$, is at present a product of past interaction with his environment, and that today's behavior is thus to some degree a reflection of the past, but *we are not tied to an historical explanation.* Open-system man can be open to the pull of the future as well as the past, to purpose as well as to drives, and to present situations as well. The open-system model thus encourages us to ask to what extent the person is oriented toward the past, the present, and the future, and permits us to recognize that persons differ in time orientations.

The model is neutral in a third sense, for it does not restrict man to being *pro*active—aggressively meeting his environment—or force him to be *re*active—waiting to be stimulated by his environment. We can consider the likelihood that any particular person is sometimes proactive, sometimes reactive. And we can also consider the possibilities that persons differ from one another in their tendencies in one direction or another. This is one point at which biological or chemical variables may plug into our open-system model of man.

But if the neutrality of the open-system model gives us important freedoms, it also contains an imperative, for it forces us to look into man's environment for his content on the four dimensions. Our model may be neutral, but the man who develops through interaction with his environment may be very much committed. If environment is an important source of man's content, we must think specifically about the conceptual tools available for thinking about man's environment.

RECAPITULATION

We started with an assumption that Behavior is a function of interaction between person and environment, or $B = f(P, E)$, and noted that in such an equation a misleading view of either person or environment would lead to error in explaining behavior. In this chapter we have concentrated on alternative conceptions of person or man, finally settling for an open-system version which posits that man has capacities to acquire content on four dimensions: goals, cause/effect beliefs, interpretations of reality, and norms. But we reasoned that such content is acquired through man's transactions with his environment, so we turn in Chapter 2 to consider conceptions of the environment.

RECOMMENDED BROWSING

Gordon W. Allport, "The Open System in Personality Theory," *Journal of Abnormal and Social Psychology,* **61** (November 1960), 301–311; and *Pattern and Growth in Personality,* New York: Holt, Rinehart and Winston, 1961. A short and a more detailed statement of the transactional approach to personality, emphasizing an open-system model.

Jerome S. Bruner, Jacqueline J. Goodnow, and George A. Austin, *A Study of Thinking.* New York: Wiley, 1956. Presents results of experiments on man's attempts to sort, categorize, and use information about his environment.

Calvin S. Hall and Gardner Lindzey, *Theories of Personality.* New York: Wiley, 1957. Compares various approaches to personality, and the assumptions of each.

Ernest R. Hilgard, *Theories of Learning* (second edition). New York: Appleton-Century-Crofts, 1965. An excellent summary of the major types of learning theory.

Clark L. Hull, *Principles of Behavior.* New York: Appleton-Century-Crofts, 1943. This volume, emphasizing drives, habits, and reinforcement, had important impact on the development of stimulus/response theories.

Barbel Inhelder and Jean Piaget, *The Growth of Logical Thinking from Childhood to Adolescence.* New York: Basic Books, 1958. Report of research by Piaget and his associates into the development of intelligence in human growth.

Ernest Jones, *The Life and Work of Sigmund Freud.* New York: Basic Books, Vol. 1, 1953; Vol. 2, 1955. An authoritative presentation of Freud's theories.

Kurt Lewin, *A Dynamic Theory of Personality*. New York: McGraw-Hill, 1935. An early and important expression of the Gestalt approach to man and behavior.

Gardner Lindzey and Elliot Aronson, *The Handbook of Social Psychology* (second edition). Reading, Mass.: Addison-Wesley, 1968. Volume I contains authoritative reviews of stimulus-response, Freudian, and cognitive theories in social psychology.

Abraham H. Maslow, "A Theory of Human Motivation," *Psychological Review,* **50** (1943) 370–396; and *Motivation and Personality*. New York: Harper, 1954. Presents a theory of the hierarchy of motives.

David McClelland, J. W. Atkinson, R. A. Clark, and E. L. Lowell, *The Achievement Motive*. New York: Appleton-Century-Crofts, 1953. A forceful statement of the importance of desire for achievement as a motivating factor.

Talcott Parsons and Edward A. Shils, editors, *Toward a General Theory of Action*. Cambridge, Mass.: Harvard University Press, 1951. An important statement by nine leading psychologists and sociologists of a framework for analyzing purposive social behavior.

Jean Piaget, *Six Psychological Studies* (translated by Anita Tenzer and edited by David Elkind). New York: Random House, 1968. An overview of the work of a pioneer in studying how children develop strategies for coping with their environments.

Herbert A. Simon, *Models of Man*. New York: Wiley, 1956. An advanced analysis of the properties of various conceptions of man.

B. F. Skinner, *Science and Human Behavior*. New York: Macmillan, 1953. Stimulus/response psychology as conceived by perhaps its most forceful proponent, the originator of "programmed learning."

Harry Stack Sullivan, *The Interpersonal Theory of Psychiatry*. New York: Norton, 1953. A leading statement of the societal approach to psychiatry.

Edward C. Tolman, *Purposive Behavior in Animals and Men*. New York: Century, 1932; and "Cognitive Maps in Rats and Men," *Psychological Review,* **55** (July 1948) 189–208. Important statements of cognition and learning aspects of behavior.

J. Milton Yinger, *Toward a Field Theory of Behavior*. New York: McGraw-Hill, 1965. A recent and excellent theoretical statement on understanding behavior by examining the interaction of person and environment.

MAN'S PATTERNED ENVIRONMENT

Man's environment is practically infinite. How can we possibly understand it, when scores of different disciplines seem constantly to find new complications in that environment? For that matter, how can the man we are thinking about understand it?

In one important sense, he does not. Certainly no one individual is able to master all that is not known about his physical, biological, chemical, celestial environment. But in another important sense, man does at least learn how to deal with his environment, by learning to find patterns in it.

Man's environment is largely patterned, not random. Although chance plays some part in man's experiences, most of what he confronts has a degree of regularity and predictability. To the extent that man learns to recognize these patterns, he need not know or respond to everything in his environment. Indeed, he cannot possibly experience consciously all the things around him. What he experiences, instead, is an environment as mediated and interpreted by other persons in whom he has confidence. He need never have gone around the world to believe that the earth is approximately round. He need not have seen a virus to believe in viruses and to fear them. He need not have toured our galaxy to believe that we are within one, and that it can be differentiated from others. He need only have been in contact with persons in whom he has faith who do believe those things.

The filters provided by others not only provide the framework for understanding what a man experiences, but also make him sensitive to some of his surroundings and insensitive to other aspects of his environment. A way of seeing is also a way of not seeing.

21

If we are to understand an open-system man and what he comes to believe about the human and nonhuman environment, we need to know more about the filters he learns to use and the processes by which he is exposed to those filters. The primary filter is called *culture,* and the study of it is the particular specialty of cultural and social anthropologists (although sociologists deal with it extensively, too).

PATTERNS OF CULTURE

Among social scientists, *culture* is generally taken to mean those beliefs, values, and techniques for dealing with the environment which are *shared* among contemporaries and transmitted by one generation to the next.

Frequently we refer to man's "cultural heritages," and this is an apt phrase, for it is obvious that if each generation had to start from scratch to invent a wheel, or cooking, or a language, none would get very far with the development and refinement of those cultural treasures. At any point in time, then, culture represents a storehouse of accumulated and more or less winnowed sets of experiences, and it is from these that our open-system man begins to acquire his content.

One of the first and most significant cultural patterns to be introduced to the individual is a language, for it is the primary key to the remainder of the culture. In being exposed to one language (or at best to a very few), man is immediately subjected to the filtering principle, for his culture is telling him about only a tiny fraction of the several hundred existing languages, and it is essentially giving him a key to *his* culture, not to all cultures.

The vocabulary of a language reflects the basic categories into which prior generations have fitted and interpreted and coded their experiences, dreams and wisdom. By means of language, the dead are enabled to contribute to the education of the living, for learning one's native language equips the individual to decode his cultural heritage. The words, idioms, and syntax of our language help as well as constrain how we come to think, to feel, and to judge. Language then facilitates communication between those who share cognitions, desires, and attitudes, for similar meanings get attached to words. But differences in language and the meaning of words can be practically insurmountable barriers to communication across cultures. Even where cultures may share the same basic language, connotative differences can severely inhibit effective communication. Through language, open-system man is exposed to the basic definitions of the environment embraced by his culture, to the basic techniques for dealing with that environment, and to the basic values to be sought in it. From culture, then, open-system man draws the content of his four basic dimensions: learning to define reality, to have goals, to have beliefs about causation, and to have norms.

> *The significance of language in thought has claimed the attention of several disciplines. Among behavioral scientists, we would look to the classifications of* ethnolinguistics *or* psycholinguistics, *and to such names as Benjamin Whorf, Edward Sapir, Dorothy Lee, Roger Brown or Clyde Kluckhohn.* <

What Is Reality?

Significant among these items of culture are definitions and explanations of the natural and supernatural environment. Culture contains the categorical distinctions which guide our perceptions of the environment, as well as the interpretations of what it is that we perceive. Culture teaches how to think about time and space, for example. How important the clock or calendar is is a cultural matter, and indeed whether clock or calendar are used at all as ways of describing or measuring man's world. Similarly, culture teaches what is dangerous, what is natural, and what is mysterious or supernatural. The division between natural and supernatural varies from culture to culture, as does the definition of supernatural. Monotheism, for example, is only one way to think of supernatural forces. Indeed, in many non-Western societies, little distinction is drawn between the natural and supernatural.

If culture provides the categories by which we perceive the environment, it also provides the explanations for the conditions we perceive. Take, as an example, the ill person. Culture tells us what symptoms to look for; temperature may be an important symptom in some cultures but not in others, and blood count may or may not be a concept in a particular culture. And whatever the symptoms observed, illness may be explained as the result of germs or of witchcraft, depending on the content of the culture. The various sciences, in contemporary Western cultures, provide definitions and explanations for many aspects of man's environment, but even in contemporary Western cultures, magic, luck, or supernatural forces are also drawn upon to explain reality.

Whatever the specific content of a specific culture, it is rather certain that open-system man learns to experience his environment—physical, social and supernatural—in terms largely supplied by his culture. His *reality* dimension will take on the content supplied by his culture.

What Is Valuable?

Another significant aspect of culture is *values*, the notions of a people about what is important, sacred, unquestioned, the things or symbols which give meaning to life. And it is from this culturally approved menu of values that open-system man is expected to select his goals or aspirations.

Biological processes may tell man that he needs food, water, shelter, and clothing, and hence that these are valuable. Beyond such subsistence levels, however, man's notions of what is valuable are learned from his culture.

Cultures generally contain some notions of wealth, and of the desirability of having wealth. Each culture has its own conception of what it means to be wealthy. In some, wealth may be measured in financial terms of stocks, bonds, real estate, and gold, but in others it is measured in terms of the number of wives owned, the number of cattle in a man's herd, or in some other fashion. In any event, the very idea of wealth is learned from the culture, and is widely shared. Wealth (as defined by one's culture) is assumed to be worthwhile or valuable.

>   *The study of values is a central focus of cultural anthropology. Clyde and Florence Kluckhohn have directed long-term research on values. Cultural anthropology contains a special division known as economic anthropology; Melville Herskovits was the individual most clearly identified with it.*   <

Cultures generally teach that it is important to be on good terms with the supernatural forces. Each culture may have its unique conception of the supernatural—ranging from monotheism to animism—and its unique prescription for dealing with those forces, but virtually all cultures present man with the understanding that a major goal is maintaining good relations ·with the supernatural.

>   *Religious beliefs and practices loom large in field reports of cultural anthropologists. The classic analyses of religion have been those of Emile Durkheim and A. R. Radcliffe-Brown.*   <

Inevitably, cultures teach that family formation or maintenance is an essential or fundamental goal for men and women. The methods by which families are formed—arranged marriages, bought brides, romance and courtship, and so on—vary tremendously from one culture to another. Similarly, methods of reckoning kinship and descent differ among cultures, as do methods of child-rearing. Nevertheless, all cultures teach that among man's more significant goals are family goals.

>   *This topic is usually classified in anthropology under the heading of* kinship structure. *A major figure in the comparison and analysis of varied kinship structures is George Peter Murdock.*   <

This list of values is by no means complete, for each culture is in some ways unique, but by identifying what is valuable, culture provides the menu of goals from which open-system man chooses, and inevitably cultures specify that among his more important goals he must consider family, religion, and wealth.

What Means Are Available?

Cultures not only define reality and values, but also provide the know-how which enables man to be purposeful in dealing with his world. Culture provides means for pursuing goals: things man can do to make a difference. Man's techniques are learned.

The means which a culture offers are derived from the explanations of reality it offers. If hunting success is partly a matter of knowing the habits of animals and partly a matter of placating the gods, then this definition of reality leads to techniques for outwitting both animals and gods. If disease is caused by germs, then man can do something to avoid or fight germs, and the culture develops sanitation know-how.

The adaptive means which a culture utilizes can be understood as *technologies*—sets of techniques—for accomplishing whatever the culture identifies as valuable or necessary. Most cultures contain sets of techniques for waging war or defending one's own group against others, for producing and preparing food and shelter, for dealing with the supernatural, for maintaining health and fighting illness. Cultures associated with modern urban life contain elaborate technologies for all those things, as well as for education, transportation, governing, and administering.

Some technologies are demonstrably more effective than others. Technologies based on atomic energy, for example, may be replacing those based on fossil-fuel energy, just as medical practice grounded in biological and chemical sciences appears to be replacing other techniques for treating illness in many parts of the world. When two or more cultures make contact, the impact on each can be profound. With increased abilities for communication and travel, the twentieth century has been shaped significantly by the interaction across cultures and by the accompanying transferral of technologies.

>   *Anthropoligists have often been interested in the process by which a technology (or value) from one culture is adopted or adapted in another. This process and the results of it are labeled* acculturation *and* cultural diffusion. *Among the leading students of these phenomena have been Alfred L. Kroeber and Ralph Linton.*   <

At another level, however, the individual has few choices of techniques, for his contact with other cultures is limited and his own never offers him the full menu. In most areas of life, in most cultures, the techniques held out to open-system man are those which have been elaborated and refined, through trial and error, by preceding genera- tions. This supplies man's basic cause/effect content.

What Are The Proper Standards for Conduct?

No culture equips its members with technologies without at the same time admonishing those adherents about the proper limits for their use. With know-how, cultures also teach standards or *norms*. The con- tents of norms vary widely from one culture to another, but all set forth some limits to the exercise of skills or power, some rules for dealing with others. In our society, for example, we learn that we as relatively strong adults are not to abuse children or old people, that we may be competitive in sports but that our competition should be limited and that we should be "good losers," if it is necessary to lose.

It is from culture that open-system man learns that he must temper ability with considerations of honesty, fairness, reliability, appropri- ateness, and taboos—and it is from culture that he learns the meaning of such concepts.

Culture, in summary, provides for its adherents a set of ready-made answers to basic questions, and thereby emphasizes what those ad- herents have in common. Although man creates and changes his cul- tures in contemporary societies (a topic we focus on particularly in Part Four), at any one point in time, culture can be viewed as im- prisoning its members in patterns of behavior and in meanings suffi- ciently distinctive that it is possible to differentiate Argentineans from Australians, and Australians from Americans. To the extent that Argen- tineans are exposed to a common culture we must expect them to be rather similar in the contents of their four basic dimensions. And to the extent that the culture to which Argentineans have been exposed is recognizably different from the Australian culture, we can readily recognize and distinguish between the two categories. It is equally obvious that those who know them well can identify significant dif- ferences among Argentineans, or among Australians or Americans, and that we shall need to consider some of the sources of such differ- ences.

PATTERNS FOR INTERACTION

So culture is a homogenizing force. But open-system man is not simply a part of a common culture, stamped without variations from a common mold, for cultures also inevitably provide for specialization. Open-system man is a specialized part of his society, and must learn how he fits.

Ascribed Statuses

At a minimum—even in the simplest of societies—man is differentiated from others in terms of age, sex, kinship. Being a child and being elderly call forth different types of behavior, and establish different expectations in the minds of others, who know something of how to interact with you as soon as they know your age category. Being male signifies a set of expectations different from those of being female. Being a Smith or Hazelton differentiates one from others, but knowing that Ahmed Smith is one of those Smiths who live at 10th and Elm really begins to tell us who he is, and how we should interact with him.

Age, sex, and kinship are *statuses* (in the sociologist's terms) and because individuals are placed in these categories by virtue of birth or biological processes, they are considered *ascribed* statuses. These are not the only statuses which can be ascribed. In a culture which recognizes slavery, for example, the categories freeman or slave may be ascribed; in a culture which recognizes caste, it too is ascribed.

Ascribed statuses are important in all societies, including yours, for they help to define how an individual fits into the society. In some of the simplest societies, most aspects of the individual's daily patterns of interaction are governed by ascribed statuses. But in all societies, and especially in the modern complicated types, achievements are also very important. For an individual to be recognized as a distinguished senator, as a master criminal, or as an accomplished artist has consequences for many sectors of his life, for such statuses tell others in various contexts how to interact with him.

Thus culture, by teaching us categories of status and the expectations attached to those statuses, teaches us patterns in the environment. By identifying persons as members of those status categories, we know what to expect of them. And by being identified as members of certain statuses, we know what others expect of us. The pervasiveness of such categories, however, leads to a certain lack of precision. They are not sufficiently specific for our open-system man to know exactly where and how he hooks into his social environment. It is the idea of *social structure* which supplies these.

> *This significance of statuses for social structure is recognized by many, but Ralph Linton is regarded as having focused attention on its importance.*   <

Components of Social Structure

Any social organization—your family, your school, your team—is considered by the social scientist to have a social structure, built out of a set of *roles*. Each role is a cluster of rights and obligations with regard to other roles.

> *The notion of* social structure *is found in several segments of the behavioral sciences, each having its own emphasis and terminological twists. One of these areas is cultural anthropology, another is sociology (under the heading of* role *theory), and a third is social psychology.*   <

Consider the embryo family: husband and wife. The role of wife consists of obligations toward the husband and rights expected of him. The role of the husband is reciprocal; its obligations are the rights of the wife, its privileges are the duties of the wife.

Note carefully three things about this illustration:

First, we are not referring to the rights and obligations of two human individuals, but of two roles. Whether the family we are describing is named Tom and Mary Jones or something very different, within our culture there are generally learned definitions of rights and obligations of husband toward the relevant spouse, and of wives toward the relevant husband.

Second, it is impossible to define the role of one without reference to the role of the other. Role is always a social unit, part of a system or network of roles, and hence is always defined with regard to other roles.

Third, the reciprocity involved in pairs of roles constitutes an essential "glue" which holds social relationships together. Only so long as each role is the source of rewards for the other role can we expect the relationship to continue.

While the two-person embryo family is one we all recognize, it is a somewhat unusual social structure, for in most families and most other social structures, more than two roles are tied together. Add a child, for example, and note that there are three sets of roles involved: (a) husband/wife, (b) mother/child, and (c) father/child. When two roles coincide or converge, such as mother and wife, the sociologist speaks of a position in a social structure. A position, then, is a location in a social structure, the occupancy of which involves the performance of a *set* of roles.

Thus social structures are orderly and relatively persistent relations among positions, which in turn are built by combining roles, which consist of rights and obligations with respect to reciprocating roles. The fact that social structures are built from roles—not from persons—allows for a flexibility and perpetuation. It means that individuals are replaceable while a particular structure persists. Your class may graduate and the faculty may turn over, but the school persists as a recognizable social structure. Anyone who has learned and is willing to perform the appropriate roles may occupy a position in a structure, and death or departure of one member need not destroy the social unit if a replacement is available. This makes possible continuity of the family in spite of the loss of a member. It makes possible substitution of one governmental administration for another without destruction of the government as such. It makes possible the persistence of the business corporation or religious congregation even though all its founding members may be retired or dead. (We should note that although the definitions of roles are fairly persistent, so that we can talk of the continuity of institutions, they can and do change, particularly in dynamic societies. This topic will be treated more fully later.)

Learning Primary and Secondary Roles

The very fact that social structure is an abstraction—that it consists of roles combined into positions lodged in networks independently of the persons occupying those positions—facilitates continuity of social organizations and societies. But at the same time social structure provides patterns that greatly simplify the social environment of open-system man. As he learns the content of a role, he learns what is expected of him as an occupant of that role and at the same time what he may expect or demand from the reciprocal role. Man therefore learns how to fit into his social environment, without the necessity of learning about all the persons in it.

Unless he knows the appropriate roles, man cannot belong to a society. Pluck him from his native society and drop him suddenly into a new one, and no matter how intelligent or how well educated he is, he will be lost in the new environment.

Transmitted as basic parts of the culture are some roles learned by virtually all members of the society: son or daughter, husband or wife, father or mother. These we refer to as *primary* roles. In each case the individual not only learns the one he or she is likely to occupy, but its reciprocal role as well. This enables women as well as men to judge the performance of male roles, and vice versa. It makes it possible for all members of the society to agree that specific items of behavior are, or are not, appropriate for a father.

Unless the individual understands such primary roles as defined by his culture, he is a "foreigner" and not ready to participate in his society. The learning of such roles constitutes the heart of what the sociologist terms *socialization,* the process whereby the individual learns those things which permit him to be a functioning part of his society.

> *The notion of socialization is another concept widely used in the behavioral sciences. In social psychology it sometimes is applied to virtually all learning. The more sociological version employed here is derived from classic work by George Herbert Mead and Charles Horton Cooley.* <

It is possible to imagine a culture so meager and a society so simple that only distinctions would be those of status and primary roles. In this case each individual would know the rights and obligations of all others, and culture would be the dominant force in daily activities. Living cultures, however, get more complicated than that, and societies become more highly structured. Division of labor becomes necessary, and therefore we find specialization of roles. At this point some if not all individuals learn roles and positions which are not taught to all. In your kind of society, for example, many learn the role of patient and relatively few learn the role of physician. Many learn the role of student while fewer learn the role of teacher. These specialized roles (and many others) are regarded as *secondary* roles, and the learning of them as secondary socialization. Generally we would expect primary roles to be learned in the family or kinship group, and to be learned rather early in life. Secondary roles, on the other hand, tend to be learned in school, on the job or in other specialized organizations, and to be learned later than the primary roles.

Secondary roles grow up around a set of highly developed techniques. Generally, though not always, they reflect an occupation or profession, and learning of these roles generally involves two kinds of things: (1) technical content, such as engineering or medical science, and (2) social structure content, such as role relationships with designers and production specialists or with patients, nurses, hospital administrators, pharmacists, and others. Generally primary roles are learned rather early in life, while secondary roles come later. The extent to which secondary roles provide recognizable patterns is something we shall consider in a later chapter, but we can note here that while primary roles are familiar to all, secondary roles are specialized and therefore provide important bases for differentiation among persons.

In highly complicated cultures, preparation for secondary roles calls for rather intense interaction with a rather narrow segment of the culture. Thus social structure in complex societies directs and limits our exposure to the total culture.

But we have been alluding to differences between societies; we need to make these differences more explicit.

Varieties of Societies

Specialists from many disciplines have pondered the differences among societies, cultures, and civilizations. Since these are such complicated entities it is not surprising that no consensus has emerged. Yet there does seem to be a convergence among sociologists and anthropologists which provides us with a useful set of distinctions, if we are careful in our usage of them. The theme is concisely summarized by Robert Redfield, who distinguishes the *folk society* from the *modern urban society.*

> We have chosen to use Robert Redfield's interpretation, but similar themes are found in the social sciences under other labels. The most widely used would include Ferdinand Tonnies' notions of Gemeinschaft and Gesellschaft; Emile Durkheim's distinction between mechanical solidarity and organic solidarity; Howard Becker's notions of sacred society and secular society. <

Redfield is careful to note that he is describing the extreme cases, that we are not likely to find any existing society which fits either extreme completely. These "pure" types nevertheless direct our attention to significant dimensions on which societies can be compared or contrasted.

The folk society, in Redfield's conception, is small and isolated; members have little contact with outsiders but intimate and frequent communication with each other. It is nonliterate; hence the culture contains only those items which can be remembered in a lifetime, and thus transmitted verbally. It has little division of labor; except for sex and age distinctions, all tend to work at similar tasks. Its members thus are homogeneous and have a strong sense of belonging together. There is no systematic pursuit of knowledge, no experimentation, no science. Custom, tradition, and convention govern behavior, with little reflection or critical examination. The sacred orientation prevails over the secular, and religious obligations together with kinship ties establish expected behavior patterns. The familial group is the unit of action. There is no money; economic exchange is based on status rights and obligations, not on a market.

Modern urban society, in this approach, is the opposite of folk society, but let's be a little more explicit about what that means. It is neither small nor isolated, which means that members do not know or communicate with all other members, but that at least some of them may communicate with those in other societies. It is literate, which means that its discoveries and experiences can be accumulated in books and other forms. Reflection, experimentation, knowledge for the sake of knowledge are important. Labor is markedly differentiated in function, highly specialized; members are thus heterogeneous and need not have a strong sense of belongingness. Custom, tradition, and convention are considered as conveniences, to be set aside as occasion demands; change is thus to be expected. The secular orientation prevails over the sacred. Economic, political, religious, and educational activities tend to be carried out in specialized positions and organizations rather than primarily in the family. Economic exchange is regulated by markets.

Out of these distinctions between the two types of societies emerges a critical difference: the bases of interdependence among members. The traditional society is held together by members' dependence on each other to maintain the homogeneity of the society, a sameness that permits and promotes personal encounters. The modern urban society, however, is integrated on the basis of functional interdependence, a differentiation and complementarity of tasks. Where the member of the folk society expects others to be doing similar tasks in similar ways, the member of modern urban society depends on others to be involved in quite different tasks and to provide much of what he requires in exchange for his own specialized products or services. Because members of the folk society face common problems with common solutions, emotional support for individuals may come from a wide range of others in the society. But because of functional differentiation in modern society, the individual depends to a large extent on strangers or casual acquaintances, and emotional support tends to come from a narrow band of members of his family and his friends.

Although your society is not a pure case of the modern urban variety, it seems clear that its central characteristics are more in that direction than in the folk-society direction. It also seems clear that the worldwide trend is away from folk societies toward modern urban societies. Finally, it seems clear that as this movement occurs, societies become more like one another than was true when folk societies prevailed.

Folk societies represent local solutions to local problems, and we would therefore expect the culture to reflect the experiences and history peculiar to each small, isolated society. A world composed of such societies therefore would be a very diverse world. Modern urban society, on the other hand, emphasizes the accumulation and extension of knowledge, the import of ideas which work, the division of labor to fit standardized and empirically tested technologies which have been studied and freed from localized versions. Abstract, generalized knowledge replaces the situation-specific knowledge of the folk society, and thus provides a base for a common culture as we move from nation to nation. As your society moves further in that direction, then we would expect ethnic subcultures to become less important and less distinctive.

And because formal knowledge is so important to modern urban society, the school becomes the crucial agency in socialization, in overcoming the subcultural distinctions so characteristic of ethnic groups. Ethnic subcultures, that is, are consistent with folk society, with emphasis on the family, religion, and tradition. As a society moves toward the modern urban category, however, family and religion and tradition yield some of their influence to school, occupational specialization, abstract knowledge, and an orientation toward change. At some stage of the movement away from folk and toward modern urban, it may be possible to discern regional subcultures, reflecting the economic specializations and agricultural bases, as well as immigration histories. America's southwest has had a distinct subcultural flavor reflecting cattle, the range, and oil; her deep south a distinct flavor of cotton, the plantation, and tobacco. But we would have to expect—with still further movement in the direction of modern urban civilization—the eclipse of such regional subcultures. The more urbanized portions of the southwest and the deep south are more like each other than they are like the more rural folk portions of their own regions.

With movement toward modern urban civilization, education becomes the major switching device for the developing individual; and from the standpoint of the society, education becomes the major device for rechanneling a generation to face the changing demands and needs of the society.

RECAPITULATION

We have been arguing that open-system man gets his dimensional content from his environment, We have also noted that man's environment is very complex, and in this chapter we have suggested that man does not experience all of it, but is exposed to those patterns revealed to him largely through human filters. The principal filtering agency, culture, supplies man with goals, means, interpretations of reality, and norms: man's dimensional content. But we suggested that, in complicated societies, man is exposed to only a portion of his culture. He is guided in his access to that culture by his location in the social structure, which determines what kind of society he hooks into, where he hooks into it, and how he relates to others. This guidance teaches him to distinguish among statuses, roles, and positions, his own and others'.

The personality develops from these experiences. How it develops is a matter to be explored in the next chapter.

RECOMMENDED BROWSING

Ruth Benedict, *Patterns of Culture,* Baltimore: Penguin Books, 1946. A small, classic statement of the meaning and impact of culture.

Yehudi A. Cohen, *Social Structure and Personality: A Casebook,* New York: Holt, Rinehart and Winston, 1961. A careful analysis of the interaction of person and social environment, built around some of the classic articles from the behavioral sciences.

Charles Horton Cooley, *Human Nature and the Social Order,* New York: Free Press of Glencoe, 1956. Re-issue of a classic early book, which helped lay the foundations for contemporary study of socialization.

Fred Cottrell, *Energy and Society.* New York: McGraw-Hill, 1955. An important analysis of man's relations to the physical world, and the social consequences of those relationships.

Emile Durkheim, *The Division of Labor in Society,* translated from the French by George Simpson. New York: Free Press of Glencoe, 1947. Presents concepts of mechanical solidarity and organic solidarity for analyzing different types of societies.

Emile Durkheim, *The Elementary Forms of the Religious Life.* New York: The Free Press of Glencoe, 1947. Re-issue of an early but significant examination of religious foundations for behavior.

Melville J. Herskovits, *Economic Anthropology: A Study in Comparative Economics.* New York: Knopf, 1960. A pioneering survey of economic patterns in non-European societies.

Clyde Kluckhohn, "Values and Value-Orientations in the Theory of Action," in *Toward a General Theory of Action,* edited by Talcott Parsons and Edward A.

Shils. Cambridge: Harvard University Press, 1951, pages 388–433. A succinct statement of the role of values in human behavior.

A. L. Kroeber, *The Nature of Culture*. Chicago: University of Chicago Press, 1952. A major scholar's selection of papers on forms and patterns of culture.

Dorothy Lee, "Lineal and Nonlineal Codifications of Reality," *Psychosomatic Medicine,* **12** (March–April 1950) 89–97. A highly suggestive analysis of the impact of concepts and language on thought.

Gerhard Lenski, *The Religious Factor: A Sociological Study of Religion's Impact on Politics, Economics and Family Life.* Garden City, N.Y.: Doubleday, 1961. An empirical study of the consequences of religious belief and practice on behavior in contemporary society.

Ralph Linton, *The Study of Man*. New York: Appleton-Century-Crofts, 1936. A classic book, which introduced concepts of "status" and "role" (although with definitions somewhat different from those we have used).

Robert H. Lowie, *Social Organization*. New York: Holt, Rinehart and Winston, 1948. Anthropological study of social organization, emphasizing kinship but including consideration of property, law, and political organization.

Bronislaw Malinowski, *Magic, Science and Religion*. Garden City, N.Y.: Doubleday Anchor Books, 1954. An important analysis of religion and other systems of belief, and their significance for behavior.

George Peter Murdock, *Social Structure*. New York: Macmillan, 1949. A major survey and comparison of world cultures, with emphasis on families and kinship systems.

Robert Redfield, "The Folk Society," *American Journal of Sociology,* **52**, January 1947, 293–308. A concise statement of the characteristics of the pure concept of folk society.

Edward Sapir, *Culture, Language, and Personality*. Berkeley, University of California Press, 1961. Selection of essays by an early pioneer.

Ferdinand Tönnies, *Fundamental Concepts of Sociology,* translated and edited by Charles Loomis. New York: American Book Co., 1940. The famous contrast between *Gemeinschaft* and *Gesellschaft* as extreme types of societies.

Stanley H. Udy, *Work in Traditional and Modern Society*. Englewood Cliffs, N.J.: Prentice-Hall, 1968. Examines relationships between technologies and forms of social organization.

Benjamin Lee Whorf, *Language, Thought and Reality*. New York: Wiley, 1956. Re-issue of a pioneering volume presenting the thesis that language constructs our perceptions of reality.

CHAPTER 3 # DEVELOPMENT AND PERSONALITY

Open-system man, in our first consideration of him, was an empty organism, having capacities on four dimensions but lacking content. We reasoned that he would acquire content through transactions with an environment, and we suggested that that environment was both patterned and filtered through culture and social structure. Now we need to take a closer look at the processes by which man acquires content. We shall argue that man's development is *patterned sequentially* in that it follows a predictable series of stages. And we shall argue that man's development is *channeled,* with early experiences providing constraints which limit possible subsequent experiences and resources which guide the individual into the next set of experiences.

Because man's exposure is channeled and sequentially patterned, we can learn quite a bit about him simply by knowing his stage of development and the channel in which he is developing. The probabilities are high that his aspirations, his definitions of reality and his understanding of causation, and his norms will be similar to those held by others in his channel and at his stage of development, and that they will be different from those in other channels or at other stages.

Developmental processes, then, result in man acquiring content comparable to others in his channel, but we must also recognize and explain the fact that development results in man acquiring a distinctiveness or uniqueness which gives him identity, which enables him and us to recognize him as apart from others. These distinguishing characteristics are summarized by the term *personality,* and it too takes shape during development.

SEQUENCES OF DEVELOPMENT

Development of open-system man generally moves from the relatively simple to the relatively complex, with each stage laying a foundation for the next. There are both physiological and social bases for such unfolding.

The Physiological Life Cycle

Maturation—changes within the individual's body which are relatively independent of environmental conditions—proceeds through well-defined states. In infancy the individual is capable only of expressing needs associated with survival, and seems to be an organism designed for eating, sleeping, and eliminating. Rapidly, however, maturation produces increased abilities: to see and hear, to remain awake for longer intervals, to exercise voluntary controls over the muscles, and later to sit, walk, feed himself, and talk. We need not summarize each year to make the central point: Infancy and childhood are marked with rapidly expanding biological competences, and it is only as these unfold that learning of more complex patterns can occur.

> *The physiological aspects of development are important topics of research in both biology and psychology.* <

Hand in hand with physical development goes cognitive development. The newborn is entirely dependent, but each month produces expansion of his awareness of the environment, his ability to distinguish elements within it, to distinguish parents from others, and to be aware of himself as a physical object. This perception marks a significant step in cognition, but at this stage the person remains "egocentric"; the world appears to be ordered around him, with him at the center. He cannot imagine another point of view, and hence is not aware that his own is a point of view. Ability to find order in the environment apart from the perceiver seems to make another important stage of cognitive development, which prepares the individual to learn a new range of more abstract concepts, and to solve more complex problems.

> *Although many have contributed to our understanding of cogni-*
tive development, the milestone research has been done at Geneva by Jean
Piaget.   <

There is growing evidence that cognitive development proceeds in
a fairly orderly sequence, new stages being reached by acquiring new
adaptations when old ones fail. We can suggest that exposure to a cognitively complex environment before the individual is cognitively ready
will have little positive effect. Likewise, lack of cognitive challenge at a
time when the individual is ready for a next stage may inhibit development. Orderly development may be disrupted or stunted if the child
is exposed to a quite limited environment or if the child is so over-
exposed that failures are overwhelming.

The physiological life-cycle not only guarantees some maturation
during the growth and development stages, but it also guarantees aging
and physical deterioration. Even as man's cognitive competence and
problem-solving abilities based on experience increase, his physical
stamina and health may be deteriorating. If nothing else, this aging
process eventually requires that certain kinds of activities be curtailed
or stopped completely. It seems inevitable, therefore, that the personality will be modified with unfolding of the physiological life cycle.

> *Research on cognitive development has focused primarily on the*
infant and the child. The more recent interest in processes of aging—in
gerentology—are only beginning to extend our knowledge beyond man's
physical peak.   <

The Social Life Cycle

Social growth likewise unfolds in a sequence, with the individual mastering at first relatively simple statuses and roles before being assigned
or admitted to complicated roles and positions. Generally the trend is
from dependent to relative independence to interdependence. There
may be more variability in the sequence of socialization and social
growth than in physiological maturation, because social structures contain more possibilities, but generally speaking the individual passes
from one status or role to more complicated ones after demonstrating

competence at prior levels and learning at least minimum requirements for the new status or role. This learning-in-advance is known as *anticipatory socialization.*

The social life cycle is correlated with the physiological one. Although each society defines these statuses in its own way, each distinguishes something akin to a sequence beginning with infancy through childhood, adolescence, marriage, parenthood, and grandparenthood. Societies with highly developed divisions of labor add at least two more categories: employed and retired. Each such socially defined stage marks a significant change in the range of roles which are considered appropriate, or significant, or mandatory. Each stage therefore colors the individual's experiences with his environment, defines or delimits or validates his competence, and hence should have a bearing on his personality.

Both physiological and social growth unfold in the direction of increased competence to meet and deal with the environment, and ultimately with a tapering off of that competence. In terms of the four dimensions of open-system man discussed earlier, this should mean that the unfolding process results in a widening and refinement of goals, broader and more accurate conceptions of reality and of the means for coping with it, and deepening understanding of norms. It also suggests that, with aging, goals may be reduced or constrained, and beliefs about causation, reality, and norms may stabilize, thus becoming outdated if the environment changes significantly.

> 	*The notion of competence as a fundamental motive in development of the personality has been stressed especially by Robert W. White, Nelson Foote, and Leonard Cottrell.* 	<

CHANNELS OF DEVELOPMENT

We made the general point in Chapter 2 that man interacts with a *filtered* environment. Now we want to combine that notion with the idea of sequential development. Our theme is that the individual's transactions with his environment are both (1) guided and (2) delimited, so that at each stage of development he is learning the content and acquiring the competence to participate in the next stage, but at the same time his learning tends to be restricted to those aspects of the environment which are relevant to his more likely future roles and statuses. Specification of one set of contents tends to be denial of exposure to others; this is what is meant by channeling. Three things must be noted at the outset of our discussion of channeling. First, in the purely folk society, where everyone had virtually the same exposure, the channeling notion would not be very important; it takes on significance as the society modernizes. Second, not every individual develops in the predicted way; some individuals become rechanneled, and we shall consider that process later in this chapter. Third, the delimited effects of channeling are not necessarily experienced as delimiting or constraining by the individual involved, for he tends to be uninterested or unaware of other content.

Subcultural Variations

One who matures in a Western civilization can hardly escape awareness of certain subcultural distinctions—such as those of the American Negro, American Indian, or Jew. Switzerland, as a classic example, is composed of four categories distinguished by language: French, German, Italian, and Romanish. Periodically the Belgians grow uneasy because some speak Flemish, others French. In Africa there are not only distinctions between blacks and whites, but each of these categories contains marked subgroups. South Africans, for example, distinguishes Afrikaaners from English and from Jews, while Blacks in Africa usually identify with one of a variety of lineages or tribes. In Southeast Asian countries, the Chinese minority is almost always set apart, although subcultures based on religious beliefs are perhaps more pervasive. India is divided into Muslims and Hindus and Christians, and this distinction was important in separating Pakistan from India. China and Japan have distinguished Christians from others, especially Buddhists. National origin—or at least ancestry—can be an important basis for subcultural distinctions, as illustrated by French Canadians as contrasted with English-speaking Canadians. Frequently South Americans distinguish Europeans from Indians from Negroes.

It seems clear that in the modern world, subcultures frequently are based on race, language, national origin, religion, or ancestry. Sometimes subcultures involve a particular combination of two or more of these factors. It is also clear that these factors *do not inevitably* result in significant differences. But where they are recognized, it means that the individual born into one such *ethnic* category is going to be exposed to an especially filtered and elaborated part of the larger, total culture.

> *The term* ethnic group *has several usages. For some authors it is synonymous with* subculture. *For others it is restricted to racial, religious, or national-origin distinctions. In any case, much relevant literature can be found under the label* ethnology, *the study of ethnic groups and their relations.*   <

Occasionally ethnic subcultures become assimilated into the larger host culture and disappear, but the tendency is usually for subcultures to be perpetuated. There are several reasons for this; when a distinctive language is involved, one's native tongue tends to unlock the subculture associated with it, but to make difficult the acquisition of content from the surrounding larger culture. Frequently subcultures exist because of emigration, and when that occurs the newly arrived tend to live and work and play together, in mutual support. Not infrequently residential segregation patterns reinforce subcultures and make assimilation difficult or impossible. Whatever the reason, ethnic subcultures often have consequences for emerging man.

Minority Subcultures

The family is a prime agent in transmitting racial and ethnic distinctions. In the ethnic group, the family is particularly important because it transmits the native tongue. In those societies in which race is significant, the family transmits cultural definitions of race as well as patterns for coping with the consequences of those definitions. The family also instills religious assumptions and beliefs and frequently a sense of identity as a member of an ethnic or racial group with distinctive history, customs, and perhaps destiny. The family also identifies for the newcomer the significant agents in the environment toward (or away from) whom action should be directed.

When the neighborhood or community is of the same racial or ethnic subculture, the child's experience in the home is reinforced by exposure to adults and other children who speak his language, share his family role models, his ascribed and achieved status definitions, and who constitute groups to whom he can refer for various interpretations of his world. Whether in a compatible neighborhood or not, his religious experiences most likely reinforce his ethnicity. Particularly if he is in an ethnic neighborhood, the child usually confronts stores or markets whcih feature ethnic services and styles and have special promotions for appropriate ethnic holidays. Neighborhood newspapers may be in his native language. All these experiences, then, prepare him in a fairly consistent, coherent way to enter school.

School frequently represents a crucial switching point in development of the individual. In many parts of the world, the school reflects the local, ethnic subculture, including the local language and customs, and thus carries forward and builds on the child's learning from home and neighborhood. Even in those cases in which the neighborhood is not a self-contained, closed unit, "parochial" schools operated by religious or ethnic organizations rather than the state may serve this reinforcing purpose. But there are other cases, especially in urban areas, in which the child enters a school which reflects primarily the larger host culture. This sudden change may produce "culture shock" and some difficulties in adjustment, as feedback from the environment tells the child that he is out of step or that his techniques are inadequate. Generally, however, we would expect the school experience to overcome culture shock, and to help the child learn a second language, a new set of role models, new expectations, and new methods of coping with the world around him.

For the member of an ethnic subculture, then, school represents a possible switching point, enabling him to gain the content which in turn prepares him for roles and positions in structures representing the larger host culture. Frequently such individuals develop bicultural lives, conforming in basic respects to the host culture but participating in family and ethnic events as well. Generally, if the switch from minority to larger host culture is to be made, we would expect it to occur with the second or third generation.

The odds are good then that the individual will reach adult status equipped with content characteristic of his subculture. Family, neighborhood, and school usually reinforce one another to teach him distinctive interpretations of his sex role and methods of courtship and family formation. These agencies usually reinforce one another in establishing occupational values and methods of building careers. They usually converge in teaching him religious values and methods of worship; patterns for political and community involvement; customary economic practices regarding consumption, saving, and investment; and forms of recreation.

Family, neighborhood, and school generally establish the channel in which the individual will proceed, yet they leave him latitude for individual variation. We can fairly well predict a man's religious preferences, given his acquaintance with a particular subculture, but not his degree of religiosity or degree of participation in religious activities. Each channel presents its characteristic "menu" of alternatives. Knowing the channel tells us the boundaries within which variations are likely to take place, but it does not tell us the specific choices to be made by the individual. For this reason ethnic *stereotypes* (generalizations applied to all members of an ethnic group) are usually inaccurate, overemphasizing and distorting some things shared within the subculture, but ignoring many dimensions on which there is significant variation.

Majority Subcultures

We tend to think of the experiences of minorities as somewhat restricting or confining, especially because members are often excluded from certain kinds of occupations or residential sections. Thus it is easy to appreciate the delimiting aspects of developmental channels, as these route the members of a minority subculture.

Development in the majority or dominant subculture, however, is equally routed. Often it is even more tightly channeled or constrained.

Although the member of a minority subculture may learn portions of both, members of the majority subculture tend to learn only their own. Members of majority subcultures may be aware of ethnic groups and be interested in them or in their unique products as curiosities, but need not seriously consider them as developmental models. Members of majority subcultures may not need to learn to cope with the minority, and indeed may be denied the opportunity to learn more than superficial aspects of the minority subculture. Majority members tend to be insulated from those occasions which might provide negative feedback and thus spur unusual learning and the widening of horizons.

> *Two of the classic studies of majority subcultures are Robert and Helen Lynd's* Middletown *and* Middletown in Transition. <

Our model of open-system man, our notions of filtered environments, and our picture of man developing in interaction with it all combine to emphasize that routing is just as real for the member of a majority or dominant subculture as for the minority member. This does not mean that the individual will experience his development as restricting or confining. The patterned, filtered experience may indeed appear to the developing person as normal or natural or even inevitable, and this may be as true for the minority subculture as for the majority subculture.

> *Extreme identification with one's own group or subculture and devaluation of others is called* ethnocentrism. *It has been extensively examined by students of* attitudes *and* opinions *in social psychology.* <

Our model as well as abundant empirical evidence indicate the great force of the family as an initial structure, giving filtered and patterned content which readies the child for the neighborhood and school, which in turn adds content for the next stage. Each experience thus increases the probabilities that the next will continue within the current channel and thereby reduces the probability of switching channels. For the vast majority of men and women in all societies, development is routed, not random.

REROUTING CHANNELS

The quickening pace of societal change, with trends toward modern urban societies, is most strikingly seen in the movement of millions of persons from rural areas into cities. World-wide, this has been one of the more significant phenomena of the twentieth century. Many millions have had to depart from the rural, agricultural, folk orientations of their parents and learn instead to live in cities, doing non-agricultural work, gearing their subsistence much more toward a money economy and markets, and relying on strangers for various essential supports.

> *The transition which urbanization reflects has been treated in the social sciences under various labels: industrialization, modernization, economic or socioeconomic development, and urbanization.* <

The fact that those millions did make the transition from rural to urban life is emphatic evidence that the channeling we have been stressing does not inevitably lead each generation to be a carbon copy of the preceding one. It is clear, for example, that the ethnic or regional subcultures which are associated with rural folk life did not and could not prepare young people for modern urban life. These subcultures did not contain the cause/effect knowledge associated with industrialized occupations and needed for coping with urban life. They did not contain the norms associated with impersonal dealing between strangers, nor the definitions of urban reality, nor the interpretations of personal goals which carried over into the city. In short, the subcultures found in rural folk societies are not geared for channeling young individuals into modern urban societies.

Then how do we account for the transition?

Generational Rerouting

Some make the move as adults, without preparation but with subcultural supports. Adult immigration—whether international or from the countryside to the city within a region—generally propels the individual or family into a subcultural pocket in the city which serves to protect and support the individual in transition, to teach him some of the new content he must have, and to help him retain a sense of self in an unknown, apparently hostile environment. Frequently the new-comer joins kin or friends from his old surroundings, who help him establish contacts, find work and housing, and generally learn his way around. Inevitably, then, there arise in cities ethnic or racial settle-ments or ghettos.

True, the child in the family undergoing transition may find that his family is itself so bewildered or unsure that it serves as a poor source of socialization for his future. Parents who themselves are learning a new culture may be changing their expectations of their children, thus affording a shifting base for socialization. And in search of anchors in the strange environment, they may emphasize the older folk culture whenever this is possible, in religious worship, in the use of the native language at home, and in kinship emphasis.

To the extent that the school is an arm of modern urban society (and not dedicated to perpetuation of subcultural distinctiveness), it presents cognitive content not available to the child elsewhere and becomes the major rerouting agency for the child in transition. Some-times the school simply extends the family's training (for clearly the family cannot be a repository of more than a small fraction of the knowl-edge available and considered necessary in modern urban society). But in the rerouting of a generation, the school may present training which is in contrast or opposition to that of the family. And the school may provide the child with much more rapid learning experience than the immigrant parents have opportunities for, thus building a genera-tion gap.

In Western Europe and North America, the educational system has for several generations been the major rerouting agency for steering rural folklike families into the modern urban middle classes. More recently the same phenomenon has occurred in Eastern Europe and it is now occuring in many other parts of the world. Clearly the develop-ment of one generation of open-system men has resulted in content different from that which the preceding generations acquired. During these periods of major societal changes, the channels themselves have been reshaped, but this does not negate our contention that man's development was channeled. We cannot predict which individuals will veer from a folk channel to an urban channel at the switching point, but we can expect that once the switch is thrown, the "menu" presented to the individual will be delimited and prescribed, and that essentially the same menu will be available to others in that channel.

Despite the weight of channeled exposure to the environment in determining the content of open-system man, he does not remain simply a reflection of his environment. There are many combinations possible from a limited array of biological and environmental factors, and these combinations permit man to develop an identity, to become a recognizable individual. This we refer to as *personality*.

PERSONALITY IN PROCESS

Because the distinctive aspects of man are so important to most of us, personality has been widely studied. But it turns out to be a complicated matter and there is no clearcut, widely accepted description or definition. Perhaps most students of the topic do agree that when we speak of personality we are referring to (1) those aspects of the person which make him distinctive, (2) aspects which persist and are rather stable, slow to change, and (3) aspects which manifest themselves in observable behavior.

Some of the earlier attempts to summarize personalities have become so well known in our culture that they are part of the everyday vocabulary (even though, in most cases, these categories have been given up by behavioral scientists as inadequate).

Among the more famous attempts to measure personalities was a scale ranging from *introversion* to *extroversion*, with the introvert being quiet, retiring, enjoying solitude, and the extrovert being friendly, enjoying interaction with others, craving excitement, and disliking solitude. Another well-known distinction sorted persons in terms of *dependence* or *independence*, referring to ability to resist pressures to conform, to work without supervision, or to express unusual ideas.

Still another distinction sorts persons into three types. In this approach the *inner-directed* individual strives for success as measured by abstract ideals implanted in him as a child. In contrast, the *tradition-directed* person looks to the past, to precedent and tradition for guidance and models for behavior. Still differently, the *other-directed* person looks to his contemporaries for guidance and direction, depending on their approval to tell him what success is.

>   *Inner-, other-, and tradition-directedness is a set of types developed by David Reisman and his associates.*   <

Perhaps the best-known and most hotly debated concept for personality assessment involved a scale ranging from *authoritarian* to *non-authoritarian,* and measured by what became known as the "California F [for Fascist] Scale." This controversial device sought to measure ways of feeling and thinking which are associated with readiness to embrace antidemocratic ideologies.

>   *Although Erich Fromm appears to have pioneered this conception in psychology, it was T. W. Adorno and associates who devised the F–scale.* <

The list could be continued almost endlessly, reflecting the many aspects of personality which we can imagine. All such measuring devices suffer from the fact that at best they represent measurements of a few of the many possible aspects, thus omitting many other possible measurements. All of us—scientists and laymen alike—are forced to choose some aspects of personality to focus on, and if the chosen aspect happens to be pertinent to our particular interests or the person's particular situation, it is useful; a bravery dimension, for example, might be quite relevant to our understanding of the policeman's behavior in a dangerous situation, but it might be irrelevant if we are considering him as a lover.

But at this stage of the behavioral sciences, we cannot settle on a small list of personality aspects which unerringly sort persons into types. There is slightly less confusion, perhaps, when we turn from types and ask about the components and functions of the personality.

Some Functions of the Personality

Because it is relatively stable and slow to change, the personality serves to give man a *continuity* as he moves through the sequences of development. It enables him to experience himself as the "same" person at different points in time. And it enables those who know him also to recognize him at different times. We would not expect a man to have one personality this year and a conflicting one next year (even though we do expect some growth or modification with experience).

>   *This view stems from the* transactional *approach to personality. Pioneers in this area were Edward C. Tolman, John Dewey, Kurt Lewin. Gordon W. Allport was perhaps the most vigorous advocate of it.*   <

Because the personality expresses the core of a person, it helps man acquire a coherence and stability in spite of segmental participation in various roles and positions. It enables man to remain a "whole" person. Thus we would not expect a man to reveal one personality at work and a wholly contradictory one at home (even though each social structure may permit him to reveal somewhat varied aspects of his total personality).

It appears then that the personality *can* function to give continuity to man over time, and coherence to man through space. But we cannot assume that the personality inevitably *does* so function. We must recognize that some personalities are stronger than others, and this raises questions about the components of personality.

Components of Personality

We can identify at least three basic ingredients to the personality which help account for the functions we have said the personality can perform. One of these is the individual's sense of *competence* in relation to his world. A second component is *motivational*, and the third is a *conception of self*. These are not unrelated.

We would expect man's sense of competence to be closely associated with his content on the four cognitive dimensions we have been con-

sidering all along: aspirations, beliefs about reality, beliefs about causation, and norms. If in general the individual's cognitive content permits him to cope with the world as he experiences it, we would expect
him to have a sense of competence, and we would expect this to be
associated with strength of personality.

We have said repeatedly that open-system man acquires goals or
aspirations, but we have not yet tackled the question of why he is goal-
oriented. What turns man on? Activates him? These questions have
long bothered people in and out of the behavioral sciences, and as
might be expected, the answers which have been offered are still controversial. There seems to be a growing consensus on two broad classes
of motives: *primary* (physiologically based and related to life itself) and
acquired (learned through interaction with others). The primary motives should be rather stable; the individual needs food and water and
other life-sustaining supports at age 60 as well as at 6 or 16. But acquired motives, being learned, can change with experience, and this
kind of reasoning has led some students of personality to suggest that
motivation has a development aspect.

A famous version of this was developed by Abraham H. Maslow,
who not only suggested an orderly sequence of learning but that the
several kinds of learned motives are ranked. Thus Maslow spoke of a
hierarchy of motives, and although his ideas are still debated, the underlying notion has stirred quite a bit of attention, making it worth our
while to take a brief glimpse at his argument.

Maslow recognized *physiological* needs as the basic, most dominant
ones, taking precedence so long as they remained unsatisfied. With
physiological needs taken care of, attention can turn to *safety* needs,
including security from physical and psychological deprivation. If
safety needs are satisfied, needs for *belongingness* and love can come into
play, and only if these are reasonably satisfied is the fourth level of
motivation significant: the level of *esteem* needs, or desire for recognition by others and for self-respect. Finally, at the ultimate level, is the
need for *actualization,* or desire for self-realization or fulfillment of one's
total capacities. It has been suggested by some students of motivation
that individuals who do not find reliable satisfactions for the more primary or "lower-order" motives have arrested personalities; they do not
develop completely through the hierarchy of motives.

> *Others who have made important use of similar concepts include Carl Rogers, who stressed* self-actualization, *and David McClelland, a student of the* achievement motive.   <

We need not settle on this specific list of motives, or this particular hierarchical sequence of them, to accept the general notion of a hierarchy of motivation. There does seem to be reasonable consensus that development of the person involves growing beyond physiological or primary motives in the direction of acquired motives, and there seems to be reasonable agreement among students of personality that this motivational growth is in the direction of some *conception of self.* We shall accept the idea that the self-concept is central to personality, without specifying whether the self-concept is measured by belongingness, self esteem, actualization, or anything else. Thus we shall concede that it may develop to include elements of altruism or it may be considerably more self-centered and selfish. At this point in the history of the behavioral sciences there is much more consensus on the general role of the self-conception than on its specific content.

The self-concept begins to emerge when the child learns to consider himself as an object. It constitutes the person's picture of who he is and who he is in the process of becoming. It is generally regarded as having two components: a private picture or estimate of the self, plus a view of the self which is reflected in the way others behave toward the person.

> *The self-concept is sometimes merely labeled the "self," sometimes the "self-image." It is an important idea in several of the behavioral sciences. Prominent among its proponents have been George Herbert Mead, Charles Horton Cooley, Erik Erikson, Gordon Allport, and Abraham Maslow.*   <

Obviously the self-conception develops and changes with experience, although it is not likely to change abruptly. It is reasonable to believe that the self-conception will be influenced by man's assessment of his physiological capacities. Believing that he is tall or fat or nimble or athletic or sickly can make a difference in man's estimate of himself. Just as clearly, the self-conception should be influenced by social locations, or positions in social structures. To be a member of the club or team or family not only results in particular behavior by others toward the person but may significantly alter his image of himself. Passing from one social status to another—often marked by initiation ceremonies such as Bar Mitzvah or a wedding—helps the individual identify himself. It also seems reasonable to believe, although this has been relatively neglected in research, that the self can be influenced by man's possession of things: pets, jewelry, money, automobiles, clothing, and so on.

>   *The significance of possessions was suggested by Thorstein Veblen's notion of* conspicuous consumption *and more recently by David Caplovitz's work on* compensatory consumption.   >

Branching points.   It may be helpful to conceive of the self-concept (as well as the publicly visible personality) as developing through the testing of a series of hypotheses. The transactions of open-system man with his environment result in feedback from that experience. The youngster explores and tests his capacities. Rightly or wrongly, he believes the feedback that he is good at some things, less able at others. Such testing applies to physiological abilities, cognitive abilities, and social abilities. Negative results the first few times may simply invite further effort, but eventually the child or adolescent comes to believe that his competences lie in some directions and not in others, and this decision serves to channel his future experiences. The realization that some prized status or skill is beyond attainment can be a traumatic experience for the individual, calling for painful reorientation of aspirations.

Realization that his talents point in certain directions and away from others helps determine man's later exposure to his environment. Realization that he is not an athlete, for example, may not convince the individual that he is a scholar, but it may encourage him to channel his energies to more cognitive or social matters. And as the individual comes to the conclusion that athletics is not "him," we would expect reduced transactions with the athletic world and increased transactions in other realms, at least to the extent that the individual can control such matters. Thus while socially defined channels delimit man's exposure to his environment and hence determine the "menu" offered to him, the self-conception helps him select items from that menu.

Therefore development of open-system man is analogous to climbing a tree. At the first main fork, one must decide on a direction. Either fork leads higher, but there are many points in the tree which cannot be reached from the other. The higher the climb, the fewer the remaining alternatives and the larger the number of unreachable points. Each branch grows from the preceding branches.

We would expect the self-conception to grow in such fashion. Each branching point serves to strengthen man's convictions about himself, and his convictions about what he is not. To the extent that he has options, we would expect transactions with the environment to be concentrated on those activities which are consistent with the self-conception, and this has a reinforcing result. As the self-conception takes shape, the individual tends to select those experiences consistent with it, and to avoid inconsistent experiences. Both the private view of self and the publicly viewable personality thus gain continuity and stability. It is possible to recognize a friend, acquaintance, or enemy after five or twenty years as the same person you knew before. And it is possible for open-system man to recognize himself as having continuity through time.

A GENERAL PROPOSITION

We find it helpful, in trying to understand day-to-day behavior of "normal" people, to assume that *man maneuvers in his environment to attain the most favorable self-conception he perceives to be possible.*

This proposition may not be adequate for conditions of extreme danger, fatigue, hunger, or thirst, but we believe that it has considerable utility for understanding the behavior of open-system man under the kinds of environmental conditions you and we face regularly.

The proposition has an important feature: It permits variation either in man's self-concept or in his environment, or in both. Thus it permits us to think of a self-confident man aggressively seeking more challenging environments, but it also allows us to picture an increasingly demanding environment which threatens to overwhelm an individual's competence, and we would expect defensive behavior or retreat. Thus we have room for the persistence and stability of personality which enables us to spot old friends or enemies years later. But our proposition also leaves room for significant changes, the kind which occasionally lead us to say that some friend has "found himself" or "bloomed" in recent years, and that another is "a broken man."

THE RECHANNELED INDIVIDUAL

The self, as the core of personality, is a force for coherence and stability and becomes especially important in a highly differentiated or fluctuating environment, or when the individual is in a developmental channel that is being rerouted. The significance of the self in steering the individual at branching points helps explain why most individuals do develop in predictable ways. Yet we cannot ignore the fact that there are enough unique cases in every modern society to make the unpredicted career notable and newsworthy. The farm boy who becomes chief executive of a modern nation; the steelworker's daughter who becomes an opera star; the coal miner's son who becomes a professional sports hero; the truck driver's son who builds a large corporation; or the tailor's son who becomes a distinguished scientist: These examples of switching from one channel to another cannot be explained simply as examples of the rerouting of a generation.

The processes by which such cases occur are not well understood, but we do have some tools which appear useful in thinking about them. How does it happen that some individuals acquire aspirations and self-conceptions different from those held out in the family, the neighborhood, and the school? After all, we have argued that the developmental experiences not only provide certain kinds of content and reinforce it by guiding the individual's contacts to others with similar experiences, but that this also denies the individual contact with the content from other segments of the larger society.

The best answer yet available is that in modern urban societies there are enough cross-cutting patterns of interaction and enough channels of communication to occasionally expose an individual to an unexpected or *atypical reference group*. By "reference group" the social scientist refers to (1) a social category which may serve the individual as a standard for comparison (keeping up with the Joneses), (2) a target for aspirations to membership (election to an honorary society), or (3) a source of perspective or orientation (a "world view" characteristic, for example, of the "new left" or the "establishment").

> 　*The notion of* reference group *was introduced by social psychologist Herbert Hyman. Among those who have explored its importance have been Robert K. Merton and Tamotsu Shibutani.*　<

Reference groups, of course, are important to all of us. The channeling aspects of development are reinforced by reference groups which are consistent and compatible with the structures we occupy and the cognitive content we acquire.　But on occasion unusual or atypical reference groups displace the expected ones.　This is relatively infrequent, even though in modern societies many persons are *aware* of the existence of social categories quite different from themselves.　Awareness of difference does not necessarily result in using the other category as a reference group, even when such a category is held in awe or in envy.

If an atypical reference group is to perform a channel-switching function for the developing person, he must imagine himself living or behaving or thinking as he believes members of that reference group do. His self-conception must be stretched.　Moreover, he must believe that there are things he can do to achieve such a result; he must perceive cause/effect connections between himself and the manner of behavior characteristic of the new reference group.　Thus it is not enough to know that others live and think and behave differently from you, or even to know how they live and think and behave.　Such knowledge must also be coupled with perceptions of ways of going about becoming like them.　If this is true, it makes such rechanneling an unlikely event, for the filters we experience in development usually preclude such connections.

Apart from chance meetings, which may certainly activate atypical reference groups but which we cannot very well anticipate, there appear to be two conditions favorable to rechanneling of individuals through atypical reference groups.

First, some individuals are especially gifted or specially endowed with abilities or potential skills which are in great demand but scarce supply.　When professional sports are highly developed and prized,

for example, talent-searching agencies seek out unnoticed or unde-
veloped talents and encourage their development. When scientists
are in short supply, teachers are alerted to identify promising prospects, stimulate children, channel their aspirations, and direct them to
scholarship opportunities. Some special endowments go unnoticed,
either because they are not appreciated in a particular age, or because
there are few agencies to discover and steer the individual into those
structures in which his talents can be developed or exploited. Only if
the individual with special endowment acquires the aspiration to develop and perceives opportunities to do so will that endowment rechannel him.

Second, occasionally historical events provide unpredicted opportunities in the form of new positions, and these opportunities are
seized by some who thus are diverted from usual channels. With industrialization and the resulting emergence of industrial unionism in
modern societies, at least one generation of labor union leaders must
be recruited from channels which otherwise would have led elsewhere.
Major wars seem inevitably to rechannel some members of the society
permanently, by exposing them to new reference groups, new possibilities for self-conception, new understandings of how to go about
pursuing new opportunities. Where modern societies produce new
"movements" based on nationalism or race, we would also expect a
generation of leaders to be recruited from other channels.

When unpredicted demands arise, reaction to them may not be
automatic. The opportunities must be perceived and translated into
terms of aspirations, and the individual must decide that there are
things he can do to take advantage of such opportunities. It must appear that the future to which the opportunity leads is both realistic and
desirable in terms of the self-concept.

The great bulk of population in any society, then, develops in the
channels of its generation, and rechanneling of the individual in isolation is unusual. This must be so, because the society cannot function
unless its socializing agencies are reasonably reliable in preparing each
generation with the aspirations, beliefs, norms, and interpretations
consistent with the realities it faces. Such preparations do not occur
through random or chance exposure of open-system man to the environment.

Keeping the development of each generation consistent with the realities it will face is clearly easier in folk societies with their stability than in modern urban societies with their characteristic tendencies to change. Folk societies can rely to a large extent on the *transmission* of culture, and for this the family is an effective agency. Modern urban societies must also rely on families for transmission of culture or sub-culture, but the family is not an adequate agency for socialization to the highly segmented and specialized positions of modern societies, nor for the invention of new knowledge. Hence the educational system becomes central.

One of the problems for modern societies is whether their families are adequately transmitting basic culture, but a second significant problem is whether families are adequately preparing the child for the crucial transition to the school. Still another question is whether the educational system is appropriately geared to changing requirements, whether it is socializing members for positions which will become obsolete shortly, and whether it functions to re-equip individuals when their cognitive content becomes outdated. These are topics to which we shall return in a later chapter.

RECAPITULATION

Emerging as an adult person is a channeled experience in every society. Modernizing societies generally contain several subcultures, each serving as a channel, but individuals are not equally exposed to all possible channels. Instead, each tends to reach maturity with goals, beliefs about reality and about causation, and norms which are characteristic of his starting channel. In periods of rapid societal change, the channel may be diverted while man is developing, but this too is patterned. Yet in transactions with his environment, open-system man does acquire a distinctiveness which others recognize as personality and which he experiences as his self. Man's concept of himself guides his interaction with the environment, thus making for continuity and orderly development in spite of physiological and social life cycles which force man to change. We have suggested as a guiding principle that man maneuvers in his environment to get the best self-conception he believes possible.

RECOMMENDED BROWSING

T. W. Adorno, Else Frankel-Brunswik, D. J. Levinson, and R. N. Sanford, *The Authoritarian Personality*. New York: Harper and Row, 1950. This controversial study has had significant impact on research into personality.

Gordon W. Allport, *Pattern and Growth in Personality*. New York: Holt, Rinehart, and Winston, 1961. A forceful statement of the transactional approach to personality.

Charles Horton Cooley, *Human Nature and the Social Order*. New York: Free Press (reprinted edition), 1956. One of the first considerations of the self-conception and its development.

Allison Davis and John Dollard, *Children of Bondage*. Washington, D.C.: American Council on Education, 1940. An important examination of the personality development of eight adolescent members of the black minority in the United States.

Erik Erikson, *Childhood and Society*. New York: Norton, 1963. An important analysis of the development of the person in interaction with environment.

E. Franklin Frazier, *Race and Culture Contacts in the Modern World*. New York: Knopf, 1957. Overview of race and ethnic factors in relation to economic, political, and attitudinal behavior, with the increased interaction of modernization.

Calvin Hall and Gardner Lindzey, *Theories of Personality*. New York: Wiley, 1957. Examination of various theoretical approaches to personality from the starting point of psychology and psychiatry.

August B. Hollingshead, *Elmtown's Youth: The Impact of Social Classes on Adolescents*. New York: Wiley, 1949. Empirical study of adolescent behavior in schools, work, religion, recreation and sex, as influenced by the family's social position.

Herbert Hyman, "The Psychology of Status," *Archives of Psychology*, 1942, No. 269. Initial formulation of the concept of reference group.

C. G. Jung, *The Basic Writings of C. G. Jung*, edited by V. de Laszlo. New York: Random House, 1959. Analysis of personality in terms of extroversion and introversion which had considerable impact on the field of personality.

Dorothea Leighton and Clyde Kluckhohn, *Children of the People: The Navaho Individual and his Development*. Cambridge, Mass.: Harvard University Press, 1947. Describes growing up in a society in which families are often widely separated, but in which the effects of this distance are modified by clan organization.

Kurt Lewin, *A Dynamic Theory of Personality.* New York: McGraw-Hill, 1935. A collection of Lewin's essays focusing field theory on the personality.

Oscar Lewis, *La Vida: A Puerto Rican Family in the Culture of Poverty—San Juan and New York.* New York: Random House, 1966. This biography of a slum family reflects cultural adaptations to deprivation and exploitation.

Ralph Linton, *The Cultural Background of Personality.* New York: Appleton-Century-Crofts, 1945. A classic statement of the impact of culture on personality development.

Robert S. Lynd and Helen M. Lynd, *Middletown,* New York: Harcourt, Brace, 1929; and *Middletown in Transition,* New York: Harcourt, Brace, 1937. Illuminates the community as a place to develop, at two periods in transition.

Abraham H. Maslow, *Motivation and Personality.* New York: Harper, 1954. An important treatment stressing a hierarchy of motives.

David C. McClelland, J. W. Atkinson, R. A. Clark, and E. L. Lowell, *The Achievement Motive.* New York: Appleton-Century-Crofts, 1953. An important book which generated considerable research.

George Herbert Mead, *Mind, Self, and Society.* Chicago: University of Chicago Press, 1934. An early classic on the relation of society to personality.

Robert K. Merton, with Alice S. Rossi, "Contributions to the Theory of Reference Group Behavior," and "Continuities in the Theory of Reference Groups and Social Structure," in Merton, *Social Theory and Social Structure,* revised edition. New York: Free Press of Glencoe, 1957. One of the major statements and review of research employing the reference group concept.

Thomas F. Pettigrew, *A Profile of the American Negro.* Princeton, N.J.: Van Nostrand, 1964. An examination of a "caste group" in a variety of realms, and the consequences of discrimination against them.

Jean Piaget, *Six Psychological Studies,* translated from French by Anita Tenzer and edited by David Elkind. New York: Random House, 1968. An introductory sample of the pioneering work on cognitive growth of Piaget.

David Riesman, in collaboration with Reuel Denney and Nathan Glazer, *The Lonely Crowd.* New Haven: Yale University Press, 1950. An important book setting forth distinctions between other-, tradition-, and inner-directed man.

Milton Rokeach, *The Open and Closed Mind.* New York: Basic Books, 1960. A study of closed-mindedness as a personality characteristic related to cognition.

Carl Rogers, *On Becoming a Person: A Therapist's View of Therapy.* Boston: Houghton Mifflin, 1961.

Tamotsu Shibutani, "Reference Groups as Perspectives," *American Journal of Sociology*, **60** (May 1955), 562–570. A useful review and evaluation of various usages of the reference group concept.

William I. Thomas and Florian Znaniecki, *The Polish Peasant in Europe and America*. Boston: Richard G. Badger, 1920. Monumental study covering the rerouting of new generations in new surroundings.

Edward C. Tolman, *Purposive Behavior in Animals and Man*. New York: Century, 1951. Reissue of a classic early statement which helped lay the foundations for the open-system model.

Jack E. Weller, *Yesterday's People: Life in Contemporary Appalachia*. Lexington, Ky.: University of Kentucky Press, 1966. Describes socializing experiences of those growing up in an almost-folk component of society.

Robert A. White, "Motivation Reconsidered: The Concept of Competence," *Psychological Review*, **66** (September 1959), 297–333.

MAN THROUGH TIME AND SPACE

To the extent that man is a product of his experiences, we gain understanding of different men by studying their environments, which mandate and delimit some important experiences. Obviously location in physical space determines the exposure of men and women to geography, climate, and similar physical and biological factors. A more subtle but nevertheless profound set of influences come from the distribution of humans in *social space,* and we need to see how social space is viewed in the social sciences.

Time, too, makes a difference. The Middle Ages afforded man certain kinds of experiences different from the experiences of the Renaissance, and the 1970s will afford experiences different from the 1960s. But calendar time is not all; we must also be able to explain different patterns in the orientation of men and women toward the future, and relate these to previous experiences. Thus we need a conception of the present which reflects man's past experiences but recognizes purpose and the future.

SOCIAL DIFFERENTIATION   CHAPTER 4

The more channels a society contains for developing its young, the more differentiation we would expect among the adults produced through these channels. In a complicated society, then, there are important differences in the ways adults perceive and respond to their environments. These patterns are referred to as styles of living, or *life styles,* and our problem now is to find some way to describe and analyze life styles.

It is in the family and in work that life style variations can best be seen. This statement may seem surprising, after the discussion in the preceding chapter in which we indicated the limitations of the family in modern developmental processes, and distinguished folk and modern urban types partly in terms of the significance given to kinship systems. For a time, some social scientists believed that the family was being eclipsed in modern societies, but the more recent view is that while the family's functions are indeed shifting, the family still is the nexus of modern social life. True, the school joins the family as a socializing agency in modern society. True, the church or temple or movement joins the family as a religious institution. True, economic production is accomplished in positions specialized in economic structures rather than within the family context.

> *Among those specializing in the study of the family are Ernest W. Burgess, Clifford Kirkpatrick, Reuben Hill, William J. Goode, and Elizabeth Bott.*   <

Yet the central role of the family in mediating and coordinating these and other activities cannot be ignored, and it is perhaps most clearly felt when the modern family disintegrates. With divorce or death of an adult member, the modern family must make significant adjustments in economic arrangements, care of the children, social participation, and emotional involvements.

We need to recognize the significance of the fact that the family deploys its members into other kinds of organizations, especially work organizations. Family and economic activity are highly interdependent in all societies, including the modern versions. With economic activity taking the form of jobs and occupations, work becomes a significant determinant of family residence; of access to education, health services, material consumption, recreational activities, and similar matters.

Types of Families

Undoubtedly the most widespread type of family is what social scientists term the *nuclear* family, consisting of one husband, one wife, and their offspring. Although polygamy (one wife, several husbands or one husband, several wives) is recognized and practiced in a number of societies, in most—and especially in modern urban societies—the nuclear family is an identifiable social unit with significance for its members. The second type of family most commonly distinguished in the social sciences is termed the *extended* family, which consists of two or more nuclear families united by blood ties: Here we are not defining the family simply in terms of genetic relationships but rather in terms of role responsibilities among kin. Which of the husband's or wife's kin become relevant is a variable determined by the culture, not just by genetic lines. Most nuclear families, however, are embedded in some kind of extended family; what kind, and how deeply embedded, are variables. Usually the extended family involves generations, with grandparents involved. Frequently the extended family involves considerable lateral interdependence: brothers and their offspring, sisters and theirs forming units within which most of the economic, religious, political, and socializing activities take place. In modern urban societies, however, family members are deployed into non-kin groups or organizations for the bulk of such activities, and the extended family becomes of less daily significance. We would therefore expect the extended family to claim a large share of the adult individual's attention in the folk society, but considerably less attention in the modern urban civilization, where attention is more likely to be divided among nuclear family, occupation, and friendship networks. The evidence is growing, however, that even in modern, urbanized, mobile societies, the generationally extended family has legitimate claims on the individual and is a source of support for him.

> *Numerous anthropological studies report societies in which the extended family (embedded in some larger clan, lineage, or tribe) forms the context or arena for most activities.* <

In very general terms, we can think of the folk society as emphasizing the extended family and modern urban society focusing on the nuclear family, but with those two kinds of focus being extremes on a continuum.

The Structure of Families

When the extended family is the basic social unit for economic production and distribution, for socialization, for religious activity, for health care, as well as for sex, then each member is likely to occupy a large variety of roles within that dominant structure. Each individual personality must relate to other individuals within the extended family in a variety of ways. Just as a competitive sports team may relate its members in one way for defense and in another for offense, the family must arrange the same individuals in one pattern for economic production, into another for socialization or religious observances, still another for health care, and so on. Each member, then, occupies many roles within the single dominant structure.

When the nuclear family emerges as the dominant type, most members are deployed by the family into other structures for specialized purposes. One or more members is assigned to economic production, to a job. One or more is assigned to the market, to organize consumption activities. One or more is assigned to school. Basic health care may be provided within the nuclear family, but beyond daily needs the individual is likely to be referred to professional health personnel in a clinic or hospital. Some or all members venture out to a religious organization for religious support. In modern urban society, many of the responsibilities to the family are fulfilled by participation in non-family organizations; the individual then has *multiple positions,* one each in several unrelated social units.

In both cases—multiple roles in an all-encompassing unit or mul-
· tiple positions in a set of specialized units—the family serves more or less well as the regulator of stress or conflict. But the manner in which this emotional support is given varies between the two types. In the extended family, support can be relatively diffuse; the loss of one member, for example, may not seriously disrupt activities. But in the nuclear family, support is a rather specific responsibility, and the loss of one member usually is a serious disruption. In the modern urban society, then, the family serves (more or less effectively) to provide meaning or reason for participation in other organizations, to handle the conflicting demands which multiple positions can place on individuals, and to integrate the activities of the several deployed members by assigning priorities. One of the high-priority items for most families in modern urban society is occupation.

Occupational Differentiation

In the traditional society, the very notion of job or *occupation* is alien. Productive activities and consumption are regulated by the kinship unit or tribe as part of the overall rhythm of life, and are not segmented into recognizably different structures. It does not make sense to ask a member of such a society what he "does" for a "living," because he does what virtually all of his sex and age do.

Even in modern urban society, the rural, agricultural component reveals something of this pattern, with productive and consumption activities tightly bound up with other activities of the family. There does appear to be a noticeable trend toward corporate agriculture (or agri-business) which introduces into farming the distinctions which elsewhere in modern urban societies have culminated in the notion of an occupation.

One basic distinction in the analysis of labor, then, is between farm and nonfarm labor, and generally it is in the nonfarm category that we speak of *occupations.* There are many ways of sorting occupations out; distinguishing blue collar from white collar, or semi-skilled from crafts from professions, or self-employed from employed. For present purposes, we shall not get that detailed, but it is important that we consider briefly two major themes which underly the proliferation of occupations in modern urban societies. One of these themes is the refinement of discretionary or decision-making abilities. The other is the routinization of activities.

Discretionary Occupations

One major reason for the specialization of occupations is the cultivation of discretionary abilities. By confining his attention to one range of illnesses, the physician is able to make refined decisions, informed both by specialized knowledge and by experience. By specializing in one kind of material and one set of tools, the cabinetmaker can make refined judgments in the selection of woods for various purposes, and in their methods of treatment. By specializing in marketing, the executive can cultivate skill in sensing market reactions to new products. The artist, the lawyer, the priest, the sculptor, the novelist, and the hairdresser are all examples of persons whose specialization permits the accrual of experience and the absorption of knowledge which permit increased competence.

> *Social scientists have been examining work under a variety of labels: industrial sociology and industrial social psychology; occupations and professions; sociology of work and organizational psychology.*   <

Routinized Occupations

A second reason for the proliferation of occupations in modern society is routinization of activities in large networks of interdependence, to obtain increased precision and reliability. This is especially well illustrated by the process of industrialization, which has segmented complicated activities into sets of relatively simple tasks, each assigned to a specialist who by repeated performance achieves the desired competence. Although the production line is the best-known example, routinization is a widespread practice in many large organizations. Its spread rests on the fact that although the total industrial process may be quite complex, the minute segments which are routinized become relatively simple, calling for little skill and being quickly learned. It is not surprising that the routinized occupations have been those most challenged by automation.

PREPARATION FOR OCCUPATIONS

Whether distilled into distinct occupations or not, work involves skills. Occupations differ from one another not only in the skills they require but also in the ways those skills are acquired. In the traditional society we would expect the skills to be acquired in the basic socialization processes within the family or kinship unit, and to be developed through practice as a member of the productive organization. We would also expect this to be an important avenue for learning for the agricultural, rural sector of modern societies, although as corporate agriculture develops, the family becomes less significant as the source of occupational learning.

Thus, in the folk setting, we expect the family to be a major avenue for preparation for work. But what happens when the knowledge required exceeds that of the family? What happens when the practice of an art or craft or profession is removed from the family setting, so that the individual has little or no opportunity to learn in that setting? The answers to such questions appear to depend on the extent to which we are dealing with discretionary as opposed to routinized occupations; and within the discretionary category, it depends on the extent to which preparation rests on tutelage or formal abstract knowledge.

Preparation for Discretionary Occupations

Discretionary occupations with a large knowledge base—requiring formal schooling—generally lodge responsibility for preparation on the members of the occupation itself. In modern societies, the medical profession usually operates or supervises medical schools and nursing schools; the legal profession usually oversees the training of lawyers; the religious professions generally operate schools of theology, and the engineering professions oversee schools of engineering. In each case, the profession controls admission to training and admission to practice after the training is completed: The doctor is formally admitted to practice, the lawyer is admitted to the bar, and the priest is ordained. Usually this control is exercised, in the name of the state, by organized bodies of the profession, on grounds that possession of the knowledge could be used to harm laymen unless carefully guarded, and only members of the profession can judge competence and ethics.

In the skilled crafts—such as printing, silversmithing, glassblowing, cabinetmaking—the responsibility for training tends to be lodged also in the occupation, but here the "professional school" is replaced by an apprenticeship system. This has a distinct parallel to the folk situation, and often the apprenticeships are awarded to the children of members of the craft, thus perpetuating family identification with it. But teaching of the skilled crafts in modern urban societies usually is the responsibility of a guild or union. The arts also rely on tutelage or apprenticeship for the preparation of a next generation.

Generally speaking, preparation of the next generation for an occupation is the responsibility of those who have the necessary knowledge or skill. Hence when the family is not able to perform this function and preparation is difficult, control of the socialization process usually resides in *colleagues*. If the knowledge component is large, colleagues control formal education channels; if the applied-skill component is large, colleagues control an apprenticeship system.

There is one large additional category of discretionary jobs for which those statements are less true, at least at present. We refer to occupations that can be labeled managerial or administrative, and that entail skill in the operation of complex organizations or major segments of those organizations. Although there are emerging—all over the world —"professional" schools of administration, it is fair to say that these do not now have the same solid foundations of abstract knowledge as have schools of medicine, law, theology, or engineering, nor have managers achieved sufficient organization as an occupational group to exercise effective control over such schools. Whether this will eventually develop is a moot point.

Preparation for Routinized Occupations

Preparation for routinized occupations is less well controlled and delineated. Routinized occupations evolve because technologies are subdivided into series of jobs calling for relatively little skill. The overall result may be considerable complexity, but the secret is in the way the simplified segments are related in the logic of the technology. Because each segment is rather precise, discretion within the job is severely restricted. Such occupations therefore do not require the long, patient, educational processes of the arts and professions and crafts. Assuming that the basic educational system is turning out literate persons able to perform simple calculations and follow instructions, the organizations using technologies calling for routine occupations can easily add the detailed knowledge of local conditions and regulations. The young man with a "normal" education in modern society can quickly be taught to operate a punch press in a factory, or pack cartons in a shipping room, or work on an assembly line. The young woman with a "normal" education in modern societies can quickly be taught to operate a supermarket cash register, or drive a taxi, or work on an assembly line. Whereas we concluded that discretionary jobs are controlled by colleagues, we now conclude that routinized occupations are controlled by the *enterprises* in which they are lodged.

Now we need to remind ourselves that developmental channels lead in different directions, and to note that this fact applies to occupations as well as to other aspects of life. In modern urban societies, it is conceivable (though not likely) that a reasonably well-educated adult might suddenly decide to enter a routinized occupation, but one does not decide suddenly as an adult to enter one of the discretionary occupations. These are entered through certain preparatory channels and not through others, and unless the decision to enter is made early enough, that path is closed.

Whatever the channels, differences in occupations together with differences in types of families result in differences in styles of living.

DISTINCTIVE LIFE STYLES

Visit in a stranger's home, and if his style of life is unlike yours, you immediately notice some of the ways in which his differs. Furniture may differ, not simply in quality but in type or style. Art objects, kinds of clothing, reading materials and musical devices may strike you as having been selected from a "menu" different from yours. Tastes in food and drink and methods of cooking may be distinctive. Speech within the home may be noticeably different from yours, in vocabulary, grammar, and topics of conversation. Stay long enough to notice, and the family may use its leisure in ways very unlike the way you use your leisure. Stay long enough and you may find that their monetary budget—not only in size but in the priorities assigned to various categories—may contrast with yours. Stay long enough and you may find that their relations with children and their methods of discipline and training are unlike those familiar to you. Most notably, the density of people in the dwelling and residential area may contrast sharply with your life style. This becomes significant in determining the amount of privacy available, noise levels, and frequency of interaction.

Or follow one of that household to work and you may quickly be struck by the patterns you find. Type of clothing or uniform may be distinctive. Attendance may be regulated by the time clock or not, and working hours may or may not be regulated to "the shift." Payment may be on an hourly basis, a weekly salary, or annual contract; settlement may be at the end of each week, biweekly, or monthly. Work may be performed in privacy or in the presence of others. It may be performed near the worker's residence, with daily trips from home to shop or office or factory, or it may necessitate periodic and sometimes extended departures, as is often the case in transport, military, and construction industries.

These and many other possible differences point up the fact that life in modern societies is significantly patterned by the family setting and the occupation, and since both of these vary considerably, the resulting styles of life do also. But these immediately obvious differences merely reflect more significant themes in life styles, and our problem now is to find ways of getting beneath the surface to find ways of describing quality and texture of various life styles. These should reflect differences in the values of the family and in the priorities attached to those values. They should reflect differences in perspectives and interpretations of reality. And they should reflect differences in interaction patterns. In short, we are looking for ways of summarizing some of the differences we have been saying were important.

Categories to tap these kinds of differences are not easy to find, and our descriptions will be imperfect and incomplete. But we can get some useful leverage by using a set of dimensions developed by Talcott Parsons and Edward A. Shils and known as the *pattern variables* (because they deal with variable ways of patterning relationships). They offer five, but we shall work with only four, each being a continuum, so that the family can be described by the degree to which it is oriented in one direction or its opposite.

One of the major distinctions we noted earlier was between families which deploy their members outward to positions in specialized structures or, on the other hand, engage their members in multiple roles within the extended kinship network. In another context we noted that industrialization was accompanied by specialization of positions. Now when relationships are highly specialized, we speak of their *specificity,* and when parties to a relationship are expected to be completely engaged in any particular encounter, we speak of their *diffuseness.* The general expectation for professors and students, in dealing with each other, is one of specificity; only those matters dealing with the educational process and the topic at hand are supposed to be significant in the relationship. But the expected behavior of friends toward one another is diffuse; good friends draw few limits to the sacrifices they will make for one another. Now we want to say that family life styles can be distinguished on the *specificity/diffuseness* dimension, giving us a summary of the degree to which the family is embedded in networks of specific or of diffuse expectations.

Another important distinction in life styles revolves around the gratification of impulses versus discipline. Some families characteristically encourage the display of emotions in various contexts, while other families emphasize restraint, neutrality, and the masking of emotions. Some permit public displays of affection, others frown on it. Some encourage grasping opportunities for satisfactions whenever available, others preach deferring gratifications while preparing for the future. We suggest that here, too, the family life styles can be distinguished on the dimension of *impulsiveness/discipline* (which Parsons and Shils label one of affectivity/affective neutrality).

Still another useful dimension refers to the degree to which relationships are governed by principles or by personalities. When it is believed that others should be treated according to abstract general principles, we speak of *universalism*; in modern societies, for example, government officials are expected to treat all citizens equally and impartially. When it is believed that relations should be guided by personal loyalties, by who the other party is, we speak of *particularism*; the government official in more traditional societies may be expected to give preferential treatment to members of his family or to his friends, for in traditional societies relationships are often guided by particularistic expectations. When families are making the transition from folklike rural society to more modern urban living, the generations may disagree over the universalism/particularism dimension, with the older generation expecting older, employed children to use their influence to get good jobs for others in the family.

Another important distinction that we noted earlier was between ascribed statuses and achieved positions. Recall that ascribed statuses are those into which the individual is born or which, by virtue of birth and maturation, he grows into. Achieved positions, in contrast, are those he acquires through effort. Now we want to argue that families differ in the extent to which they defer to others because of ascribed characteristics or because of achievements, and they differ in the extent to which the family itself expects to be regarded on one or the other of those criteria. We shall refer to this dimension as one of *ascription/achievement*.

To these four pattern variables, we shall add a final dimension which should help us appreciate differences in life styles, this one having to do with spatial orientations, and called a *local/cosmopolitan* dimension. For the family with a local orientation, significant events are primarily those which happen nearby, significant persons are those seen and interacted to or with regularly. Place—habitual and traditional location—sets the boundaries within which friends and spouses are found, work is carried out, and life cycles are expected to unfold. Virtually everything perceived in the locality has significance. Uprooting of families with this local orientation (for example, in urban renewal programs) is usually a traumatic experience. Families with the cosmopolitan characteristics, however, place less emphasis on location as a permanent matter. They tend to find significance in and pay attention to more distant matters—to national or international developments, or to the arts and sciences more generally—and to be only selectively concerned with local matters. The occupational career may carry them from one community or city to another, and hence they may have networks of friends scattered over a wide territory. For families with the cosmopolitan orientation, geographic location is subordinate to ideas, events, or career.

>   *Robert K. Merton introduced this distinction in a study of community influence. Alvin W. Gouldner extended the notion to occupations.*   <

Now we can suggest that the family is not free to simply choose a comfortable position on each of these five dimensions. The culture or subculture from which members of the family emerge instills an outlook and a definition of appropriate orientations, and part of the developmental process involves learning them. Furthermore, these five dimensions are interrelated, and we would expect consistency among them. They tend to go together as depicted below:

Folk society	*Modern urban society*
Diffuse relationships	Specific relationships
Impulsive	Disciplined
Particularistic	Universal
Ascription	Achievement
Local	Cosmopolitan

Thus the consistency we note among positions on those five dimensions has a functional basis. It is reinforced by channeled learning during the developmental process, and by the fact that new families are seldom formed through marriage of partners whose orientations on these five dimensions are radically different. Hence if we observe that a family is highly cosmopolitan or disciplined, we can usually infer

that it is also specific and universal and achievement-oriented. Likewise, knowing that a family is impulsive and particularistic also tells
us that it is probably diffuse, ascriptive, and local.

Because most societies currently are in some stage of modernization,
they reveal evidence of both life styles, with many families somewhere
near the midpoint, but some more oriented toward either of the two
poles. Now if families can be differentiated, they can also be evaluated
and ranked, and this brings us to the topic of social stratification.

STRATIFICATION

Some form of stratification exists in all societies, but there is a wide
variety of stratification systems. We would have to expect this, because
we have said that the basis for stratification is evaluation, and evaluation by members of a society reflects the basic standards or values
prevalent in that society. To the extent that each society has developed a distinctive culture, reflecting local conditions and problems
and unique traditions associated with them, we would expect a distinctive set of standards for ranking. Thus the factors which would result
in high ranking in one society may not yield high evaluation in a neighboring one.

> *Among those specializing in the study of stratification have been
Joseph Kahl, Gerhard Lenski, Pitirim Sorokin, and W. Lloyd Warner.* <

Nevertheless it is possible to find patterns in stratification systems
by placing them on the folk-society/modern-urban-society continuum.
In the former, stratification reflects ascribed traits or qualities, with
some families inheriting the status of rulers and others of ruled; some
inheriting the status of freeman, others of slave; some inheriting priestly
statuses, others being commoners. Where such status differences are
inherited and this is reinforced by religious or moral sanctions, we
speak of a *caste* system of stratification, and in the pure case no individual or family would be able to change its status. Even as a society
moves in the direction away from the folk end of the continuum, with
more elaborate differentiation of labor, education, residence, and

wealth, its stratification system may be basically one of caste, as in India until recently and among the ancient Incas. Not infrequently caste differentiations are based on race or ethnicity, and such distinctions may indeed hold over into societies which are otherwise rather far on the continuum toward the modern urban type.

At the other end of the continuum, stratification is based on performance or accomplishment. Here, too, status reflects the standards of the society and can vary from one society to another; but as we indicated in an earlier chapter, modern urban societies tend to converge, and hence the bases for stratification seem rather similar. Such societies, moreover, are characterized by *social mobility*, the movement of families from one location to another in the stratification system. The bases for such movement, in the pure case, are achievement or lack of it; hence mobility may be upward or downward. And in the pure case—sometimes termed the "open society"—upward mobility is a possibility for every family.

Multiple Bases of Stratification

We have indicated that most of the world's societies are in transition, with the more modern, urban societies still containing vestiges of ascribed criteria, and the less modern, more rural societies taking on some of the characteristics of an achievement orientation. Thus even in our kind of society, there exist multiple (and sometimes inconsistent) standards for stratification. Inherited wealth, for example, elicits deference from many, even in the most modern of current societies. Distinguished ancestry may yield status, just as race or ethnicity may prevent the attainment of status. Even in the most modern of contemporary societies, the differences in bases for stratification are noticeable if we compare rural areas with metropolitan ones, the former emphasizing ascription more than the latter.

Contemporary urban societies, then, are characterized by multiple bases of stratification because they are in transition. But there is another important reason for the multiplicity of standards, which would persist even if the society were fully in the modern urban state. Multiplicity of standards also results from the extensive diversity of activities and life styles. With so many different things to be done—achieved—and with each family limited in its ability to comprehend the total, there is no single standard against which all families can be compared. Is accomplishment in the medical field equal to achievement in business? Or in the military or educational fields? Different families have different answers to such questions, and even if there is consensus on the relative importance of one field in relation to the others, specific degrees of accomplishment within one may not be easily compared with specific degrees of achievement in another.

With the multiplicity which results from diversity and lack of total comprehension of differences, performance or achievement must be evaluated through indirect evidence.

Indicators of Status

It has become customary (both for sociologists and for members of modern societies generally) to judge accomplishment in terms of three variables which tend to be associated with accomplishment but are not inevitably linked with it. The three are: education, occupation, and income. One reason for the wide use of these variables is that families can be sorted into a relatively few categories on each (blue-collar, white-collar, professional; or high school, college, postgraduate) and this greatly simplifies the problem of comparison. Another reason for the wide use of these three variables is that evidence for them is relatively visible (or inferrable).

These three variables are usually related, so that knowing a family's rank on one gives a clue to its rank on the others. This is so because in modern societies education is so closely associated with ability to perform, and because income is generally correlated with performance. But education, occupation, and income are by no means perfectly correlated, even in the most modern of contemporary societies, and this appears to be due largely to the fact that such societies reflect ascriptive as well as achievement standards. The perfectly open society, with mobility opportunities for all, would afford equal education opportunities for all, and we have seen in our consideration of channels for development that this is not the case. Even though rerouting does occur, educational exposure is to some extent a matter of inheritance. Some occupations can be passed down from generation to generation, thus precluding entry by those whose ancestors were not in it, and impeding mobility. Wealth can be inherited in contemporary societies, and since economic wealth is a basis for income, income is not automatically a reflection of the accomplishments of a particular nuclear family; it may reflect instead the accomplishment of an earlier generation.

Those close enough to particular families to be able to know the details behind the generally visible evidence may indeed discount that evidence. Nevertheless, since such specific knowledge is not often available, we turn to the three general variables with reasonable confidence in the accuracy of our predictions. These three variables also serve to guide the mobility-inspired family. By asserting that status is gained through increased education, or by rising in the occupational ladder, or by gaining greater income, these general stratification variables serve to channel aspirations for families in contemporary societies. Thus stratification and the emphasis on social mobility direct attention toward the future, a topic we examine in the next chapter.

RECAPITULATION

Because different channels of development in modern societies afford different opportunities and experiences, individuals emerge from them as adults with different styles of living. These differences are best seen in the kinds of families formed and the kinds of occupations entered. Whether the orientation is toward an extended or a nuclear family has significant impact on other aspects of the life style. Whether the occupation is routinized or discretionary has an influence on the family and other aspects of the life style. Hence in modern urban societies families differ considerably in many ways, five of which we have identified. But these differences are not random; they are patterned. The resulting life styles can therefore be compared and evaluated and ranked, resulting in social stratification. Although there is a wide assortment of bases on which societies stratify their members, modern urban civilization emphasizes those indicators which usually go with achievement. The thrust of modern society thus focuses attention on the future, and we turn now to an examination of the impact of the future on man.

RECOMMENDED BROWSING

Bernard Barber, *Social Stratification: A Comparative Analysis of Structure and Process.* New York: Harcourt, Brace and World, 1957. A useful overview of the reasons for and consequences of stratification systems, and how they change.

Reinhard Bendix and Seymour M. Lipset, editors, *Class, Status and Power: Social Stratification in Comparative Perspective* (second edition). New York: Free Press of Glencoe, 1966. A significant collection of theoretical and empirical studies.

Peter Blau and Otis Dudley Duncan, *The American Occupational Structure.* New York: Wiley, 1967. The major examination of occupations and stratification in the United States.

Elizabeth Bott, *Family and Social Network.* London: Tavistock Publications, 1957. Comparison of family structures and processes in two classes in London.

T. B. Bottomore, *Classes in Modern Society.* New York: Pantheon Books, 1966. Examination of the impact of industry on stratification.

Urie Bronfenbrenner, "Socialization and Social Class Through Time and Space," in *Readings in Social Psychology,* edited by Eleanor E. Maccoby, Theodore M. Newcomb, and Eugene L. Hartley. New York: Holt, Rinehart and Winston, 1958. Analytic summary of changing values and resulting changes in child-rearing customs, over a long period.

Theodore Caplow, *The Sociology of Work.* Minneapolis: University of Minnesota Press, 1954. An analysis of occupations and the institutions governing work in modernized society.

Harold Christensen, editor, *Handbook of Marriage and the Family.* Chicago: Rand McNally, 1964.

E. Franklin Frazier, *The Negro Family in the United States* (revised edition), Chicago: University of Chicago Press, 1966. Reveals how Negro families historically attempted to adjust to new and uncertain trends in America.

Herbert J. Gans, *The Urban Villagers: Group and Class in the Life of Italian-Americans.* New York: Free Press of Glencoe, 1962. Insight into life as experienced in an ethnic subculture.

William J. Goode, *The Family.* Englewood Cliffs, N.J.: Prentice-Hall, 1964. An overview of family structure and functions in societies around the world.

Alvin J. Gouldner, "Cosmopolitans and Locals: Toward an Analysis of Latent Social Roles," Parts I and II, *Administrative Science Quarterly,* 2 (December 1957), 281–306 and 2 (March 1958) 444–480. Application of the local/cosmopolitan distinction to organizational roles.

Everett C. Hughes, *Men and Their Work*. New York: Free Press of Glencoe, 1958. Insightful essays on various occupations.

Joseph A. Kahl, *The American Class Structure*. New York: Rinehart, 1957. A useful summary of what is known about social structure in the United States.

Melvin Kohn, "Social Class and the Exercise of Parental Authority," *American Sociological Review*, **24** (June 1959) 352–366. An empirical study of different methods of punishing children, with the conclusion that these differences express different values of the parents.

Gerhard Lenski, *Power and Privilege: A Theory of Social Stratification*. New York: McGraw-Hill, 1966. Considers various bases for stratification and the changes accompanying modernization.

Robert K. Merton, "Patterns of Influence: Local and Cosmopolitan Influentials," in Merton, *Social Theory and Social Structure*, revised edition. New York: Free Press of Glencoe, 1961. Introduces the distinction between local and cosmopolitan orientations, and relates them to community influence patterns.

D. R. Miller and G. E. Swanson, *The Changing American Parent*. New York: Wiley, 1958. Shows that families from bureaucratic and entrepreneurial work settings favor different ends and means of socialization.

George P. Murdock, *Social Structure*. New York: Macmillan, 1949. A controversial but important cross-cultural comparison of the family.

Sigmund Nosow and William H. Form, editors, *Man, Work, and Society*. New York: Basic Books, 1962. Assembles various writings about nature and significance of occupations.

Talcott Parsons and Edward A. Shils, editors, *Toward a General Theory of Action*. Cambridge: Harvard University Press, 1951. Identifies and describes the pattern variable distinctions of ascription/achievement, diffuseness/specificity, universalism/particularlism, and impulsiveness/discipline.

Ethel Shanas and Gordon F. Streib, editors, *Social Structure and the Family: Generational Relations*. Englewood Cliffs, N. J.: Prentice-Hall, 1965. A rich collection of papers on families in modernizing societies.

Martha Strum White, "Social Class, Child-Rearing Practices, and Child Behavior," *American Sociological Review*, **22** (December 1957), 704–712. Reports evidence of class differences in methods of training small children, and suggests that they are associated with quite different reference groups.

CHAPTER 5

SPHERES OF ACTION AND THE FUTURE

Man's behavior is influenced by the future, or more precisely, by his cognitions of the future. Achievement, ambition, the pursuit of goals, purpose—all these notions involve some anticipated or hoped-for future state of affairs. And in those societies which underscore achievement, we would expect views of the future to be conspicuous. Even in the traditional folk society, with its emphasis on ascription, continuity, and stability, we would expect some cognitions of the future, for there are seasonal rhythms to be anticipated and social and biological definitions of the life cycle to make members aware of change.

At a minimum, then, most people are occasionally aware of the inevitability of changing future states for themselves, and to the extent that they can conceive of themselves in those future states, they conceive of a future *life space*. By this we are referring to the individual's anticipated self-conceptions. We said in Chapter 3 that the self-concept is the individual's private view of his personality, a view significantly affected by others' judgments and reactions to him. The future life space thus contains one's private expectations of who he will be in the future, what positions he will occupy, what he will have done, what others will think of him.

> *The term* life space *was introduced by Kurt Lewin and has been used to some extent by Gestalt psychologists. We are using it in a way slightly modified from the traditional.* <

For some, the future life space will be quite extensive, perhaps including even their own obituaries. For others, the time horizon is considerably more restricted; the future emphasized is more immediate and extends perhaps only to the next stage in the life cycle: marriage for the teenage girl, retirement for the sixty-year-old executive, or a first job for the college senior. For still others, the future life space may be predominantely the imminent future: tomorrow, next week or next month. Clearly one important variation in life spaces is the time horizon.

We should expect the time horizon to be affected by one's stage in the life cycle. For the adolescent it may be virtually impossible to imagine the self in old age; even middle age may be only a fuzzy notion, and a career may appear interminable. For the grandparent, on the other hand, much of life is in the past, and the future may appear relatively brief and determined. Even the young adult with considerable foresight is likely to alter or revise his future life space as his experiences reveal more about his self, about what is possible and desirable. This, of course, is more likely to be true in the rapidly changing society than in the more stable one. The folk-oriented person is likely to be less future-oriented than the urban-oriented. For the former, the future is little differentiated, with the exception of ascription—what age will bring. For the latter, not only is it expected that he will grow older and thus experience changes, but that the environment will change as well.

Life spaces also vary in terms of precision or clarity, partly reflecting individual differences in intelligence and imagination, but to a large extent reflecting societal differences. In stable, relatively undifferentiated societies, the individual may see himself previewed in the lives of many others, and he may therefore have rather crystallized and precise expectations for himself in the future. In rapidly changing and highly differentiated societies, the projection of the self is more difficult because of the wide range of possibilities together with the inability to anticipate accurately what opportunities and constraints will arise.

To the extent that an individual has developed a future life space, it can serve to establish directions for aspirations and thus to help the person select among perceived paths to alternative futures. The future life space can serve as a set of criteria for rejecting some paths as incompatible with the self-conception. The more precise and clear the future life space, the more we would expect it to help him in choosing among paths to the future.

But even the most definitive future life space is not sufficient to guide everyday activities. At best, it can guide the person at critical junctures or turning points. We cannot expect the future life space conception to be turned on every morning when we arise. The many episodes of daily life cannot be constantly reflected against the future life space, for at least two reasons: (a) the ultimate consequences of today's actions for the total life frequently are ambiguous (if not trivial), and especially so in modern society, in which activities are segmented and specialized and changing, and (b) even when daily actions can be linked to the future life space, the difficulties of constantly calculating the connections and net results would immobilize us. Limitations on man's cognitive capacities call for some frame of reference less extensive and ultimate than the future life space concept. Yet if man is to have aspirations and take purposive action, he must have a cognitive context for dealing with these daily activities. He must have an arena in which to act, or a *sphere of action.*

SPHERES OF ACTION

How can we begin to deal with the cognitive context for activity which we label an "action sphere?" How can we understand the action sphere for a particular person? We shall begin with some conceptual tools introduced earlier, in our first considerations of man's environment. There we said that individuals occupy *roles* which are built into *positions.* These reciprocal sets of rights and obligations help us identify the kinds of contexts in which daily activities unfold, but the concepts of roles and positions were designed to analyze social structures and by themselves they are not precise or specific enough to define a sphere of action.

Open-system man cannot operate simply by knowing that he is a father and husband, an accountant, a citizen, and a churchgoer. He needs to know—and our concept of action sphere needs to deal with— whose father and husband he is, where and with whom he employs his accounting skills, what political unit he is a citizen of, and which church or temple he attends. Because our open-system man occupies the role of husband does not mean that his rights and obligations are reciprocal to any or all who occupy the role of wife, even if he is man enough to try! He occupies roles in specific positions, lodged in specific social units, and these determine not only which roles are reciprocal to his, but also which other persons respond to him, recognize the legitimacy of his claims on them, and in turn place demands on him.

Now if we map *all* the roles and positions occupied by an individual at a particular period or stage of his life, and identify all the roles and positions as well as persons reciprocal to him, we have described his sphere of action.

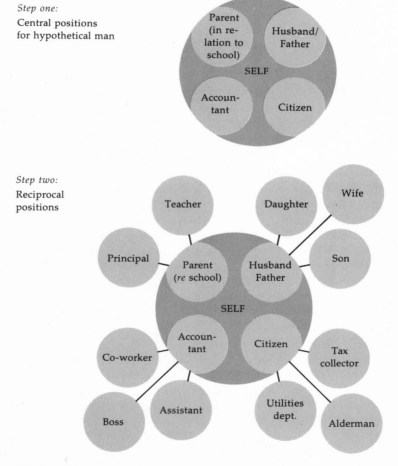

Step one:
Central positions
for hypothetical man

Step two:
Reciprocal
positions

FIG. 5.1   *Schematic construction of a hypothetical (simplified) sphere of action.*

Step three: Action sphere, persons and positions connected to self at one stage in life

FIG. 5.1 (continued)

Figure 5.1 is a much simplified description of a hypothetical sphere of action. (In modern society, it is extremely difficult to display graphically all the roles and positions and other persons of significance to a particular person.) Step 1 in the figure shows a few central positions held by a hypothetical man; step 2 identifies the reciprocal positions; and step 3 displays the action sphere, including the persons with whom the individual's present positions connect.

As can be seen from step 3, the action sphere shows where man fits in society. It tells him (and us) what he does not belong to as well as what he does. It shows whether and where he hooks into medical, education, economic, religious, military, political institutions. It determines who has significance for him, and for whom he is a significant person. The action sphere thus is a social arena in which to seek satisfaction of his needs and aspirations. It therefore defines resources and opportunites and constraints for the person.

Variations in Action Spheres

One source of variation in action spheres has already been touched on, in Chapter 3. The channels for development discussed there can be seen as affording sequences of action spheres: first, for the child, in the family and neighborhood, later changing to include the school, and still later to include job structures. Each action sphere presented certain opportunities and constraints which made entry into the next action sphere both possible and likely and precluded others, and it was this orderly sequencing of action spheres which made it possible to identify routes or channels for development. This sequencing—of learning and of action spheres—continues into and through the adult life as well, with the action sphere delimiting access to various kinds of learning and directing opportunities for putting learning to use.

One significant kind of variation of action spheres is the richness or breadth of opportunities they offer. Some put man in touch with most of the major institutions of society, giving him the opportunity to penetrate deeply into educational, medical, business and financial, religious, and political streams of his society. Some action spheres, on the other hand, afford a relatively meager set of opportunities, leaving the individual on the periphery of those same institutions. Generally speaking, opportunities in these several directions are correlated; if opportunity to participate in educational or economic affairs is great, then opportunity to participate in the others is also great. Conversely, if constraints are strong in educational or economic directions, they usually are also strong in the others, except for religion. This fact of configuration is consistent with our earlier observations on life styles and stratification. Achievement in educational or economic institutions generally provides resources—both financial resources and resources of knowledge of appropriate roles—for other institutions.

Another important way in which action spheres differs from one another is in the degree to which the significant other persons in the action sphere are themselves interdependent. In the folk society, for example, an individual may have 15 other persons in his sphere of action, all of whom are interdependent and acquainted with each other. In the modern urban society, on the other hand, an individual may have 30 significant others in his action sphere, and aside from his family members, few if any of the others may know each other.

This matter of independence or interdependence among the significant others in one's action sphere has many consequences, particularly for one's room to maneuver. Although this is a topic we shall consider in detail in a later chapter, we can illustrate it here. In a small, rural town, it is likely that most if not all of the residents know each other, or at least know about each other. The consequence is that an individual's behavior in one position or role becomes communicated to others significant to his other positions and roles. When a teenager is picked up for reckless driving, it is not unlikely that his principal and teachers will hear about it, as well as the corner grocer, his minister, and of course, his family. And each may apply negative sanctions of some degree, thus imposing multiple jeopardy for deviance in one role. Similarly, though, if an individual is cited for commendable behavior in one role in the same small town, he may be rewarded by persons reciprocal to him in other positions as well. The outstanding athlete in school may receive small favors from town merchants, or his absence from or lateness to part-time jobs may be overlooked.

Maneuverability in action spheres also varies in the degree to which there is a repetition of persons in reciprocal positions. In the small town, not only are the residents acquainted, but each can appear in a number of different contexts with the same individual. Relatives may also own stores used by the individual; neighbors may also be aldermen; co-workers may be lay officials in the individual's church; and the judge hearing the reckless driving case may be a friend of the teenager's parents. The action sphere of an individual living in an urban area is such that persons do not appear in many different reciprocal relationships; rather they interact with the individual in one role relationship and in no other. Step 3 in Figure 5.1 more nearly depicts this kind of action sphere, for no persons appear in more than one reciprocal relationship with the individual. Because of this lack of repetition of persons in different role relationships, and because persons in the action sphere are not acquainted with each other, anonymity is more likely for urban residents.

Perhaps the most crucial way in which action spheres can vary is in their vulnerability to the actions of others. In an interdependent world, action spheres overlap. As each of us acts in his own action sphere, our actions have consequences for the spheres of action of those adjacent to us. Thus we may deliberately control or unknowingly influence others, and by the same token we may be controlled or influenced by others. But the degree to which others may constrain us or curtail our opportunities is a variable; and at the same time, there may be considerable variation in the resources offered by different action spheres to counter or offset such vulnerabilities.

>   *The vulnerabilites afforded by various types of interdependence have been analyzed at the society level by Robert A. Dahl and Charles Lindblom* (Politics, Economics and Welfare, *New York: Harper, 1953) and at the small group level by John W. Thibaut and Harold H. Kelley* (The Social Psychology of Groups, *New York: Wiley, 1959).*   <

Cognitive Maps of Action Spheres

We have said that we would find an individual's action sphere at a particular period in his life by mapping all the roles and positions he occupies and the roles, positions, and persons reciprocal to him. Now we must also note that there is a psychological version—a cognitive map—which represents open-system man's interpretation of his self in his sphere of action. Because his conception of self reflects the fact that he is purposive, has beliefs about causation, interpretations of reality, and norms, we expect him to attach meanings to what he perceives in his sphere of action. Though we would expect his cognitive map to approximate the scope of the action sphere as structurally defined, we must allow for the inevitable selectivity involved in perception. Therefore man's cognitions of his action sphere will be some (slight or perhaps major) distortion of the roles, positions, and persons actually in that action sphere, interpreted in terms of his goals, his causation beliefs and interpretations of reality, and his norms.

The major figures in the action sphere of a college student may be his roommate, girl(s), classmates, parents, a brother, and teachers. Out of this configuration, the student must proceed toward the target of a degree, or knowledge, or both. But he must also attract love and respect, achieve the necessary grades, have fun, and gain financial support (perhaps by enlarging his action sphere to include an employer). His several roles give him the possibility of making certain demands on those in his action sphere, but those roles also lead the others to expect certain satisfactions from him. Somehow using this configuration of resources and obligations, the student must learn to maneuver: to know and acknowledge the prevailing norms, to establish realistic priorities for the allocation of his time, to learn what works and what doesn't, and to manage the conflicts which arise from the varied expectations of those in his sphere of action.

Clearly there are differences in the action spheres of college students, in terms of the roles and positions included as well as in the personalities of the reciprocal role-players. Yet even if two action spheres were approximately the same structurally, we would expect variations in the cognitive maps of the students. Some students not only have multiple goals but perhaps incompatible goals. Some may lack the prior experience to maneuver effectively in the college-student action sphere. For some the norms of equity and honesty seem inconvenient. Some will sense reality differently and attribute threatening motives to those in reciprocal roles.

As any college student knows, the action sphere surrounding higher education can be difficult, for several developments may be underway simultaneously. The student may be preparing for an occupation, but also actively engaged in courtship, maintenance of friendship, and the search for self-understanding. Usually the college is demanding enough that the student who fails to give the academic requirements high priority is unsuccessful, but few students can be single-minded about the college experience.

Our hypothetical illustration of the action sphere of a college student serves to point out several features of most action spheres: (1) because open-system man is a multipurpose organism, he usually perceives of his sphere of action as a multipurpose arena, but (2) because multipurpose and multiperson action spheres may place competing demands on his time and energy, man must frequently establish priorities (which may change over time), and (3) in complex changing societies, some action spheres may be seen as temporary or transitional, affording preparation for entry into other spheres of action. The degree to which action spheres are seen as stepping stones to other action spheres is a significant variable, and raises important questions about how the individual perceives the articulation between present action and the future.

UNFOLDING CAREERS

We shall consider any *sequential* set of relationships to or *participation in* a social *institution* as a *career*. Thus the individual in modern urban society penetrates more deeply into the educational institution as he moves from elementary grades through secondary ones and then perhaps into technical or collegiate ranks, and we say that this constitutes an educational career. The sequences of occupational experiences from table waiter to restaurant owner or from private to colonel constitute occupational careers. And the sequences of positions from confirmed member of the church through church elder or deacon constitutes a lay church career.

Careers can unfold without conscious planning by the individual, but frequently, in a society that emphasizes achievement, individuals perceive that present action spheres afford opportunities to promote careers. To the extent that the individual seeks to grasp perceived opportunities, thus acting in the present action sphere so as to enhance that action sphere or move into a better one, we can speak of a *career strategy*. This applies to careers in any of the institutional fields, but is especially notable in the occupational field.

Variations in Work Careers

We noted in Chapter 4 that occupations could be contrasted as routinized or discretionary, and now we need to consider what kinds of job sequences are associated with each kind of occupation. While seldom is a career sequence guaranteed to an individual, various occupations usually hold out to those who enter them *career prototypes*: fairly clear expectations of what the individual may reasonably anticipate if he is reasonably adept and motivated. Occupations differ in the extent to which career prototypes have been crystallized, because the prototypes are based primarily on precedent and some occupations have longer and more stable histories than others. Yet most occupations tell their newcomers something about probable opportunities and directions for achievement.

Routinized and discretionary occupations differ considerably in terms of the *opportunity structures* they present, and we can see at least two types of opportunities involved in occupations. One is *opportunities to learn*, and the second is *opportunities for visibility*—to have performance noticed by significant others.

> *The concept of opportunity structures was developed by Richard A. Cloward, who applied it to the study of criminal behavior.* <

Once the individual has mastered a routinized job, his opportunities to learn skills in preparation for a better job are severely constrained. In the discretionary job, on the other hand, the individual has opportunities to continue learning, for at least two reasons: (1) exercising discretion permits him to learn the consequences of his choices and thus affords cumulative experience, and (2) exercising discretion usually brings him in contact with others holding greater responsibility and permits him to observe them in action, thus affording him some understanding of the performances required in better jobs. Usually the career prototypes for discretionary jobs call for each job to be built on the preceding one, and to be preparatory for the next.

The second significant difference in opportunity structures for the two kinds of occupation lies in the *visibility* attached to performance in those jobs. Routinized jobs are highly prescribed, performance standards are well established, and the individual is expected to adhere to recognized procedures. His task is to adhere, to conform, and not to exercise discretion. Under these conditions his successful performance is similar to the successful performances of others in similar jobs, and he becomes differentiated and visible only if his performance is substandard. Thus jobs in routinized occupations deny one the opportunity to distinguish oneself from others in terms of positive accomplishments. Because these occupations lack opportunities for distinguishing oneself and opportunities for learning, they generally are associated with the lower part of the stratification system.

Discretionary occupations, on the other hand, afford greater opportunities for visibility because discretion calls for individual choices and the consequences of those choices reflect (more or less) on the individual. Visibility of performance rests on the ability of others to perceive those consequences, and hence the direction in which one is visible is determined by the significant others in one's action sphere. This visibility may be with the work group itself, in an office or team; it may be with customers or clients; or perhaps with professional colleagues at large. Whatever the direction, we would expect it to be important in determining strategies for promoting the career. Because of this visibility and the presence of opportunities to learn, these occupations often afford upward mobility in the stratification system.

Multiple Careers

For many in modern societies work careers are of crucial significance, but we must not lose sight of the fact that many have additional careers in other institutions and these may be important parts of the action sphere. Many people in modern societies develop careers in voluntary associations and community affairs, often in addition to occupational careers. Some develop political interests, take part in campaigns and party affairs, and thus develop political careers, even though they never run for office. Some develop avocational careers, participating in amateur sports, garden clubs, hobby associations, or art programs. Many develop careers with respect to the financial segment of society, having savings accounts, insurance coverage, retirement programs, and investment plans. As a family member, moreover, the individual invariably has a family career, with an unfolding sequence of positions such as husband, father, father-in-law, grandfather, etc.

Multipurpose man, then, acts in action spheres which afford opportunities and establish constraints for progress in several careers simultaneously. Not infrequently, the requirements of one career act as constraints on others, forcing the individual to establish priorities and requiring conscious management of the action sphere. Because the occupational career often significantly influences access to other careers, the occupational career is crucial in the spheres of action of many, and affords criteria by which choices are made in the development of other careers. But possibly more significant in establishing priorities and in managing action spheres is the family.

CAREERS AND THE FAMILY CYCLE

The family provides a nexus or intersection for the unfolding careers of its several members, and invariably the family style of life reflects the changing careers of its members. It also reflects the life cycles of those members. For both reasons, then, we must expect the family to display a patterned cycle of its own.

The Nature of Family Cycles

The most obvious feature about the family cycle is the addition and subtraction of members. The nuclear family begins with husband and wife, grows by the addition of one or more children and eventually by their marriages, and dwindles as those marriages siphon attention into new nuclear families and by death or divorce of original members. But the family cycle is also significantly influenced by the fact that each of its members is pursuing several careers. As changes occur in each component career, the family also changes. As a result, resources needed by the family shift through time, and we must expect that these shifts will be patterned.

When the family is filled with young children, for example, resources in the form of physical stamina can be quite important, whereas emphasis may shift from that type of resource at a later stage. Demands for certain types of knowledge and information may shift as members' careers develop and choices must be made. Various other resources become important at different times, but in modern urban society eonomic resources frequently become the key to others. It is in the economic sector of modern society that family and occupation become significantly interlocked (a fact reflected in our earlier consideration of family life styles and stratification systems). The demands on the family for economic resources change in response to changes in composition, in the relative dependence of members, and in the stages of development of the several careers of family members. In modern urban society, then, economic demands on the family generally begin modestly, increase as the family grows and more careers are launched, and then perhaps stabilizes or declines somewhat as the family dwindles.

Variations in Family Cycles

Because family cycles reflect perceptions of responsibility of members, they vary with differences in cultural definitions of status and role. We would expect, then, important variations in family cycles from one folk society to another, reflecting local differences and histories, but all of them should be different from the family cycles to be found in modern urban societies. Even when we confine our attention to modern urban society, important differences in family cycles show up, and we can identify at least some of the reasons for this. The matter of age has considerable bearing on other factors.

The age of husband and wife at time of family formation is one important variable, and tends to be associated with the amount of education these individuals attain, and hence with types of occupations and work careers. There is also an association between the ages of husband and wife at the time the family is formed and their ages when new members are added. And the earlier the marriage, the longer the remaining period of fertility for the female, thus increasing the possibility of a larger family and of a longer period in the family cycle in which additions are made.

Age of husband and wife at marriage has significant economic implications. Early marital responsibility also increases the likelihood of early parental responsibilities, but decreases the amount of education and occupational preparation the members are likely to receive. Thus in modern societies the earlier the assumption of serious economic responsibilities the fewer the resources available at the time of family formation, and the smaller the prospects for resources in the future.

The ages at which children become independent and self-supporting is also a significant variation, and is ordinarily associated with position in the stratification system. In families lower on the socio-economic scale the children tend to get less education, to leave school, enter the labor market, and to become economically self-sufficient at an earlier age. Indeed, they may make positive economic contributions to the family until marriage, and in the rural sector of modern society, children may be expected to be economically productive while still in school.

The ages at which families are formed, expanded and contracted, then, establish constraints and opportunities within which the several careers of family members can unfold. Thus, for example, the first child in a family faces a set of constraints and opportunities different from those faced by the third or fourth child in the "same" family. The last child in a large family experiences a collection of older brothers or sisters, together with older parents who are better versed in the art of child-rearing, but busier and perhaps less physically energetic. Similarly, the number and spacing of children in the family sets constraints on the mother's opportunities for pursuing occupational or community careers.

> *The influence of birth order and the number of children in the family on socialization processes have been important topics in the general field of child development.* <

Interlocking Careers of Family Members

The unfolding careers of each member of the family likewise act as opportunities or constraints on other members. Educational careers for the children, for example, or political or religious careers for the parents, may be significantly influenced by shifts in economic careers which call for relocation.

The interlocking of careers with each other and with the family cycle is most dramatically illustrated by drastic disruptions. Such disruptions include premature death of a parent, divorce, disabling illness or accident, or disruption of the occupational career through economic depression. These involve losses of members or of roles, but the interdependence of careers is also illustrated by the reunion of family members following dissolution of the marriage of a son or daughter, or the expansion of the nuclear family to incorporate a widowed grandmother or grandfather.

Premature removal of the father from the nuclear family, for instance, may curtail some careers and expand some careers for other members of the family, and thereby alter the family cycle. Removal of the father, in modern societies, may mean reduction of economic resources without necessarily reducing economic responsibilities. Indeed, for some members of the family, economic responsibilities may be increased significantly. The wife, for instance, may begin an occupational career and forsake community or political careers, and the children may begin working earlier than they would have without loss of the father. Educational careers may be curtailed for the same reasons. Premature loss of the wife may have a different—but no less significant—set of consequences. Her coordinative and child-caring functions may need to be parceled out to other members of the family or to hired help, her shopping and other consumer activities may be reassigned to the father or older children, and responsibility for providing emotional support may have to be redistributed to others within the family.

RECAPITULATION

Everyday activities occur within a context which is meaningful for open-system man. We have called this context a *sphere of action,* and defined it as the sum of the roles and positions—and persons—impinging on the person at a period in his life. We have also argued that open-system, purposeful man may perceive his action sphere as affording him resources and opportunities and constraints, and that he may visualize an unfolding sequence of action spheres associated with his life cycle, and thus he may visualize a future life space. An action sphere, then, not only reveals linkages in the present, but, as well, linkages into the future. And we have said that because the action sphere is multipurpose, linking man to several social institutions, there may be within the action sphere several linkages into the future, several careers being developed simultaneously. The family usually constitutes an important segment of an individual's action sphere, and it also serves as the major arena for the coordination of the several careers of its several members.

In a contemporary society, then, many individuals and families face complex worlds that require the establishment of priorities among activities and careers, and the development of strategies to meet present and future demands.

RECOMMENDED BROWSING

Howard S. Becker and Anselm Strauss, "Careers, Personality, and Adult Socialization," *American Journal of Sociology* **62** (November 1956), 253–263. Explores the relationships between occupational careers and personal identities.

Howard S. Becker, *Outsiders.* New York: Free Press of Glencoe, 1963. Shows how "deviant careers" can unfold from interaction of the individual and others in his environment.

Leonard D. Cain, Jr., "Life Course and Social Structure," in *Handbook of Modern Sociology,* edited by Robert Faris. Chicago: Rand McNally, 1964, 272–309. A comprehensive review of concepts and research related to the life cycle.

Eli Chinoy, "The Tradition of Opportunity and the Aspirations of Automobile Workers," *American Journal of Sociology* **57** (March 1952), 453–459. Evidence that cognitive maps of meager action spheres tend to be rather accurate.

Charles H. Coates and Roland J. Pellegrin, "Executives and Supervisors: Contrasting Self-Conceptions and Conceptions of Each Other," *American Sociological Review* **22,** (April 1957), 217–220; and "Executives and Supervisors: A Situational Theory of Differential Occupational Mobility," *Social Forces* **35** (December 1956), 121–126. Reports of a research project contrasting the perceptions and aspirations of two categories with rather different objective opportunities.

Richard A. Cloward and Lloyd E. Ohlin, *Delinquency and Opportunity.* New York: Free Press of Glencoe, 1960. Presents and elaborates the concept of differential opportunity structures.

Kai T. Erikson, *Wayward Puritans: A Study in the Sociology of Deviance.* New York: Wiley, 1966. Emphasizes the impact of the society in determining which types of careers are deviant or acceptable.

Bernard Farber, "The Family as a Set of Mutually Contingent Careers," in *Household Decision-Making,* edited by Nelson Foote. New York: New York University Press, 1961. A unique conceptual model of the family.

Robert H. Dahl and Charles Lindblom, *Politics, Economics, and Welfare.* New York: Harper, 1953. Includes an important discussion of varieties of interdependence and the possibilities of each for the control of behavior.

Melville Dalton, "Informal Factors in Career Achievement," *American Journal of Sociology* **56** (March 1951), 407–415. Evidence from an industrial plant in the United States of the influence of ethnic origin, religion, and other informal factors in occupational advancement.

Kurt Lewin, *Field Theory in Social Science: Selected Theoretical Papers*, edited by Dorwin Cartwright. New York: Harper, 1951. An overview of the theoretical position of a pioneer, including his conception of life space.

Simon Marcson, *The Scientist in American Industry*. New York: Harper, 1960. Empirical research revealing problems in the fit of scientific careers and the requirements of industrial bureaucracies.

Arthur B. Shostak and William Gomberg, editors, *Blue-Collar World: Studies of the American Worker*. Englewood Cliffs, N.J.: Prentice-Hall, 1964. A collection of articles which throws light on the life spaces and action spheres of the American working class.

John Thibaut and Harold H. Kelley, *The Social Psychology of Groups*. New York: Wiley, 1959. Contains insightful analysis of vulnerability to the control of others, rooted in various forms of dependence.

PRIORITIES AND STRATEGIES

In modern urban societies, the number of careers the individual is involved in—and thus the variety and depth of his interaction with his society—is a variable. Some participate in a quite limited range of social institutions and thus experience a paucity of careers, but no matter how many or how few careers the individual unfolds, virtually all members of modern societies have the problem of budgeting resources, of establishing priorities for the allocation of time and energy.

Each action sphere contains a configuration of one's own careers, and thus requires the budgeting of resources among those careers. The college student, for example, may have to adjust his educational and family careers simultaneously. The housewife may have to balance family and community-action careers; the husband may have to budget time and energy between family and occupational careers. One of the reasons why the family remains a fundamental social unit in modern urban society is that it is the arena in which action spheres of the several members become contingent on one another, and hence the arena for establishing priorities not only among careers within one's action sphere but also for the careers among family members. As the nexus for several action spheres, it is the family which is the most likely vehicle for collecting resources and distributing them, thus influencing the priorities assigned to various careers.

By assigning priorities to careers, the family directs current energies toward some careers and thereby defers development of others. Because families differ in the volume of their resources (as well as their responsibilities), some find the problem of priorities much more severe than others find it. And because family life styles differ, including their time horizons, some emphasize present use of resources without much consideration of strategies, while others stress not only present priorities but deferred gratification and the development of long-range career goals. But to the extent that the future is important at all in present behavior, some strategies for career development are necessary. In modern societies, careers in the economic institution are so crucial that we shall consider, first, family economics and their implications for occupational career strategies.

> *The notion of* deferred gratification *has been widely used in social psychology and industrial sociology.*   <

ECONOMIC STRATEGIES

In discussing family cycles, we suggested that demands on the family for economic resources change in response to changes in family composition, in the relative dependence of members on the family, and in the stages of development of the several careers of family members. In modern urban society, we said, economic demands on the family generally begin modestly, increase as the family grows and more careers are launched, and then perhaps stabilizes or declines somewhat as the family dwindles. If these statements are true, we should be able to sketch "demand curves" for economic resources through the family cycle, to show at each stage of the family cycle the kinds of economic demands placed on the family, and to translate these into financial statements.

Family Financial Demand Curves

In modern urban societies, a family cycle might entail the following kinds of financial responsibilities:

Family formation: General subsistence costs (food and rent and transportation) plus purchase of household furniture and appliances.

Arrival of child: Expanded general subsistence costs, medical expenses, additional furniture and equipment.

Additional children: Increased subsistence costs, including purchase of home and acquisition of mortgage, more furniture and equipment, increased medical costs.

Children maturing: Increased subsistence costs and, perhaps, educational commitments; wedding costs.

Children grown: (and self-sufficient): Declining subsistence costs, but perhaps mounting medical expenses as parents age.

This hypothetical family cycle, translated into financial demands, might yield a financial demand curve somewhat like the one shown in Fig. 6.1.

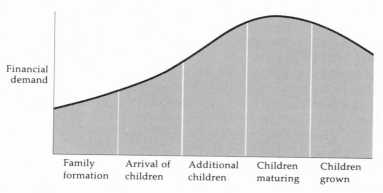

FIG. 6.1 *Hypothetical financial demand curve for nuclear family.*

Variations in Financial Demand Curves

Position of the family in the *stratification system* is a major determinant of the responsibilities leveled on parents in the family, and thereby a major determinant of the family's financial demand curve. Position in the stratification system influences the kinds of reference groups recognized by the family, and thus indicates the standards of achievement to which the parents are expected to respond.

In modern societies, for example, the vast majority of parents might hope or *aspire* to provide higher education for their children, but the degree to which this would be considered realistic and a definite responsibility clearly varies according to position in the stratification system. For those high in the stratification system, responsibility for providing higher education is taken for granted and the issue becomes the proper location and type of education; failure of the children to obtain degrees from elite institutions is interpreted as failure of the parents to meet the standards held out by their reference groups. In the middle of the stratification system, failure of the children to obtain degrees from *some* institution of higher education becomes failure of the parents. Lower in the stratification system, the wish for higher education may be just as strong, but failure of the children to obtain it is not considered failure on the part of the parents. Thus when educational responsibilities are translated into financial demands, they become one component in the family's financial demand curve, which in turn reflects the differences in financial responsibilities stemming from differences in stratification.

Education is only one component in which stratification makes a difference. The type of housing deemed "necessary" for the family varies with position on the stratification scale, as does type of clothing, transportation, and recreation. The occasions on which professional medical and dental treatment are sought vary by socioeconomic class. And stratification predicts the size and nature of financial reserves deemed appropriate at various stages of the family cycle, but whether such reserves take the form of cash savings, insurance, contributions to retirement funds, investments in real estate or corporate securities, or otherwise, is a reflection of the reference groups impinging on the parents at different levels of the stratification system.

> *Some light is thrown on this topic by students of stratification, but our insights have come primarily from those in psychology, economics, and sociology who are identified as students of* consumer *behavior. A pioneer in this field has been George Katona.* <

Societal differences also make for variation in the family's financial demand curves. Whether medical costs, for example, are borne by a government or union, by voluntary insurance agencies, or by the family directly has significance for the shape of the family's financial demand curve. Similar variations from one society to another (or within one society at different times) apply also to questions of emergency welfare costs, educational costs, retirement programs, and even recreation.

We should also note that the absolute amounts of financial demands may be significantly influenced by *inflation* or *deflation*. Especially in cases of inflation, families may be pinched if resources are lodged in fixed financial quantities which have less purchasing power as the family progresses.

In general, therefore, we would expect families in modern societies to have financial demand curves corresponding to Fig. 6.1, but we would also expect the curve for any particular family to reflect the influences discussed above: position in the stratification system, societal variations, and inflationary/deflationary trends. These factors—together with the family cycle and composition—determine the specific *shape* and the absolute *height* of the family's demand curve.

Generally speaking, the age at which economic responsibilities are begun is younger for lower-class families than for upper-class families, and the absolute height of the curve is less for lower-class families than for upper-class families, within the same society. In hypothetical terms, the curves for the two families—plotted by ages of the husbands —might be contrasted as shown in Fig. 6.2.

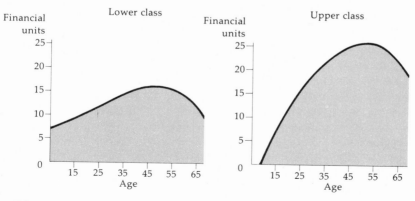

FIG. 6.2 *Hypothetical financial demand curves for lower- and upper-class families.*

The above discussion has concentrated on the demands for financial resources experienced by the family. An equally important question is how those financial demands compare with the financial resources available to the family as the family cycle unfolds. The most crucial factor in determining financial resources, for most families in modern societies, is the occupation of the head of the household. To understand the fit between demand and supply, therefore, we must return to occupational career prototypes.

Occupational Career Progression

Earlier we suggested two kinds of career prototypes. One is associated with routinized occupations, provides few opportunities, and usually is found in the lower half of the stratification system. The other is associated with discretionary occupations and provides opportunities to learn and to accumulate knowledge, together with opportunities to have performances seen by others; these usually are found in the upper portion of the stratification system. An important distinction between the two kinds of career prototypes rests on the number of steps from entry into the occupation until ultimate achievement in it. Routinized occupations generally require little specialized training and movement from entry to ultimate achievement may occur in two or three advancements. Because specialized learning is not elaborate in these occupations, the ability to progress from bottom to top of these occupations may be gained in a matter of months or a few years. Thus the individual in a routinized occupation can reach the ceiling of his occupation fairly quickly, and unless he moves into a different occupation, he can expect to remain at that level indefinitely.

Career prototypes for discretionary occupations, on the other hand, tend to be less specifically defined, to have more rank or categories between entry and ultimate achievement, to be more dependent on the accumulation of experience and training, and thus to stretch the time between entry and ultimate achievement over a period of years, often decades.

The speed with which an individual may expect to reach the peak of his potential in an occupation is thus an important variable from one occupation to another. But an equally significant variable is the relationship of those career prototypes to the financial demand curves of the family.

The career prototypes for *routinized* jobs contain few steps in the progression ladder and rather rapid progression through those steps. Hence the individual may arrive at the top of his occupational career before his family financial responsibilities reach their peak. When this occurs, we refer to *early-ceiling occupations,* as illustrated in Fig. 6.3.

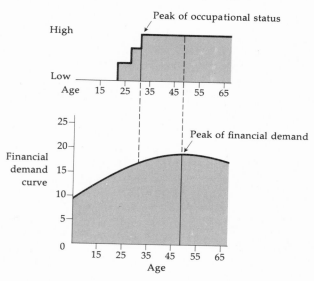

FIG. 6.3 *Definition of* early-ceiling *occupations: comparison of occupational status and financial demand curves in routinized occupations.*

In discretionary occupations, on the other hand, the prototype suggests continued increments of occupational status until or beyond the peak of economic responsibilities to the family. We shall refer to these as *late-ceiling occupations,* as illustrated in Fig. 6.4.

We would have to expect family activities to strongly reflect the impact of occupational ceiling. If the head of the family is in an early-ceiling occupation, family financial planning and career strategies should reflect the growth of financial pressures while the individual is stabilized on a career plateau. If the head of the family is in a late-ceiling occupation, on the other hand, financial planning and career strategies should take a very different course.

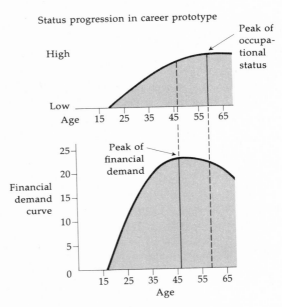

FIG. 6.4   *Definition of* late-ceiling occupations: *comparison of occupational status and financial demand curves in discretionary occupations.*

We need to remember that we are working with a dichotomized distinction between routinized and discretionary occupations, while in reality occupations differ by degree on that continuum.   Likewise, some families undoubtedly find that they reach the occupational ceiling at about the time their demands for financial resources also peak. In such instances, questions of strategy may not seem very important. Nevertheless, we believe that the distinctions we have drawn are significantly akin to reality for the majority of families in modern societies, so we turn now to an examination of family and career strategies.

Family and Career Strategies: Early Ceiling

Early-ceiling occupations contain little opportunity to learn the skills needed for more promising jobs, and provide little or no opportunity to become visible or build a reputation for unique abilities. Without new learning, the individual tends to be constrained to his present occupation, and without visibility he tends to be constrained to his present job. In spite of mounting economic responsibilities in the family, then, his occupational future may look very much like the present; he has reached a plateau.

Unable to gain increased economic resources by *personal* work performance, but under pressure to increase economic resources, the individual, we would expect, would turn to *cooperation* with others in similar circumstances, to get increased returns for the occupation as such. The worldwide tendency, in response to these conditions, is *collective action* through labor unions or occupational associations or professional societies. In order to protect members of these occupations from arbitrary or uncertain preferential treatment, unions tend to emphasize *seniority* as the basis for whatever distinctions become necessary.

There are other conceivable routes for those in routinized occupations to close the gap between resources and economic demands. The most effective, at least during periods of labor shortage, is for the individual to hold a second job (or "moonlight"), or for other members of the family to work. The working wife is not unusual in the family's middle years. Frequently individuals in early-ceiling occupations aspire to self-employment, and occasionally they get out of the early-ceiling occupation to become self-employed; usually, however, this requires economic capital which is difficult for persons in an economic squeeze to accumulate, and it often requires education not possessed. Prolonged part-time educational programs may ultimately result in switching to a different occupation with a later ceiling, but this requires sustained attention and resources.

Family and Career Strategies: Late Ceiling

Because late-ceiling occupations require the exercise of discretion, they permit the individual to accumulate experience and expertness as well as visibility. With increasing ability and reputation, the individual may expect opportunities to branch off into other but related occupations or to transfer his abilities to other employers. Late-ceiling occupations thus afford alternative opportunities and provide their members with individual bargaining power; the more personal visibility and competence, the greater that power to negotiate.

The able energetic individual in a later-ceiling occupation can expect to develop his career by differentiating himself through *personal* performance in *competition* with others. In spite of collegial cooperation to protect and advance the occupation, the emphasis in these jobs is usually on individual accomplishment; unionization is resisted.

For late-ceiling occupations, the gap between economic resources and economic demands tends to come early in the family cycle, especially because of the extended education usually required. Not infrequently the individual holds temporary jobs in other types of occupations, while preparing for the late-ceiling occupation. Not infrequently, the wife works during this early stage of the family cycle.

Family Strategies Compared

The working wife and "moonlighting" are thus likely to occur at different stages in the family's cycle, depending on the type of primary occupation engaged in by the head of the family. When the primary occupation is an early-ceiling one, second jobs and working wives—together with debt accumulation—tend to come in the middle of the family cycle. When the primary occupation is a late-ceiling one, second jobs and working wives tend to come early in the family cycle, and debts accumulate early but are gradually reduced as the career gets underway.

When the head of the family has an early-ceiling occupation, in which his personal efforts do not distinguish him from others or earn economic returns, work is not likely to be a central ingredient of the self-conception nor is it likely to be a "central life interest." We would expect, therefore, that the individual and his family would derive central satisfactions from other types of careers: recreational, community, political or labor union. At the other extreme, when the head of the family is building a successful late-ceiling career, we would expect work to be a central theme for the family as well as a central life interest for the individual. When such a career is being launched, the wife may well be involved in employment, but later we might expect her to develop careers in community affairs which supplement or bolster the husband's career, but may or may not involve economic returns.

Thus the type of occupation influences the degree to which aspirations are channeled into occupational pursuits for the household head, but in addition, type of occupation of the household head is important in guiding the career developments of other members of the family. Not only are the wife's careers within the family and in employment affected, but children's educational careers may be closely tied to the distinction between early- and late-ceiling occupations. The parents' experiences may be translated directly into aspirational goals for their children, with resulting pressures for or against formal education, and especially in the kinds of educational programs encouraged. Even if parents, in families revolving around early-ceiling occupations, stress the economic or other values of education for their children, the likelihood is that limited economic resources will result in less interaction with the educational institution than in families oriented to late-ceiling occupations.

It is sometimes asserted that individuals in early-ceiling occupations, seeing little hope for occupational advancement, adopt an impulsive life style instead of the disciplined life style required for development of a strategy. There does indeed appear to be some empirical association between type of occupation and the impulsive/disciplined variable, but we feel safe in predicting it in only one direction, not both. We would not expect to find the impulsive life style displayed by those with successful careers in late-ceiling occupations; absence of a disciplined strategy would be likely to preclude success. On the other hand, the individual in an early-ceiling occupation may be embedded in other family careers which indeed call for discipline and strategy, however routine the occupational prototype appears. In the early-ceiling occupations, then, we would expect to find those with the impulsive life style, but also those who carefully plan strategies for paying off a mortgage, getting the children educated, or acquiring a fund for early retirement. Thus, while impulsiveness may prevent a late-ceiling job, we cannot predict that an early-ceiling job will preclude the disciplined life-style.

Type of occupation of the household head thus has quite an impact on family life style and family strategies. The impact is so strong, generally, that type of occupation of the father is still a good predictor of the son's type of occupation. The channeling processes discussed earlier clearly reflect this.

>   *This phenomenon emerges from studies of inter-generational* mobility, *by students of* social stratification.   <

In contrasting early- and late-ceiling families, we have, of course, neglected those occupations which fall somewhere between those extremes. Such middle-range occupations do exist, and we would expect family strategies in these cases to reflect the blending of two styles of adaptation. The important point is not that all families adapt in one of the two ways we have described, but rather that family financial demand curves, occupational progression, and family income combine in particular ways to determine family life styles and career patterns, and to establish the boundaries within which family strategies can be decided.

There remains one more important consequence of occupational types which we have not yet considered. This concerns the geographic extensiveness of the sphere of action.

Local and Cosmopolitan Action Spheres

Because routinized occupations provide few opportunities either for learning or for visibility, careers in such occupations tend to be played out in one geographic setting and, frequently, with one employer. Although standardization means that workers are virtually interchangeable, with the possibility therefore of quitting in one location and moving to another, the likelihood of loss of seniority rights is a strong deterrent. Such movement is more likely to occur in areas and at times of extreme labor shortage than under other conditions.

Discretionary occupations, on the other hand, afford both opportunities to learn career-cumulative knowledge and to become visible, and both these conditions make possible geographic mobility as the career unfolds. While some learning is pertinent only to the site, discretionary experience is often transferable to other sites. And to the extent that the individual manages his visibility, his reputation may gain him opportunities for career advancement at other geographic locales. Thus, for discretionary occupations, the action sphere may well include persons at considerable distances from present jobs.

The action sphere may contain persons in other organizations whose recognition may lead to job opportunities outside one's present organization. Indeed, some occupations require this kind of visibility and contact for the ambitious individual; this generally is true for city managers, school superintendents, hospital administrators—all positions for which career development channels are not available within a single community. Other occupations, such as university professor, afford opportunity for career development within a single organization, but career progression can be enhanced either by moving or threatening to do so.

For some occupations, visibility may be within scattered divisions of a single organization, with the same consequences for a cosmopolitan sphere of action. The military is a good example of such extended visibility, but many national or international business corporations and national governmental agencies afford career-building opportunities through a succession of jobs at various locations.

The fact that the head of a household is in a discretionary occupation does not *necessarily* mean that he adopts a cosmopolitan career strategy. There is always the possibility of the family becoming so emotionally involved in a given locality that opportunities for occupational advancement elsewhere are not seriously considered. Such factors as friendship or kinship ties, local climate, or access to special geographic features such as ski slopes or the ocean may operate to keep the family immobile. But there are several other situations, all revolving around other careers in the family, which can lead the individual into a discretionary job to elect a local career strategy: (a) educational careers for the children may lead the family to the conclusion that a geographic move would be detrimental; (b) medical history of some member of the family may preclude change of climate; (c) wife's occupational career may be so promising in the present location that family movement would be too costly; (d) the family's financial career may be tied to local investments (such as real estate) and be expected to suffer if the family moved, or (e) obligations to the extended family (in death or chronic illness, for example) may preclude moving any distance. For a particular family, some of the conditions may be temporary, leading to the possibility of readopting the cosmopolitan strategy after a period of time.

Career prototypes for some discretionary occupations include a switching point at which the individual must choose between further progress via the cosmopolitan strategy and geographic mobility or switching to a different occupation for which the local strategy is reasonable. Professional occupations in the setting of complex organizations—engineers and scientists in business corporations, or professors in large universities—typically contain such switching points; the individual may choose to follow the professional career on a cosmopolitan basis or to move into a managerial occupation and build the career within the host organization.

>   *The sociology of professions describes a number of professions which are practiced in organizational settings and which may present such career switching points.*   <

For those who elect the cosmopolitan strategy, we would expect it to permeate the family life style. With geographic mobility, frequency of interaction within the extended family is reduced; visiting parents or grandparents now requires a trip, and vice versa. Geographic mobility also means that friends are dispersed; the family has friends in various locales but sees them only occasionally. Geographic mobility means a wider set of experiences for the developing children, and broader subcultural contacts for both children and parents.

Under these conditions, we would expect the family to have a more cosmopolitan viewpoint than would be true for families which develop careers in a single location.

LEVELS OF MEANING AND PRIORITIES

We began Chapter 5 by suggesting that the individual has a life space —an impression of one's self into the future—which serves more or less as a criterion for selection among alternative paths of development. But we also suggest that the individual finds it impossible to relate each daily episode, each alternative, to the life space. We then suggested that the *sphere of action* served to link daily *situations* or episodes with the more enduring conception of *life space*. These can be viewed as three levels of meaning for the individual.

The life space, however clear or ill-defined, helps the individual establish priorities, helps him decide which of alternative possible action spheres is meaningful, helps him assign value rankings to the several possible careers. The use of the life-space concept for this purpose may be infrequent, and once decisions have been made they remain in force until for some reason the sphere of action is called into question. This feature removes the necessity of consciously calculating the ultimate consequences of immediate actions; it ties current behavior to the future without overloading his calculating capacities.

The action sphere, in turn, establishes priorities and premises for action in immediate situations. Many episodes in daily life—especially perhaps in highly segmented and specialized modern societies—lack intrinsic meaning or challenge. Family chores and job routines, for example, may be tolerable only because they are part of longer-range strategies; they acquire meaning only because of their context.

Generally speaking, we would expect the more distant or encompassing level to provide meaning for the less encompassing ones, but on occasion events can reverberate in the other direction. Occasionally a climatic episode has unforeseen consequences for action spheres and life spaces, calling into question previous criteria for choices and perhaps suggesting previously unimagined conceptions of life space. Although infrequent, such crucial events do sometimes result in rerouting of the individual's developmental path.

RECAPITULATION

Particularly in modern societies, economic strategies are important ingredients of life space and spheres of action. This is particularly visible within the context of the nuclear family, in which expectations of future financial demands and occupational career progression intersect. We have suggested that career and family strategies vary, depending on whether the head of the household is involved in an early-ceiling or late-ceiling occupation, and further that different family life styles are associated with local versus cosmopolitan action spheres.

Thus we have been considering the interaction between life space and action spheres. We need now to consider in more detail the activities of man in more immediate contexts, and we turn to this task in Chapter 7, with examination of the structure of situations in which episodes unfold.

RECOMMENDED BROWSING

Robin Barlow, Harvey E. Brazer, and James N. Morgan, *Economic Behavior of the Affluent.* Washington, D.C.: The Brookings Institution, 1966. A rare look at wealthy families and how decisions are made about their work, savings, and investments.

Peter Blau and Otis Dudley Duncan, *The American Occupational Structure.* New York: Wiley, 1967. Important collection of data shedding light on occupational opportunities, mobility, careers, and the family.

Elaine Cumming and William E. Henry, *Growing Old: The Process of Disengagement.* New York: Basic Books, 1961. A theoretical approach to the social and psychological aspects of aging.

Melville Dalton, *Men Who Manage.* New York: Wiley, 1959. Includes important materials on the importance of visibility in building managerial careers.

William R. Dill, Thomas L. Hilton, and Walter R. Reitman, *The New Managers.* Englewood Cliffs, N.J.: Prentice-Hall, 1962. A provocative empirical study of the early stages of careers in management, and of the importance of opportunities to learn and to be visible.

Robert Dubin, "Industrial Workers' Worlds: A Study of the 'Central Life Interests' of Industrial Workers," *Social Problems* **3** (January 1956) 131–142. An empirical study of the world of blue-collar workers, with the conclusion that work and work place are not central life interests.

James S. Dusenberry, *Income, Savings and the Theory of Consumer Behavior*. Cambridge, Mass.: Harvard University Press, 1949. A major formulation of factors determining economic behavior.

Alvin Gouldner, "Cosmopolitans and Locals: Toward an Analysis of Latent Social Roles," *Administrative Science Quarterly*, Parts I & II 2 (December 1957) 281–306, and 2 (March 1958) 444–480. A study of college faculty members, indicating different career strategies.

Robert H. Guest, "Work Careers and Aspirations of Automobile Workers," *American Sociological Review* **19** (April 1954), 155–163. Affords insight into the significance of seniority benefits in encouraging local action spheres.

Reuben Hill, "Decision-Making and the Family Life Cycle," in *Social Structure and the Family: Generational Relations*, edited by Ethel Shanas and Gordon F. Streib. Englewood Cliffs, N.J.: Prentice-Hall, 1963. Empirical investigation of family decisions about residence, occupation, purchasing, saving, and retirement.

George Katona, *Psychological Analysis of Economic Behavior*. New York: McGraw-Hill, 1951. Pioneering research including family planning, spending, and saving patterns and the reasons for them.

Gerald R. Leslie and Arthur H. Richardson, "Life Cycle, Career Pattern, and the Decision to Move," *American Sociological Review* **26** (December 1961), 894–902. Emphasizes the joint importance of career pattern and life cycle in the decision to change residences.

Eugene Litwak, "Occupational Mobility and Extended Family Cohesion," *American Sociological Review* **25** (February 1960), 9–21; and "Geographic Mobility and Extended Family Cohesion," *American Sociological Review* **25** (June 1960) 385–394. Examination of the relationships of family and mobility in contemporary societies.

David Riesman and Howard Roseborough, "Careers and Consumer Behavior," in *Consumer Behavior*, Vol. II, edited by C. H. Clark. New York: New York University Press, 1956, pages 1–18. An exploration of a number of factors related to the life cycle of consumption.

James D. Thompson, Robert W. Avery, and Richard O. Carlson, "Occupations, Personnel, and Careers," *Educational Administration Quarterly* (Winter 1968), 6–31. Elaborates on the notions of early- and late-ceiling occupations, and of career strategies.

Ralph H. Turner, *Social Context of Ambition: A Study of High School Seniors in Los Angeles.* San Francisco: Chandler, 1964. An empirical study of mobility and its impact on personality and values.

Harold Wilensky, "Orderly Careers and Social Participation," *American Sociological Review* **26** (August 1961), 521–539, and "Life Cycle, Work Situation, and Participation in Formal Associations," in *Aging and Leisure,* edited by Robert W. Kleemeier. New York: Oxford University Press, 1961. Reports of an empirical study which explored bases for "orderly careers" and "disrupted work patterns," and considered relations between occupational and family developments.

BEHAVIOR HERE AND NOW

Much of day-to-day behavior takes place in social contexts. We need ways of thinking about interdependence among persons in day-to-day episodes, and how these influence men's actions. We can recognize that persons *adapt to* many of these interpersonal situations, but also that they may seek to *rearrange* relationships with others, to adjust their interdependence and expectations. We also need to understand how decisions are made when situations present alternatives. In everyday behavior, too, there may be considerable opportunity for personality variables to make a difference, and we need to be able to take this into account.

CHAPTER 7

ENCOUNTERS IN EPISODES

INSTRUMENTAL EPISODES

Much of man's day-to-day activity occurs in episodes, in short bursts of action which have beginnings and ends separated only by seconds, minutes, or possibly hours. Although the reasons for engaging in episodic activities generally are supplied by the action sphere (as we indicated in Chapter 6), the overt action can be observed to have a beginning and end. Some of these episodes are strictly personal or private: man gets dressed in the morning, drives to work, mails a letter, visits the rest room, or mows the lawn. But many of man's daily activities—and especially the more problematic ones—involve other persons. Man may have breakfast with his family, participate in a meeting, negotiate for a loan, visit the dentist, entertain friends.

Man may interact with others for either of two reasons, and often they are combined. Some interactions are sought for their intrinsic qualities, because it is pleasant or rewarding to the personality to be in the presence of the other. Friendships and love are built on this base. Some interpersonal relationships are instrumental, with the other parties seen strictly as agents for the attainment of some goal. Customers may be interested only in a druggist's abilities to fill their physicians' prescriptions. Some relationships formed initially for instrumental purposes can gradually, however, take on intrinsic qualities as well. A regular customer at a drugstore may become friends with the druggist, and interact with him on other than purely instrumental bases. Alternatively, relationships which are basically intrinsic usually have some instrumental transactions. Husbands and wives each fulfill

121

instrumental needs for each other as well as intrinsic ones. In the folk society, most relationships would have large elements of both instrumental and intrinsic qualities. It is in the modern urban society—with notions of specificity, achievement, universalism, and discipline—that specialized instrumental relationships occur.

>   *Work on this topic can be found under the general label of interpersonal relations.*   <

This distinction results in modern urban man often being frustrated in trying to transact business in less modern, more folk types of social situations; round-about transactions interwoven with discussions of family, weather, or gossip seem inappropriate and time-consuming. By the same token, the individual socialized to folk ways may be dismayed by the more abrupt and less personal style of transaction characteristic of modern societies.

Because this volume is concerned primarily with man as purposive, our attention in this chapter will be focused on instrumental episodes and relationships, although we shall find it necessary to consider expressive aspects. In instrumental episodes, the other persons the individual may encounter may be in either an *adversary* relationship or a *cooperative* one. The adversary situation would occur, for example, when the other party is a competitor for some scarce resource, or in bargaining, when one's gains are achieved at the cost of the other. The cooperative episode, on the other hand, emerges when the parties perceive that their costs can be reduced or their energies conserved by coordinated action, or when certain desired effects can be obtained only in concert.

Whether they involve adversary or cooperative relationships, man maneuvers in these instrumental episodes in pursuit of his goals. Other persons—and therefore other personalities—are involved in daily episodes, but the individual in complex societies cannot know very much about very many of the personalities he encounters. He comes to episodes anticipating that others will behave in fairly predictable ways based on the obligations of the roles they and he occupy. Some roles leave little room for discretion and hence for the play of personality. Others—such as boss, wife, or teacher—may be significantly influenced by the personalities of those occupying the roles. But in both cases, activities are bounded and guided by the prescribed rights and duties of the roles. This structural guarantee rests on interdependence.

With functional specialization, each person becomes a resource (or an obstacle) to persons in roles reciprocal to his. By meeting the demands of his own role he is therefore able to make demands on others. Thus interdependence and role reciprocity provide structure for the episodes of daily living and place boundaries around the operation of personalities. If we want to understand episodes and man's maneuvering in them, it becomes necessary to examine more closely how roles are put together.

NETWORKS OF ROLES

We said in Chapter 2 that a role is always defined with reference to at least one other role. Social scientists distinguish three basic types of role networks: the *dyad,* the *group,* and the *role-set.* When only one other role is involved, the social scientist speaks of a dyad, and we shall begin our analysis with that.

The Nature of Dyads

The father and his son at a ball game constitutes a dyad. The doctor and patient at the clinic do, too, just as do the teacher and student in an office conference, the salesman and customer in a department store, and the cabdriver and his passenger. In all these cases, there is the potential for adversary stances as well as for cooperation. The dyad is especially vulnerable if one of the parties has not been well socialized to his role or lacks self-confidence, for the other party is then free to take advantage. The dyad also is precarious if one of the parties has no reasonable alternative. The patient who cannot choose his doctor, or the salesman who must negotiate with all potential customers, are more likely to feel the constraints of the dyadic relationship than those who have voluntarily selected a particular dyad. When neither party has options—a case of bilateral monopoly—interaction in the dyad can be especially difficult.

> *The German sociologist Georg Simmel pioneered in the analysis of*
> *dyads and triads, as well as larger groups.*   <

Dyadic relationships may be *fleeting*—as in the taxicab case—or
repetitive, as in the case of father and son. In many fleeting relationships, the constraints are almost entirely those of role expectations.
The relationships of the bank teller and his customer and the city bus
driver and his passenger are examples. But some fleeting relationships
are less instrumental and less governed by rules, and thus more open

		Dyad contact	
		Fleeting	*Repetitive*
Content of interaction largely controlled	*By role expectations*	e.g., bank	Some in-law relationships; some couples married by family arrangement
	By personalities	Fellow train passengers (strangers)	Friends, lovers, some married couples

FIG. 7.1   Variations in dyadic relationships.

to the imprint of personalities (see Fig. 7.1). Fellow passengers on a
train, strangers in a waiting room, or customers at an airport cocktail
lounge need not interact, but if they do, their relationship is largely
shaped only by their personalities. The importance of some of these
encounters far outweights their duration, in part because they afford
the opportunity for a relationship based on intrinsic qualities, unhamp-
ered by any history, and frequently by any future. These chance encounters can be so significant that the course of the individual's life is
strikingly altered.

Many repetitive dyads are also subject to heavy involvement of
personalities, but others are greatly endangered by large dosages of

personality. Sometimes in-law relationships are of this character. A husband may feel compelled by tradition or his wife's insistence to maintain cordial relationships with his wife's mother, but because there is potential volatility in the relationship, personalities are suppressed and role expectations strictly adhered to. Some business transactions, though routinely and frequently entered into by the same two parties, are ritualized so as to protect the integrity of the transaction against disruption by personalities. Marriages, particularly where arranged by parents or entered into at an early age before full personality development, may come to be largely governed by role expectations, with little room for the open expression of the unique personalities. We would expect these marriages to be more likely to break up when the necessities for their continuance are removed. Frequently this is when the children have grown up and have left the home.

Those repetitive dyads that do permit a wide expression of personalities may be subject to brittleness. Even those dyadic relationships that involve highly compatible personalities and thus a basis for working out disagreements and misunderstandings exhibit some volatility. This is illustrated by lovers' quarrels and family spats. A prime reason for the brittleness of some repetitive dyads is that each person is a source of potential rewards and punishments for the other, and each person is making the judgments about the appropriateness of the other's behavior. Each is both judge and jury and if one applies sanctions which the other thinks unwarranted, retaliation is to be expected. Failure to meet role obligations or disagreement about what constitutes failure can lead to escalation of conflict. To help protect against this, dyads may be enlarged temporarily to include an impartial third party who can adjudicate the dispute, as in the use of parents to settle quarrels between children, or of friends to negotiate between lovers in a quarrel, or of the court to resolve disputes over a business contract. The simple presence of a third party in a third-party role may help prevent the conflict from ever arising, as in the case of the referee at the tennis match, the supervisor at the office, or the patrolman at an intersection.

Dyads can be bolstered not only by the actual presence of a third party, but also by the potentiality of a third party whose presence can be called forth if necessary. Generally the latent third party is provided by a social institution, especially the legal institution. Simply knowing that the role expectations can be enforced through legal channels facilitates action in many dyads without actually invoking legal sanctions. The legal contract which precisely defines reciprocal role expectations permits the later entrance of a third party who neither knows the participants nor has personal interests in the outcome. Parties to the dyad may develop quite precise and detailed expectations of each other without legal contract, but commitment of those expectations in a legal document facilitates the role of the third party if required. Resort to a written contract seems more likely if the parties are involved in complicated activities than otherwise, but seems less likely when the parties have a history of trustworthy relationships.

The importance of the legal institution in facilitating dyadic relationships is emphasized when we contrast folk and modern urban societies. Legal institutions within a modern urban society permit the formation of dyadic relationships and the transacting of business across a nation, or internationally. In the folk society, on the other hand, trust and the possibility of adjudication of differences traditionally remain within the boundaries of the folk society, and therefore are localized.

When folklike societies do transact exchanges across their boundaries, they frequently do so through marginal members of one or both their societies. Minority group members who are essentially outsiders in their own societies can often be found, for instance, in the merchant class acting as third parties in trade negotiations between societies. Presumably because they are not full members of either society, they can act more impartially and be trusted in the negotiations. However, when a society comes to embrace formerly autonomous folklike units, and is in transition toward being a more modern urban society, we would expect one of its problems to be establishing and gaining trust in an impersonal legal system which can function as the third party to facilitate society-wide transactions.

It should be clear, however, that third parties are not always facilitative for a dyad. The eternal love triangle with its conflicts is an instance. The third party can be a divisive and disruptive influence, promoting instability in a relationship. This can also apply to the legal institution as a third party. Laws and legal procedures may institutionalize conflict by defining a dyadic relationship as an adversary one, thus preventing possible cooperative arrangements. Divorce laws, for instance, may require the construction of evidence demonstrating the spouse's immorality or incompetence as a marriage partner, thus making reconciliation even less likely.

The Structure of Groups

Although in such primary groups as the family and work team, episodes often occur in the form of dyads, face-to-face groups are more than a collection of dyads; they have distinctive properties of their own.

> *Recent work on groups can be found under the labels of* small group analysis *and* group dynamics. <

For one thing, third parties are built into the relationships between any two members of the group, and can be either disruptive or facilitative. It does mean that there are usually more observers of any individual's behavior and therefore greater likelihood of insistence on his fulfillment of his role obligations. At the same time, this means that there are more to insist he receive his rewards. For both reasons, the face-to-face group can be less brittle than the dyad. And because the group is a repetitive set of social relationships, there are opportunities for rectification tomorrow or next week of injustices which may slip in today. But larger groups also have built into them the potential for instability, for as the group increases in size and in complexity, problems in communication and coordination may increase. Personally costly problems may continue for some time before they are solved to the satisfaction of those involved.

In comparison with the dyad, the group can offer more possible sources of personal satisfactions—of enhancement of the self-conception—as well as instrumental results. The individual may find that while he can barely tolerate some of the personalities he must work or live with, he can form close bonds with others. For such reasons, we would expect to find the formation of subgroups of friends in both families and work teams, where they are often called *cliques*. We would expect these to be stronger psychologically than other relationships in the group because they represent free—and mutual—choice. Another reason for subgroups is the nature of the interdependence involved in the work of the group. Technologies may call for particular combinations of specialized skills, or their configuration at particular locations, and these requirements may dictate who must interact in getting the tasks done. Subgroupings also emerge as the result of pooling of resources to gain power; these are regarded as *coalitions.*

> *Subgroupings within primary groups were a major theme of* sociometry, *especially as pioneered by J. L. Moreno. (Recently the term has been applied to a wider range of phenomena.)* Communication networks *in task subgroups have been analyzed particularly by Alex Bavelas and Harold Leavitt and associates. The analysis of* coalition *phenomena, stimulated by game theory, has gone forward in the fields of* international relations *and* political sociology.   <

Instrumental groups frequently exhibit what has come to be known as the *dual process*: on the one hand, group activity is concentrated on solving task problems, and on the other hand, maintaining the integrity of the group as a social unit. It is easy enough to observe that instrumental groups must accomplish both things, but complications arise as soon as we note that these things are not independent. Action taken to solve one of the two problems can add to the other. As members of the group take action or make suggestions to aid in task accomplishment, but others counter by pointing to the limitations of those suggestions or offer competing alternatives, feelings may be hurt, status may be challenged or undermined. Thus when the group is trying to solve task problems, interpersonal tensions may mount.

> *In the study of small groups, there has been considerable research into the dual-process phenomenon and group* leadership. *This field was pioneered by Robert F. Bales, who developed* interaction process analysis, *which has been used for much of the research.*   <

One way that this dual problem is handled is by alternating between task problems and the rebuilding of group solidarity. The coffee break may afford an opportunity for this, or the picnic, the beer bust, or the hunting trip. Another solution to the dual-process problem of instrumental groups is through the emergence in the group of two leaders, one specializing in task-accomplishment and the other in management of interpersonal relationships. On occasion the two leadership functions are combined in one role: in formal organizations, for example, in which an individual is appointed to an authority role. In some cases, the personality of an individual enables him to lead in both the group processes, but frequently this is not the case, and even in formal organizations, informal leaders emerge in work groups, either to supplement or to combat the formally appointed authority.

>   *The emergence of informal leaders—and other aspects of* informal organization—*is widely reported and analyzed in* industrial sociology *and in the field of bureaucracy or* complex organizations.   <

The evidence is well established that the dynamic processes of groups as social units are intertwined with their dynamics as instrumental units.

The Role-Set: An Extended Network

In Chapter 2 we pointed out that roles usually cluster into positions. The person occupying a position is involved in reciprocal relations in several different directions and with several different role partners. This collection of roles reciprocal to a particular position has been called a *role-set.* (To be sure that there is no confusion with the concept of action sphere introduced in Chapter 5, let us emphasize that the role-set focuses on *one* position and its reciprocating roles. The action sphere focuses on one individual and *all* the positions he occupies at a period in his life, including the reciprocal roles and persons occupying them. Essentially, then, the action sphere is made up of a number of role-sets.)

>   *The concept of role-set was introduced and has been analyzed by Robert K. Merton.*   <

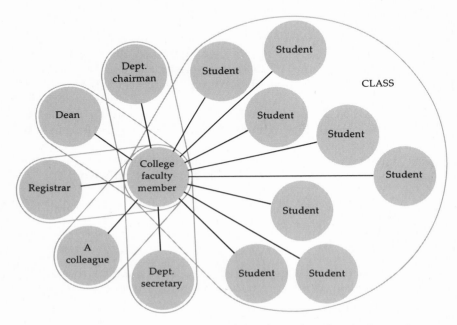

FIG. 7.2   *A partial schematic portrayal of the role-set of a college faculty member.*

Obviously the reciprocating roles in the dyad are part of the role-set, and the reciprocal roles in the group are part of the role-set. But in complicated structures, the role-set may include dyadic and group role relationships that are separated from each other. The position of college instructor, for example, involves dyads with departmental chairmen, colleagues, the dean, registrar, and departmental secretary, as well as a group when the instructor interacts with a class (see Fig. 7.2). And none of these are necessarily in interaction with each other.

Although we have argued that many episodes unfold in dyads or groups, the notion of role-set reminds us that a man's episodic behavior may be constrained and supported by roles out of sight during the episode. The instructor's behavior in class with the students may be significantly influenced by his role relationships with colleagues or administrators. The son's relationship with his father is similarly influenced by his relations with members of his peer group as well as his relations with other members of his family, and family episodes frequently reflect this fact.

A more extreme case of the group's influence on behavior in other role relationships involves being deployed by the group as its agent in dealing with persons not members of the group. The negotiator deployed by the union to deal with management, the lawyer deployed by the corporation in a lawsuit, the policemen deployed by the department to a tough beat—all are both constrained and supported by the group, even though the group is not present during many episodes.

Thus open-system man is involved during a typical day in a variety of episodes, many of which involve encounters with other persons. These encounters, generally speaking, are not understandable simply in terms of personalities or in terms solely of the immediate context, but rather are constrained and facilitated by the fact that open-system man and the persons he encounters are locked into networks of roles. Thus networks of roles shape the terrain in which man maneuvers on a day-to-day basis.

THE CALCULUS OF COSTS AND REWARDS

The notion of role, defined in terms of reciprocal rights and obligations, implies an exchange. Presumably this exchange in role relationships rests on the *norm of reciprocity,* but inevitably a question of balance is implied. Although the specific content of the norm of reciprocity varies from culture to culture, such a norm is found universally. It tends to assure the party in one role that his proper performance will bring a proper response. The presence of such a norm does not guarantee that the performances of persons in reciprocal roles will have equal rewards for the others, only that some rewards will be exchanged. Open-system man need not be coldly calculating (although some may well be Machiavellian) in order to be interested in the score. The family may be vaguely aware that it has an entertainment obligation to neighbors or that there is an imbalance in gift exchanges with friends. The individual may, without formally keeping score, be aware that another has done several favors and that some obligation has thereby been incurred.

In some episodes, the accounts may be balanced at once; but where the relationship is repetitive, debts may accumulate through a series of episodes before they are reciprocated. In such situations, score-keeping may be covert and only be mentioned once the imbalance seems to be getting out of hand.

Distributive Justice

The norm of reciprocity does not necessarily require that the benefits exchanged be equal or equivalent. The question of the values of benefits involved in exchanges raises another norm, that of *distributive justice,* which requires that those with equivalent claims will receive equivalent rewards. The content of this norm also varies by culture. In the folk society, with emphasis on ascription, two persons who make similar contributions may be judged and agree that rewards should be unequal because they have unequal claims based on inherited status. In modern urban societies, with emphasis on achievement and universalism, the norm of distributive justice tends to require that similar contributions receive similar rewards.

> *Notions of* distributive justice *and* equity *are fundamental to theories of social* exchange *in sociology and social psychology. Major contributors have been Peter Blau, George Homans, Harold H. Kelley, and John W. Thibaut.*   <

> *The notion of* relative deprivation *has been researched by a number of sociologists and social psychologists, probably the most notable being Samuel Stouffer and his associates.*   <

Even in modern urban societies, there is no requirement of equal distribution and indeed rewards are not equally distributed. All parties may be agreed that some members of the group contribute more to the total welfare of the group than others and that in exchange a larger portion of the rewards are justly theirs. Obviously some participants may consider a distribution of rewards unjust and thus feel deprived relative to others. This situation can divide the group seriously and recast what were originally cooperative relationships into adversary ones. With complicated activities in specialized roles, it becomes more difficult to arrive at consensus about the relative contributions of persons in role networks. For the sports team, is the offensive star more valuable than the defensive star? Is the design engineer more important than the construction foreman? One of the problems in a modern urban society is that the participants have available multiple criteria by which to assess the performances of others with whom they are involved. Prior socialization for roles may establish understandings of the appropriate criteria, but in dynamic and complicated situations questions of criteria and their application must be worked out by the participants as episodes unfold.

In his daily activities, then, open-system man may face questions about whether the rewards he is receiving are fair when compared to the rewards received by those with whom he interacts. Perceptions that he is being taken advantage of can be threatening to his self-conception.

The Inducements/Contributions Bargain

Whereas distributive justice raises the question of equity among participants, open-system man's accounting scheme must also consider whether his returns—equitable or otherwise—are sufficient to warrant continued participation. It is quite possible for man to believe that he is fairly treated and yet to be dissatisfied with his participation in the role network. On the other hand, it is equally possible for man to feel himself unfairly treated and to resent it, and still to participate because he lacks more attractive alternatives. A second major function of man's system of calculus, then, deals with what we can identify as the *inducements/contributions* contract. This involves consideration of the inducements or rewards that the parties in the role network are prepared to offer in exchange for the individual's contributions. While this may raise questions of distributive justice, the central question now is whether the inducements/contributions bargain struck with the group is at least equal to the bargains available in other groups. Thus perception of alternatives is an important ingredient in the negotiations of the contract. (Because of the availability of alternatives, some are in a better position to negotiate an attractive bargain which may result in perceived inequities by others in the group.)

> *Chester Barnard, James March, and Herbert Simon have treated this question from the point of view of the group or organization in terms of* inducements/contributions theory.   <

The balance of rewards and costs inducing membership at one point may not be sufficient at another time because of changes in action spheres associated with life cycle, or because perceived alternatives suggest that a new and better self-conception can be realized elsewhere.

Instrumental action thus propels modern man into networks of roles calling for his conformity and adherence to the rules of the game (or roles) in exchange for the benefits the role network can offer. And because the relationship is one of exchange, score-keeping becomes important. But we cannot be content to believe that man simply conforms to immutable roles or that the calculation of costs cannot be influenced by his efforts. There is often room for man to maneuver.

MANEUVERING THROUGH EPISODES

Purposive man becomes involved in role networks—dyads, groups and role-sets—especially because he is trying to accomplish something. He is building a road, curing a disease, buying a house, publishing a book, negotiating a loan. Each of his goals is associated with a body of beliefs about cause and effect relationships, identified perhaps as engineering, finance, medicine, or economics. In complex modern urban society, these bodies of knowledge usually can be applied only by becoming embedded in role networks. Accomplishment thus rests on a combination of technical and social skills and this raises the question of such maneuvering through episodes.

> *An insightful and entertaining analysis of maneuvering through episodes, which overemphasizes the social skills at the expense of the technical achievement—gamesmanship—is provided by Stephen Potter.* <

Socialization prepares individuals to assume roles, but no matter how well socialized, the individual who enters a role network is naive about local interpretations of roles, and about the personalities of those involved, and the others involved are likewise naive about him. Except in the simplest situation, then, socialization is insufficient and there is a certain amount of learning that must take place as episodes unfold. For open-system man to learn these nuances he must be sensitive to the clues provided by others; if he is not, he runs the risk of unknowingly violating local ground rules and offending others. This is a potential source of embarrassment, and may seriously impede attainment of instrumental objectives. Even if the newcomer is alert, these problems may occur unless the other participants in the role network convey accurate clues. When all the members of a network of roles are newcomers, this problem is magnified. Therefore we would expect that when a new group is formed—no matter how competent the members are as individuals—it will be relatively ineffective initially; military organizations are particularly vulnerable and therefore cognizant of this. Combat maneuvers or shakedown cruises facilitate this kind of learning.

Impression Management and Feedback

Others respond to open-system man in terms not only of the role he occupies, but also the impressions he manages to convey in that role. He may not deliberately engage in what has been termed *impression management,* but to the extent that he is striving for the achievement of some instrumental objective and is sophisticated in these techniques, he can deliberately offer clues about himself on any relevant dimension: his goals, his interpretations of reality, his beliefs about causation, and his norms. The elected official may carefully control his facial expressions during a press conference in order to convey his coolness, and his preparation for and control over his job. The musician at a public concert will assume a manner that will demonstrate the seriousness of his purpose. The nurse will do some visible things to appear to be busy while she is observing a patient's condition—his color, respiration rate, shallowness of breathing—in order that the patient is not disturbed by her surveillance and others do not charge her with wasting time.

> *How man manages himself—and particularly his impressions on others in interpersonal relations—is the particular focus of* ethnomethodologists, *most notably Erving Goffman and Harold Garfinkel.*   <

Whether an individual attempts to give an honest impression is a variable. Any attempt to manage impressions is fraudulent to some degree, for inevitably some things about the individual are omitted, while others may be exaggerated. The stereotypical example is the party-goer who attempts to impress others with his familiarity with the esthetic world by dropping names of artists, musicians, and actors—only some of whose work is actually familiar to him. The college freshman may for hours practice the way he holds, lights, and draws on his pipe in order that he publicly exudes the proper degree of social sophistication. Some performances, of course, are almost entirely fraudulent. The best examples can be found among con-men who assume a variety of poses in order to fleece their victims.

Generally speaking we would expect that if an individual's participation in the role network is strictly utilitarian he will give those clues which he believes will most facilitate the achievement of his goals. To the extent that man's self-conception is at issue, however, we would expect him to put his best foot forward, selectively affording clues which he considers to be status-enhancing. The professor is likely to tell his students about those of his studies which paid off in contributions to his field, and ignore those that were failures. Often instrumental and status objectives are interwined so that the attainment of status within the network of roles is an important step toward instrumental objectives.

Impression management may be aimed at enhancement of the status of others in the role network, rather than or at the expense of oneself. On an occasion in honor of his coach, the athlete may recall games in which he blundered badly, but the coach evolved a new strategy to bail the team out. By offering status through such things as deference, the instrumentally oriented individual may induce others to be more favorably disposed to him. Thus the calculus of rewards and costs may result in paying the price of status within the role network in exchange for rewards in the future or in other social contexts. One may ingratiate himself through low status in a high-status group, in order to maintain membership in that group and thereby achieve high status in other social groups through such devices as name-dropping. An individual may prefer to remain a reserve player on a strong sports team rather than an outstanding player on a weak team.

There is always a subjective element in impression management; one can never be certain how the clues he affords will be perceived and interpreted by others. Therefore if he is deliberately managing impressions we would expect him to also be sensitive to *feedback,* and adjust his performances accordingly.

It is not only the newcomer who must manage impressions and observe feedback. The established member of the network confronts this problem as participants in the network leave and are replaced by new members.

Gaining Support

The learning which takes place in role networks is not confined to the level of interpersonal expectations, or to the level of personality. Frequently members of role networks teach each other cause-and-effect connections which are pertinent to the utilitarian objectives. Where tasks are complicated, members of the role network cannot be expected to be thoroughly familiar with every aspect of the group's activities. If relationships are cooperative, members may pool information and experiences so that each individual's performance is strengthened. This feature is especially critical when some members are deployed to hostile environments. Thus cabdrivers, policemen, clergymen, or salesmen spend what time they can with their respective coworkers learning new ways of handling old problems, or how to deal with difficult situations which they have not themselves yet faced.

The fact that individuals meet hostile environments as agents of the group and then rejoin the group has other supportive consequences. Members of the role network may help the individual maintain a balanced perspective by reminding the defeated that all agents sometimes meet defeat, or by reminding the elated that victory strings end.

To the extent that the individual contributes his experiences— failures as well as accomplishments—to the pool of knowledge, he can expect to share in that pool and thereby gain the support of the group.

Conformity and Credit

To win others' support, the individual must conform, to some degree, to their expectations. In addition to mastering the technical know-how associated with his goals, he must maneuver to gain cooperation and do so without incurring unreasonable costs. Some persons may conform simply for the sake of conformity; others because it is a means of achieving utilitarian ends. In the latter case, a history of conformity may result in expanding freedom within the role network through the accumulation of what has been called *idiosyncrasy credits*. This seems to occur when an individual has so demonstrated loyalty to the group and fidelity to its norms that he has earned the right to occasionally default on expectations without paying a penalty. Group leaders are often chosen on demonstrated adherence to group norms, and are given latitude to behave in ways that if done by other members would raise questions about loyalty. Obviously it is possible for the individual who has earned idiosyncrasy credits to squander them.

Reducing Costs

So far we have concentrated primarily on the rewards that can be gained by maneuvering in episodes. But the person can also experience considerable costs, and some of his maneuvering within the network of roles may be designed to reduce these costs. In order to reduce them, he may have to call to the attention of others in the network the fact that he believes he is the victim of inequities or that he is tempted by alternatives.

Complaining is not an easy task, expecially because groups may develop norms which discourage frequent complaining. There are a variety of indirect methods of complaining, however. The individual, without registering a complaint, may find opportunities to lead others to the conclusion that inequities do exist. Sometimes it is possible to make sure contrasts are visible, so that others decide for themselves that inequities exist. The second way of registering dissatisfaction without complaining is to withhold some contributions or, more frequently, to meet expectations grudgingly. This is frequently a tactic in family squabbles. Alternatively, the individual may deviate from expectations by actually overconforming to one aspect of the role relationship or another, and through this, call attention to the fact that something is unsatisfactory. When they are constrained from striking, workers may resort to abiding rigidly to every rule in the books, a tactic which will frequently so slow down an organization that complaints are recognized.

Valued members of a role network may reduce costs (or gain relative advantages) by developing alternatives, a tactic which works only if others in the present role network learn of these alternatives and if they consider them to be competitive. As we indicated in Chapter 5, work visibility is an important factor in developing job alternatives and in enhancing occupational careers. The value of visibility is not confined to the occupational sphere, however, but applies to such varied situations as courtship, bargaining dyads, and international politics. Still the individual who constantly threatens to withdraw may soon find his threats ignored, and if he continues he may jeopardize his standing in the group. The more efficient tactic may be to arrange for others in the role network to learn of the individual's alternatives as if by accident. This tactic avoids some of the risks of bluffing, which is an alternative way of indicating dissatisfaction. Bluffing involves a direct confrontation with other members of the role network, raising the possibility of tension, and has the further disadvantage that a called bluff either forces the individual out of the group or reduces his status if he remains.

Another major way that costs are reduced is at the psychological level and involves the reduction of *cognitive dissonance*. Cognitive dissonance arises when an individual perceives that two or more of his cognitions—beliefs, attitudes, or norms—are inconsistent. The high school valedictorian may conceive of himself at the head of his college class, only to find that he is among the rank and file, and these two cognitions are incompatible. His father, meanwhile, may be learning that someone else has been assigned to the coveted position of general manager, resulting in a cognition inconsistent with previous expectations. Dissonance theory generally holds that dissonance is psychologically costly, and that the individual will seek to modify one or more of his cognitions to bringing them into agreement. One way in which this can be done is to lower aspirations, thereby reducing or eliminating the discrepancy between accomplishment and expectation. This process is sometimes referred to as "becoming realistic," and is difficult because it involves reformulation of the self-concept. The college student may convince himself that he should seek a less competitive career than he envisioned. Another psychological way to reduce cognitive costs is for the individual to alter his norms. The same college student may resort to cheating rather than lower his aspiriation for a high-status career. The ability to reduce dissonance by altering norms appears to be a personality variable; some find it entirely too costly because adherence to the norms is central to their self-conceptions. Instead they may withdraw from the role network.

>   *The theory of cognitive dissonance has been developed by Leon Festinger and his associates. It is one form of a broader category,* balancing theories, *whose major contributors include Fritz Heider and Theodore Newcomb.*   <

RECAPITULATION

Regardless of man's time dimension or his life space, much of his daily action occurs in short-burst episodes, many of which require interaction with other persons. These others are encountered not simply as personalities or at random, but within networks of roles—dyads, groups, or role sets. If man wants the benefits these others can offer he must pay the price of meeting their expectations. But depending on his skills—managing impressions, sensing feedback, gaining support, earning credits, or reducing costs—he may be able to maneuver to gain more favorable terms and thus achieve instrumental or intrinsic results. If these maneuvers do not result in a satisfactory balance of rewards and costs, open-system man may have to suspend action within episodes and instead direct his attention to changing the parameters for future episodes. In Chapter 8, we turn to consideration of this topic.

RECOMMENDED BROWSING

Robert F. Bales, *Interaction Process Analysis: A Method for the Study of Small Groups*. Reading, Mass.: Addison-Wesley, 1950. Sets forth a method for observing and analyzing activity in groups which has been employed by many others.

Chester Barnard, *The Functions of the Executive*. Cambridge, Mass.: Harvard University Press, 1937. Written by an accomplished executive, this book sets forth the "inducements/contributions theory" widely used in the study of formal organizations, as well as a penetrating analysis of "informal organization."

Peter Blau, *Exchange and Power in Social Life*. New York: Wiley, 1964. An important sociological version of exchange theory as a basis for social relations.

D. C. Cartwright and A. Zander, editors, *Group Dynamics: Research and Theory* (second edition). Evanston, Ill.: Row Peterson, 1960. A balanced collection of articles on the processes of small groups, especially emphasizing social-psychological approaches.

Fred Davis, "The Cabdriver and His Fare: Facets of a Fleeting Relationship," *American Journal of Sociology*, 65 (September 1959) 158–165. An analysis of a dyadic relationship virtually devoid of socially integrating devices.

William R. Dill, Thomas L. Hilton, and Walter R. Reitman, *The New Managers: Patterns of Behavior and Development*. Englewood Cliffs, N.J.: Prentice-Hall, 1962. A penetrating study of how careers are started, stressing the management of visibility and sensitivity to environment or feedback.

Leon Festinger, *A Theory of Cognitive Dissonance*. Evanston, Ill.: Row, Peterson, 1957. The initial presentation of a theory which has since claimed major attention in American psychology.

Harold Garfinkel, *Studies in Ethnomethodology*. Englewood Cliffs, N.J.: Prentice-Hall, 1967. A collection of articles by one who has been pioneering in the field.

Erving Goffman, *The Presentation of Self in Everyday Life*. Garden City, N.J.: Doubleday Anchor, 1959. A classic analysis of man maneuvering in social episodes; a forerunner to ethnomethodology.

A. Paul Hare, E. F. Borgatta, and R. F. Bales, editors, *Small Groups* (revised edition). New York: Alfred A. Knopf, 1965. A useful collection of articles on processes in small groups, emphasizing sociological as well as psychological approaches.

Fritz Heider, *The Psychology of Interpersonal Relations.* New York: Wiley, 1958. An important formulation of *balance theory* in psychology.

E. P. Hollander, "Conformity, Status, and Idiosyncrasy Credit," *Psychological Review,* 65 (March 1958) 117–127.

George C. Homans, *Social Behavior: Its Elementary Forms.* New York: Harcourt, Brace, 1961. One of the basic statements of exchange theory in social psychology and sociology.

Harold J. Leavitt, "Some Effects of Certain Communication Patterns on Group Performance," *Journal of Abnormal and Social Psychology,* 46 (January 1951) 38–50. A classic experiment on the effects of different communication networks on task groups.

Stewart Maccaulay, "Non-Contractual Relations in Business: A Preliminary Study," *American Sociological Review,* 28 (February 1963) 55–67.

James G. March and Herbert A. Simon, with the collaboration of Harold Guetzkow, *Organizations.* New York: Wiley, 1958. An important extension of the inducement/contributions theory, taking into account behavioral science developments in the two decades following Barnard's original formulation.

Robert K. Merton, "The Role-Set: Problems in Sociological Theory," *British Journal of Sociology,* 8 (June 1957) 106–120.

J. L. Moreno, editor, *The Sociometry Reader.* Glencoe, Ill.: The Free Press, 1960. A compilation of articles, collected by the man who pioneered in this field.

F. J. Roethlisberger and W. J. Dickson, *Management and the Worker.* Cambridge, Mass.: Harvard University Press, 1939. The classic study of formal organizations, which found pervasive informal organizations, and opened the field of industrial sociology.

John W. Thibaut and Harold H. Kelley, *The Social Psychology of Groups.* New York: Wiley, 1959. A major analysis of small groups, emphasizing the exchange and transactional aspects of participation.

Kurt H. Wolff, editor and translator, *The Sociology of Georg Simmel.* New York: The Free Press of Glencoe, 1950. Contains chapters on the dyad and triad, as well as insightful materials on such topics as sociability, social gatherings, secret societies and coquetry.

RESTRUCTURING ROLE NETWORKS

A sphere of action presents open-system man with sets of role networks in which episodes unfold. Because interaction with others within these episodes involves interdependence and reciprocity, there inevitably are involved aspects of both costs and rewards, and possibilities of imbalance. Some of these imbalances can be handled through interpersonal maneuvers such as we considered in Chapter 7. Not infrequently, however, reward-cost imbalances are built into the role network rather than being due to the personalities of the participants, and it becomes important to have mechanisms for restructuring of dyads, groups, or role-sets.

We would expect interpersonal maneuvering to be the first resort of the individual who is dissatisfied, because this manner of coping demands less energy and time than alternative measures for redressing imbalances—either the restructuring of relevant role networks by the reworking of role expectations or by changing dependence and power, or finally by withdrawing from these networks and seeking a more favorable sphere of action. We would expect withdrawal to be the most costly in terms of time or energy. Hence where interpersonal maneuvering is not enough we would expect attention to shift to the restructuring of the role network, thereby changing the parameters of episodes. The methods available for such restructuring depend in part on the nature of the imbalances.

FORMS OF STRUCTURAL IMBALANCE

The social sciences have identified several sets of conditions which usually result in perceived descrepancies between rewards and costs. These include *role-set conflict, multiple-position conflict,* and *status inconsistency.*

143

Role-Set Conflict

In introducing the concept of role-set, we said it consisted of all of those roles reciprocal to a given position. Each of these imposes a set of demands on the person occupying the position, and in complicated and dynamic role-sets it is not unusual for some of these demands to be incompatible and conflicting. The children and the husband may compete for the wife's attention and collectively demand more attention than she can possibly give. It is not uncommon for the husband/ wife relation to be renegotiated following the arrival of the first child, for example. The industrial foreman has been termed the "man in the middle," signifying the conflict which may arise in expectations of subordinates and of superordinates.

> *Traditionally* role-conflict *has been used to refer to both role-set conflict and multiple-position conflict. More recently the distinctions have become clearer through the research of Neal Gross, Robert Merton and Frederick Bates.*   <

Conflict Between Multiple Positions

In contemporary societies, individuals tend to occupy positions in several different structures which may impose incompatible demands on the person even though there is no internal conflict (role-set conflict) within any one of these structures. Thus the woman may occupy a position in a very smooth-running office, and be a mother in a well-ordered family, and still experience conflict betweeen the requirements of the occupation and the family. Even if the foreman escapes role-set conflict at work, he may find that the night-shift requirements conflict with the family's recreational demands. The college student may experience conflict between the dyadic demands in courtship and the demands placed by professors on students.

Status Inconsistency

As noted in Chapter 2, man is differentiated from others in terms of ascribed categories such as age, sex, and kinship, as well as achieved categories, both of which we identified as status categories. Status categories, being less specific than roles or positions, may be applied in a variety of role networks. The boss may also be identified as old, the legislator may also be identified as male, the student also as young. This application of status categories to persons in positions need not cause complications, but if expectations are divergent there arises the problem of *status inconsistency*. Thus for the boss to be young where the workers are older involves status inconsistency in cultures such as ours; for the legislator to be a woman results in ambivalence as to how she should be treated; and for the older student to face a young instructor leads to conflicting expectations. Status inconsistency also appears in the family, especially in the case of the adolescent—who sometimes is expected to behave as an adult but who is also treated as a child—and in the case of the aging father who is becoming dependent on his son.

> *As in other topics within the social sciences under current explora-tion, this topic has been approached from a variety of perspectives under varying labels including* status consistency, equilibrium, incongruence, discrepancy, *and* crystallization.   <

Mitigating Conditions

Even though these forms of structural imbalance are present, the epi-sodes they contain may not reveal conflict. Role-embedded problems may sometimes be alleviated by sophisticated and cooperative persons.

In cases of status inconsistency, for example, thoughtful persons may carefully avoid incidents which aggravate the inconsistency. The junior boss may treat the older subordinate with special respect, and the older subordinate may reciprocate. The family is vulnerable to all three types of structural imbalance, but frequently the parents tactily or overtly cooperate to minimize the episodes in which conflict might be stimulated. In some families, the husband and wife may agree, for the benefit of the children, to remain together and to avoid contact with each other's relatives, or discussions of politics or religion.

A second condition under which a structural imbalance may not become manifest is a situation in which adherence to conflicting de-mands is not detected. If he can otherwise satisfy his role obligation to both family and mistress, the husband who can keep them apart has it made. The foreman may talk one way with subordinates and another with his bosses, and perhaps get away with it if bosses and workers do not have direct communication. The politican who can segment his constituents and tell each what they want to hear may also get away with it, but only so long as each segment does not know of his contradictory statements to others. Behavior which meets one set of expectations and violates another may be easier in the relative anonymity of the city than in the village; on the other hand, the technologies of modern urban society, such as television, may add considerable complications for the politician.

A third situation in which an individual may escape the costs of a structural imbalance comes about when another person, whose expectations have been violated, fails to levy penalties, either because the damaged person finds using those penalties offensive, or concludes that the offender had no choice. On some occasions, the injured person may be seriously disappointed, but be so powerless that he cannot apply sanctions and thus cannot force the conflict to the attention of the offenders.

The fact that social contexts may enable an individual to meet conflicting expectations but escape the penalties which others may levy does not necessarily mean that he incurs no costs. If the individual is psychologically committed to the roles involved, then we would expect him to experience cognitive dissonance and the associated psychological costs. The internalization of norms (which results in a "conscience") thus provides an observer even when the individual is alone. The internalized norms, however, may be such that the individual is able to compartmentalize his cognitions and psychologically deny that conflict exists even though others believe it does.

>   *Cognitive compartmentalization is an important aspect of the theory of cognitive dissonance.*   <

Escaping the costs of structural imbalance is not easy. Probably all of us avoid some costs due to these mitigating conditions. But in modern urban society, it is highly unlikely that any of us regularly and constantly escapes from the costs of conflict associated with role networks. Modern man does therefore employ devices designed to restructure role networks in which unsatisfactory episodes unfold.

REWORKING ROLE EXPECTATIONS

Restructuring of role networks means that a new set of role expectations has to be worked out with the other participants; roles must somehow be redesigned. In reworking role expectations, open-system man may try (1) to expand or contract the role network, thus avoiding one set of the expectations in conflict, (2) to transfer responsibility to another party, (3) to negotiate compromise.

Expanding or Contracting the Role Network

Perhaps the most obvious way of escaping the costs when under cross-pressure in different social positions is to withdraw from one of the positions. The wife who finds that her job or her voluntary community work conflict with her family obligations may resign; or priorities may be reversed and she may shed her family in order to protect her professional career. Withdrawal from a position is an effective means of escaping conflict but it may not be a practical possibility. The family cycle and its associated financial demands may preclude resignation from the second job, for example.

When conflict arises within a role-set rather than between positions, contraction is again a possibility. But role-sets are networks of interdependence; thus elimination of one of the roles is difficult because it requires redefinition of one or more of the remaining roles and therefore cannot be done unilaterally. In divorce (or death of a family member), the roles of the remaining family members must somehow expand to take up the responsibilities of the departed member. In work groups, arbitrary elimination of a conflicting role is precluded because the role is essential for the accomplishment of the tasks for which the group is held responsible. One of the advantages of work organizations with formalized authority is that they embrace criteria against which responsibilities can be redivided and reassigned; when conflict within the work group interferes with accomplishment of the tasks, responsibilities may be shifted and the organization restructured so that work roles are compatible.

>   *The significance of* **authority** *structures for work organizations has received much attention in the social sciences, particularly by Max Weber,*

Chester Barnard, and Alfred Chandler. The relation of technology *to social structures is likewise an important topic and has been examined by Stanley Udy and Joan Woodward. Conflict in formal organizations has been analyzed by James March and Herbert Simon.*   <

Another way of handling conflict is to enlarge the role-set. Some couples with marital conflict may seek to solve their problems by expanding the family to include a child. This third party may add a positive link in the family, may divert attention from disagreements over role obligations, and may provide a basis for compromise. The university departmental chairman may expand his role network, thus incurring obligations which he can then use to explain to departmental faculty members why he cannot meet their expectations; we would expect this tactic to work if his position is ambiguously defined and if he can convince the faculty that his new role benefits them.

Conflict within a role-set may be alleviated by becoming involved in an additional position. Thus the henpecked husband may take on a second job to escape discord in the family, and indeed the expectations of family members may be changed as a result.

Transferring Responsibilities

Rather than adding or subtracting a role, an individual may use another tactic: He may abdicate a portion of his role with the assurance that another will assume it. Thus the mother may avoid disciplining her children on the assumption that the father will perform that chore for both. The boss may delegate certain onerous responsibilities to an assistant or a secretary, or he may refer responsibilities which would conflict to his boss for settlement.

When the requirements of a position overtax the resources of the person, he may shift some of the burden to persons reciprocal to him in another position. Thus the wife who becomes overactive in community affairs may induce her husband to take on some of her obligations to community agencies, for example. The boss who takes on administrative responsibilities in a religious organization which are too time-consuming may have his wife or his secretary attending to some of the paperwork.

Negotiating Compromise

The most direct, though not necessarily the easiest, way to repair conflicting structures is to get those holding incompatible expectations to redefine or compromise them. Whether the conflict is within the role-set or between positions, the victim can either attempt to negotiate directly with one or more of those holding conflicting expectations, or he may get them to negotiate among themselves. Thus family quarrels which reveal costly role conflicts may result in patching-up sessions in which roles are redefined. And the husband may steer his wife into a conversation with his boss in order that she can be briefed on the sacrifices she needs to make in support of her husband's new promotion.

All of these—expanding or contracting role networks, transferring responsibilities, negotiating compromises—are devices for reworking roles to relieve them of strain. These often work but are by no means foolproof. Even when they work, they are essentially defensive, helping to correct disadvantages. But if man has aspirations—if his goals require participation in role networks—he may wish to take the offensive, to achieve an advantage with respect to others. Whether on the offense or defense, he may find it necessary to manage his dependence.

CHANGING DEPENDENCE AND POWER

Open-system man cannot escape being interdependent with some others. If he lacks acceptable alternatives and is dissatisfied with the cost/reward balance in his present role networks, then he must find ways to restructure role networks by altering his dependence on others or their dependence on him.

A Conception of Power

Power in social relations has been widely considered. Perhaps the most straightforward but broadly applicable way of thinking about power has been offered by sociologist Richard M. Emerson. Emerson begins with the notion that the power of one person resides in the dependency of another; the more dependent the other, the more power the first person has over him. Power thus rests on supply and demand. If you need something which another person can provide, you have demand and he has supply, and he thereby has a potential base for power. Whether in fact his power materializes depends on the availability of supply elsewhere. The degree of your dependence—and thus the degree of the other's power—is related to the intensity of your need or demand as well as the difficulty of finding other suppliers. Where your need is of extremely high priority and the other has a monopoly on the supply, he is in a very powerful position relative to you. Where your need has high priority and there are many suppliers, or alternatively where your need is only moderate but there are only a few or one supplier, you will be somewhat dependent and the other will have some power.

> *Social power not only has been viewed through several frameworks, but in several different disciplines. Prominent among psychologists have been John Thibaut and Harold Kelley, and John R. P. French, Jr.; among political scientists, Robert Dahl and Harold Lasswell; and among sociologists, Peter Blau and Talcott Parsons.* <

One important advantage to Emerson's conception is that it permits us to consider interdependence or mutual power; in view of the fact that role relations involve reciprocity, a conception of power which allows for reciprocal exercises of power is realistic. Large amounts of power held by each participant do not cancel each out; in fact, this characterizes many relationships which have solidarity. Neither does an increase in your power necessarily decrease the power of the other, because your dependence on him may remain constant. In fact, it is quite possible for relationships in a role network to increase in interdependence, and for this to result in more power for each dependent. Each ally in an alliance may be stronger for being a member than he would have been as an independent. Indeed, this is what accounts for alliances or partnerships, and it can be seen at all levels from international relations to domestic political parties to courtship and marriage.

This version of power is nonspecific enough to be widely applicable. It does not confine our attention to power based on personality variables, or economic or political dependence—although all these may be in the picture. Emerson's formulation permits us to consider the relative supply of anything in demand. Demand is thus determined by open-system man's aspirations and those cause-and-effect routes which he believes will achieve his objectives. If he demands love or respect, then those who can provide love or respect may have power; if he demands money, information or knowledge, or privacy, those who can supply such needs may acquire power.

This conception of power, it should be noted, focuses on the potential for power, whether or not exercised. If exercised, power may be employed deliberately or quite innocently, and the other party may or may not be cognizant that the other has exercised power. Changes in the power relationships may be either deliberate or unintentional. If you desire to deliberately restructure role networks and cannot renegotiate role expectations, then you must alter dependence relationships, hence power relationships. Therefore let us turn our attention to the ways in which power relationships are changed.

Tactics for Changing Power Relationships

Within this conception, power relationships may be changed either by increasing your power relative to others' or by decreasing their power relative to yours. This presents several possibilities, which are illustrated in Fig. 8.1.

Change in a power relationship may be achieved by operating on either demand or supply, your own or the other's. Perhaps the most

Determinants of Dependence

Participants	Supply	Demand
You	Develop alternative sources (I)	Reduce (II)
Other	Cut off alternatives (III)	Stimulate (IV)

FIG. 8.1 *Tactics for changing power relations.*

direct or immediate device is to work on these variables as they apply to you. Thus you may reduce your dependence on the other by developing new sources of supply (I), or by shifting your priorities, thus reducing your demand for the rewards he can supply (II). Either of these tends to equalize power by reducing the power that the other can exercise. Alternatively, disadvantage may be rectified by increasing your power with respect to the other. This may be done by cutting off his alternative sources for benefits that you can provide (III), or it may be done by stirring up his interest in benefits you can provide (IV).

Altering the Supply Side of the Equation

The development of alternative sources of supply (I) is a widespread tactic in modern society. The possibility of dealing with alternative suppliers may be just as effective and less costly than actually doing so. Thus, in courtship, being popular may increase your power with your partner, whereas dating others would accomplish the same thing but would add further complications. As we discussed in Chapter 6, power with respect to an employer may be increased by maintaining visibility in the labor market and thus keeping alternatives open. Again the potential may be more important than the reality, but the individual who constantly threatens to leave may expend his potential. There are many occasions when deliberate cultivation of alternatives makes possible the profitable renegotiation of relations.

Perhaps the best illustration of reducing the other's alternative source of supply (III) occurs with early-ceiling occupations. In Chapter 6, we pointed out that the combination of financial need and an occupational early ceiling leads to collective action through unions or associations. These are coalitions which serve to reduce or eliminate for employers alternative supplies of workers, thereby increasing the relative power of employees. Or the father's power may be threatened by the birth of several girls and by the possibility of a female coalition in the family.

An important tactic in reducing the other's alternatives is, paradoxically, the reduction of your own. By irrevocable commitment to a particular position or stand, you tell the other person that there are no alternatives left open for you, and therefore he must deal with you on a take-it-or-leave-it basis. This tactic, which has been practiced under such labels as brinkmanship by politicians, has been analyzed in the social sciences by Thomas Schelling. When successful, this tactic is quite effective, for it forces the other to make all the concessions, but for this reason it may also inspire the other to seek revenge. The brinkmanship tactic also requires a judgment of just how dependent the other is on you, and if you misjudge the degree of this dependence, the relationship may be aborted.

> *The processes of* negotiation *and* bargaining *have only recently become a research focus for social scientists, among them Thomas Schelling, Kenneth Boulding, Anatol Rapoport, and Sidney Siegel and Lawrence Fouraker.* <

Altering the Demand Side of the Equation

When you are building power by stimulating the other's demand for items you can supply (IV), the basic tactic is to offer to enhance the other's self-conception. One of the most important devices by which to do this is to offer the other person status. The lover by lavishing the girl with compliments and attention which can be withdrawn may increase her dependence on him. The university by offering the status of an honorary degree may gain power by incurring an obligation on the part of an important person. Demand may be stimulated through promises of enhanced status as well. Advertising may hold out the promise of an improved self-image if a particular product or service is used; an individual may do volunteer work in a political campaign in the hope of socializing with the candidate.

The power deficit can also be brought into line by reducing your demand for what the other party has been providing (II). This involves establishment of a new set of priorities which moves you toward indifference and may ultimately result in complete withdrawal from the enterprise. This appears to be an unstable tactic. If it does not bring a response from the other party and thus a new power balance, we would expect ultimate dissolution of the relationship.

WITHDRAWING FROM ROLE NETWORKS

Withdrawing from important role networks means altering the individual's sphere of action and thus is not a matter to be lightly undertaken, but it does happen, and to virtually all of us. It involves shifting of priorities, which can occur for either of two reasons. After trying interpersonal maneuvering, reworking role expectations, and changing power/dependence relations, the individual who still experiences dissatisfaction with the reward/cost balance is likely to shift his priorities by lowering his aspirations or by redirecting them. The second reason for withdrawing from a role network stems from changes in the life cycle or in the family cycle which may change values and needs and thus call for new priority schedules.

New priorities for the action sphere call for assessments of reward/cost balance of present role networks as compared to possible alternative ones, and this makes important the collection and evaluation of information about those possibilities.

Costs of Foregone Opportunities

Participation in certain role networks precludes participation in certain others. Selection of some among alternative role networks thus involves not only the rewards associated with the chosen alternative, but also the loss of rewards which might have been achieved by participating in other role networks. This cost is known by those who calculate such matters as *the cost of foregone opportunities.*

The individual faced with alternative role networks may thus be forced to consider various inducements/contributions balances. When a new alternative is perceived to be clearly better, we would expect the individual to resolve the discrepancy by shifting. Likewise, where the alternatives are clearly less desirable, we would expect them to be dismissed. It is in those cases in which it is difficult to determine the *net* balance of rewards and costs that we would expect conflict to be experienced. An interesting job, for example, with good career opportunities but in an undesirable location may be difficult to compare with a boring job in a pleasant location with good career opportunities.

The woman with a promising career may be tempted by a proposal from a promising man which would require occupational retirement. Such perceived alternatives may ultimately be accepted or rejected as a result of decision processes (which we shall consider in the next chapter), but it is possible for perceived alternatives to be left dangling for a considerable length of time and to cause problems for the person in his role networks.

This problem may persist in cases in which one's situation is not particularly satisfying, but in which perceived alternatives are not clearly better. On the other hand, the individual may take deliberate steps to determine the rewards and costs that would be incurred in moving, and thereby force clarification of relative advantages.

Gathering Information

The process of gathering information about alternatives may be quite straightforward, involving simply the asking of questions, but when relationships are complicated and cannot be predicted adequately in question-and-answer form, trial periods may be involved. Employment often involves a probationary period, and couples may have a trial marriage, or a trial separation. Often, however, the exploration is too delicate for such direct dealings and the parties resort to a sounding-out process.

The sounding-out process occurs when the possibility of a new set of relationships exists but the parties involved are constrained from fully disclosing either their interests or their dependence. The sounding-out process can be illustrated by the problem of the boss with amorous designs on his secretary in an organization that taboos such relations. He must find some means of determining her willingness to alter the relationship, but he must do so without risking rebuff, for a showdown might come at the cost of his dignity or his office reputation, at the cost of losing her secretarial services, or in the extreme case, at the cost of losing his own position—and certainly with costs to his self-conception. But the sounding-out process occurs in a number of other contexts: the buying and selling of major items such as homes and automobiles, the development of political alliances, corporate mergers, and negotiating for new jobs. In each of these cases, the problem is to stimulate the other to yield information without yourself giving more information than is necessary, or without prematurely committing yourself. Usually the deliberate use of ambiguity is involved in the movement toward new clarity, with each party supplying information that may have several meanings and looking for responses as clues to which meanings to pursue.

The History of Withdrawal

The process of withdrawal may be rather abrupt if the role network is not very important to the individual, but when it involves significant alteration of the sphere of action or the life space, the path to withdrawal is probably long and painful. When family relations are seriously strained, for example, or when the occupational career is not progressing satisfactorily, we would expect the individual involved to go through a sequence of experiences before making the torturous decision to withdraw. When the individual is forced to the realization that interpersonal maneuvering is not solving his problem, we would expect him to try renegotiation of role expectations, and when frustrated with this, to seek redress through power manipulation. Only after this attempt too has met with ultimate frustration would we expect the final withdrawal. At each step, as costs and frustrations mount, he might give increased attention to foregone opportunities and to information about these.

Married couples experiencing conflict, after they realize that interpersonal maneuvering is inadequate, may engage in a series of arguments designed to alter role expectations. Failing in this, one or both may seek to increase power by getting the children or friends to take his or her side in disputes, or may try to reduce dependence by lowering aspirations for marital satisfaction. One or both may begin to consider what life would be like without this marriage or perhaps what another marriage would be like. Thus final dissolution of the marriage may follow only after a long series of escalating attempts and frustrations. The changing of jobs may follow a similar history of mounting frustrations.

RECAPITULATION

Episodes unfold in structured contexts, and interpersonal skills may not be sufficient to overcome structural imbalances, which result in role-set conflict, multiple-position conflict, or status inconsistency. Some potential conflict is mitigated by social or psychological processes, but restructuring of role networks is sometimes required. This can be achieved through renegotiations of role expectations, or by changing power and dependence relationships. When satisfactions still do not flow from these attempts, individuals withdraw from the role network and modify their spheres of actions.

RECOMMENDED BROWSING

Stuart Adams, "Status Congruency as a Variable in Small-Group Performance," *Social Forces* 32 (October 1953), 16–22. One of the early empirical studies of the effect of status congruency on individual and group performance.

Chester I. Barnard, *The Functions of the Executive.* Cambridge, Mass.: Harvard University Press, 1938. One of the most insightful analyses of work organizations, including the bases of authority.

Frederick L. Bates, "Some Observations Concerning the Structural Aspect of Role Conflict," *Pacific Sociological Review* 5 (Fall 1962), 75–82. One of the first studies to distinguish and analyze conflicts stemming from role-set versus multiple positions.

Peter Blau, *Exchange and Power in Social Life.* New York: Wiley, 1964. A thorough consideration of exchange theory applied to sociology.

Kenneth E. Boulding, *Conflict and Defense: A General Theory.* New York, Harper and Row, 1962. An important interdisciplinary and formal analysis of conflict and its resolution.

Alfred D. Chandler, Jr., *Strategy and Structure.* Cambridge, Mass.: M.I.T. Press, 1962. A major historical study of the impact of technology and environmental conditions on authority systems in four industries.

Richard M. Emerson, "Power-Dependence Relations," *American Sociological Review* 27 (February 1962), 31–40. A formal statement of a general theory of social power.

John R. P. French, Jr., and B. Raven, "The Bases of Social Power," in Dorwin Cartwright, *et al.*, editors, *Studies in Social Power*. Ann Arbor: University of Michigan, 1959. An important social psychological perspective on social power.

William J. Goode, "A Theory of Role Strain," *American Sociological Review* **25** (August 1960), 483–495. An analysis of strain and its resolution in role-sets and multiple positions.

Neal Gross, Ward S. Mason, and A. W. McEachern, *Explorations in Role Analysis*. New York: Wiley, 1958. A pioneering study of the sources and consequences of conflict stemming from the role network of the school executive.

William Kornhauser, with the assistance of Warren O. Hagstrom, *Scientists in Industry*. Berkeley, Cal.: University of California Press, 1962. A study of strain between scientists and organizations in industrial research.

Harold D. Lasswell and Abraham Kaplan, *Power and Society: A Framework for Political Inquiry*. New Haven, Conn.: Yale University Press, 1950. Presents a political science conception of social power.

Gerhard Lenski, "Status Crystallization: A Non-Vertical Dimension of Social Status," *American Sociological Review* **19** (August 1954), 405–413. An exploratory study of the relations of status inconsistency to political attitudes and behavior.

James G. March and Herbert A. Simon, *Organizations*. New York: Wiley, 1958. An important application of the inducements/contributions theory to work organizations, with attention to conflict.

Robert M. Merton, "The Role-Set: Problems in Sociological Theory," *British Journal of Sociology* **8** (June 1957), 106–120. A classic treatment of the role-set and procedures for dealing with its conflicts.

Anatol Rapoport, *Fights, Games and Debates*. Ann Arbor, Mich.: University of Michigan Press, 1960. An analysis of three types of conflict and the circumstances in which they are likely to occur.

Thomas C. Schelling, *The Strategy of Conflict*. New York: Oxford University Press, 1963. An analysis of advantageous moves that can be made in bargaining situations.

Sidney Siegel and Lawrence Fouraker, *Bargaining and Group Decision Making: Experiments in Bi-Lateral Monopoly*. New York: McGraw-Hill, 1960. A pioneering laboratory approach to bargaining under bilateral monopoly conditions.

John W. Thibaut and Harold H. Kelley, *The Social Psychology of Groups*. New York: Wiley, 1959. A social-psychological perspective on power relations in groups.

James D. Thompson, "Organizations and Output Transactions," *American Journal of Sociology* **68** (November 1962), 309–324. An analysis of transactions under different conditions of interdependence.

Stanley H. Udy, Jr., "Technical and Institutional Factors in Production Organization," *American Journal of Sociology* **67** (November 1961), 247–260. An empirical study of the interrelations between technology and authority structure.

Max Weber, *The Theory of Social and Economic Organization*. London: Wm. Hodge, 1947. The original formulation of the theory of bureaucracy and its relationship to different types of authority.

Richard E. Walton and Robert B. McKersie, *A Behavioral Theory of Labor Negotiations: An Analysis of a Social Interaction System*. New York: McGraw-Hill, 1965. While emphasizing labor/management transactions as social processes, this volume goes beyond, in the direction of a wider theory of negotiation.

Joan Woodward, *Industrial Organization: Theory and Practice*. London: Oxford University Press, 1965. A report of important research on the impact of different technologies on authority relationships.

CHAPTER 9

MAKING DECISIONS

One of the primary functions of culture is its provision of "frozen answers" to recurrent problems, problems faced by all'or most members of the society, and faced by succeeding generations. Having such answers simplifies life tremendously, and social life would be inconceivable without them. The folk society offers a quite limited range of alternatives, relative to the ready-made answers it provides, whereas the modern urban society permits or requires decisions regarding marriage partners, educational channels and locations, occupational careers, housing and household equipment items, and savings and investment patterns, as well as where to spend the next vacation or which new automobile to trade for.

Yet in every society some range of options is left to the individual or to the family unit. It is in the modern urban society, with its emphasis on achievement, that "better and better" decisions are sought through the pursuit of *rationality*. In such societies, an identifiable idealized model of rationality is held out.

THE SIMPLE VIEW OF RATIONAL DECISION

The process of choosing rationally is simple in the abstract. In economics (which has been the academic discipline most directly concerned with rationality models) decision-making traditionally has involved considering all the alternatives and selecting that one which will maximize profits or welfare. Hence it is not very difficult to describe in simple terms the steps involved in making a decision, or at least the steps which would be involved if we wanted to make a careful one. Somehow we would (1) take stock of our situation, (2) determine the alternatives available to us, (3) predict the outcomes of each of the alternatives, (4) compare those predicted consequences against our desires or values, and, having identified the most desirable or possible outcomes, (5) pick that alternative which will lead to it.

But that abstract version of decision-making is deceptively simple, a fact which has led to considerable controversy. Part of the complication arises from the fact that it is *man* who makes decisions, and a model of decision processes must reflect that fact if it is going to help us understand the process. Another part of the complication lies in the fact that often it is man deciding in *social contexts*. For both reasons, we must consider the problematic issues in decision-making.

> *Within the traditional social science disciplines, controversy over rationality models has been mainly between students of decision-making in economics and psychology. Some complexity has been added with the emergence of such fields as* statistical decision theory, operations research, *and* management science.   <

DIMENSIONS OF DECISIONS

The Preference Dimension of Decisions

Prevailing models of decision focus on means to given ends, on the selection of alternatives, not on the selection of ends or goals. In terms of frequency this may be the typical decision problem, but in modern urban society man from time to time may also choose between alternative values, ends or goals. This does not mean that each individual or family unit is free to choose among all patterns of society or even among very many of them, for as we have seen social structure serves to channel experiences and contact with subcultures. Yet contemporary society does offer to many of its members the notion of alternative future states of affairs, including future *selves*, and this poses goal or value questions. (In the pure folk society asking the child what he wanted to "be" when he grew up would perhaps be a nonsense question. In the modern urban society this is one of life's major decision issues.)

One kind of issue for man, therefore, involves alternative future states: what kind of environment he wants to bring about, what kind of relationship to his environment he wants to achieve, or what kind of self he wants to become. It is not unusual to speak of such issues as issues of goal, although it may be more descriptive to speak of issues involving *perceived possible outcomes,* for on some occasions none of the alternatives are desired and the choice becomes one of the least harmful alternatives.

Variations of the Preference Dimension

Cultures provide general standards of desirability. In our kind of culture, for example, it is considered normal to prefer health to illness, wealth to poverty, life to death, rationality to irrationality, success to failure. Those who would reverse the ratings are considered abnormal.

There are no conceptual problems here so long as we are working in a one-dimensional sphere, so long as the question is whether we prefer health to illness or wealth to poverty. But difficulties can arise when we are asked to choose between health and wealth, for this involves a comparison of two dimensions rather than high and low points on a single dimension. In practice the problem becomes even more difficult, for often the choice is not between absolutes but between, for example, some degree of health and some degree of wealth, and here the individual often experiences ambivalence.

It is not unrealistic, therefore, to conceive of preferences for possible outcomes as varying along a dimension from *crystallized* to *ambiguous.*

The Causation Dimension of Decisions

More frequent, perhaps, are decisions involving choices among alternative means to a crystallized preference. Although such choices are required in all societies, tradition, habit, or custom frequently reduce the alternatives available to or perceived by members of folk societies. Modern urban society, however, often offers a menu of options regarding what action will bring about the desired outcomes. There is more than one way to treat an ulcer, or find a job, or beat the system. Or at least try to do these things.

Yet even in modern urban society, it is somewhat misleading to pose decision issues as issues of means, for this tends to focus attention too narrowly: on whether an intended result obtains. It thereby distracts attention from additional results or side effects. A more general term—and the one we shall use—is *cause/effect relationships,* or simply causation. So long as our preferences are clear, our decision problem is to find or select an action which will produce results we consider desirable: to select an appropriate causation.

Variation on the Causation Dimension

In simple situations, knowledge of cause/effect relationships may be complete. In the complicated situation, however, causal actions may have multiple effects which ramify in different directions; some consequences may be known, some suspected but not proved, and still others unnoticed.

Realistically, then, we must consider that understanding of cause/effect relationships can vary from complete to incomplete. But even more realistically, the individual decision-maker may *believe* that his understanding of cause/effect is *complete* or *incomplete.*

Types of Decision Issues

Clearly the two variations in decision-making that we have been discussing are each dimensions and not simple dichotomized variables, but for the purposes of our analysis here, we can focus on the extreme values only. Then, by combining the two dimensions, we have the four possible decision issues shown in Fig. 9.1. We have numbered the resulting cells, for ease of referring to them.

Beliefs about cause/effect knowledge

Preferences regarding perceived outcomes		Complete	Incomplete
	Crystallized	I	II
	Ambiguous	III	IV

FIG. 9.1 · *Types of decision issues.*

Now we can see that the simple version of decision-making is realistic for one, but only one, of our four types of decision situations. The simple examination of all alternatives and selection of the best one is realistic if you believe that you have complete understanding of alternatives and their consequences, and if you know precisely what you prefer. This is Cell I, and it applies only if the decision issue is simple relative to man's capacities. We now turn to consideration of man's capacities (we shall return to Cells II, III, and IV later).

MAN AS DECISION-MAKER

Whether man is rational, or can be, has been hotly disputed within and among the social sciences and humanities for a long time. Gradually the helpful distinction has emerged between *objective rationality* and *subjective rationality*. Objective rationality exists when the alternative chosen is in fact the very best one, and in a complicated world it is virtually impossible to have the kind of knowledge needed to attain it. While objective rationality is an important idealization, it has trivial applications. Subjective rationality refers to the situation in which the best of known alternatives is chosen, considering the information available to the decision-maker at the time, his understanding of causation and interpretation of reality, and his norms.

Subjective rationality is a concept that is much more realistic for complicated situations than objective rationality is. At the same time, it helps us see that the question of man's rationality is not a very meaningful question. Subjective rationality simply means that man makes the best choices he can within his perceptions of his situation. And most of us most of the time do this. But in realistic situations, we seldom have the information or the understanding to enable us to determine whether objective rationality has been used, so that concept is of little use. Finally, since some of man's most important choices involve not means but goals (for which rationality is not an appropriate concept), it appears that there are much more meaningful questions to raise about decision-making than the question of rationality.

For the present, then, we shall set the question aside on the reasonable assumption that when man is being purposive, he also hopes and tries to be rational. In the subjective sense, he is likely to be rational.

He may also be rational in the objective sense, but neither he nor we will know it except under some extremely limited conditions. Only if man is *self-sufficient* (with respect to the issue at hand) and *independent* is there a chance of determining objectively whether he is rational. Seldom, in reality, is man either self-sufficient or independent.

Cognitive Complexity

If man is realistic he must often realize that he does not know *all* possible courses of action. In some relatively simple situations we may be presented with a "menu" of alternatives, but often we must *search* for alternatives; "shopping" is one example. "Dating" is another. Even then, there are costs to searching, in terms of both time and effort. If man waits to consider all possible mates, for example, he will never get married. If he tries to consider all possible colleges, he will never get his application completed. And if he samples all possible occupations, he will be forever getting ready but never actually producing. In a complicated society, the variety of alternatives potentially available to answer those kinds of questions approaches infinity, at least relative to man's abilities.

Under these circumstances, if man insists on "maximizing"—on finding the very best alternative—he is immobilized. As a practical matter, he must at some point stop searching and choose, but where is that point? Our best answer so far is that practical man searches until he finds an acceptable alternative, or a satisfactory one. This behavior has been termed *satisficing* (in contrast to *maximizing*), and there can be little doubt that it is an accurate description of human behavior in many decision situations. At a minimum we would expect it in our Cell II in Fig. 9.1.

>   *The notion of* satisficing *was introduced by Herbert Simon, and utilized by James March and Richard Cyert. This group has pioneered in focusing the behavorial sciences on decision-making and identifying cognitive limits on rationality.*   <

Even in situations less complicated than those mentioned above—situations in which the number of alternatives is more finite—man may well believe that his knowledge of cause/effect relations is incomplete (Cells II and IV in Fig. 9.1), and evolve some procedures for shortcutting the evidence-gathering problem.   Which automobile, for example, will provide better tire wear, gasoline mileage, repair records, comfort, trade-in values, and sex appeal over the course of the next two or three years?   When he is faced with such a decision as this, no matter what kinds of calculations he makes, man can only make estimates or forecasts; if he is realistic he knows that his knowledge of the consequences of choosing one car rather than others is incomplete.

>   *The use of general principles or rules for reducing alternatives to a manageable number, or reducing cognitive complexity, is sometimes labeled "hueristic decision-making" by students of* management science.   <

Not only are there different consequences for each alternative, but any single alternative may have different impact over varying time periods.   Today's "hot item" may mark its owner as avant-garde today, but as definitely passé next year.

The Arousal of Emotion

Man with finite cognitive capacities must find some devices for reducing the cognitive complexities of his world.   If he is unable to do so, he will be inefficient, anxious, or perhaps immobilized, and we would expect emotional responses.   Thus, if man tells himself, or is told by significant others, that a less-than-maximum result is intolerable, he is likely to avoid a decision by making a prolonged search for the perfect solution, out of fear.   And if his decisions are evaluated out of context by others who after-the-fact have information not available at the time he made his decision, he is likely to be angry or defensive.

>   *Connections between decision-making and emotions have been relatively neglected by behavioral scientists, although there has been some work on the effects of fear of failure on selection of alternatives.   The more serious inroads of emotion on decision-making capacity are hinted at in* clinical *and* abnormal psychology.   <

Whenever man is judged according to the idealized version of rationality but faces a highly subjective reality, we would expect emotions to intrude into the decision process. On many occasion, however, emotions do not intrude because complexity is reduced to manageable proportions, to something equating man's abilities.

The Reduction of Complexity

Faced with the frequent complexities of modern urban civilizations, man cannot hope to be objectively rational. Subjective rationality, in which man makes reasonable choices within the scope of his knowledge, is a realistic hope, but it requires that boundaries somehow be established around decision issues; that is, it requires that complex situations be reduced in size, scope, or in the range of variables. Simon has suggested the term *bounded rationality* for this.

Now if complexity must be simplified before man can make (subjectively) rational decisions, the processes of simplification become important. We have already touched on one device for simplification: satisficing. Satisficing requires that the search for alternatives proceed not through all alternatives, but only until a satisfactory one is found. Man often—usually—attaches time "boundaries" to his decision situations. If consequences ramify with time, simplification occurs by ignoring longer-term outcomes or downgrading their importance.

A second device for reducing complexity is to accept the cause/effect statements of others as authoritative. If we realize the inadequacies of our own understanding of causation, we can turn to the "pros" or experts. Indeed under some conditions man may attribute authority to others who are in fact as ignorant as he.

> *Persons who are overwhelmed by complexity and uncertainty may welcome authoritarian figures as providing solutions. This tendency has led some students of personality to focus on* authoritarianism, *as we mentioned in Chapter 3.* <

Complexity can also be reduced by restoring to probabilities, and this is a widely practiced device for simplifying decision issues when repetitive events are involved. One form of this emerges in modern societies as insurance, wherein a share in the known losses for large numbers is traded for the unknown chances of the single individual. In the case of insurance, in which actuarial sciences are developed and employed, the probabilities—say, of residential fire—can be computed quite precisely and are considered *objective probabilities*. Even in insurance, however, there are important subjective elements. Life insurance tables of life expectancy do require judgments or estimates (or guesses) about advances in medical science, accident rates, and other factors, and for that reason it often turns out that experience is different from the predictions. Still, the concept of insurance rests on phenomena associated with large numbers, and we have rather elaborate statistical manipulations for dealing with probabilities under these circumstances.

The large-number device need not involve other persons, but may instead refer to one's own repeated experiences. The corporation or government agency operating a fleet of automobiles or trucks may forego automobile insurance because it can pool its own experiences and "self-insure." The individual trying to drive home from the office may draw on his own experiences to conclude that during the rush hour one route is probably faster than the alternatives.

Economists and statisticians refer to decision situations in which probabilities are known as *risky* situations (in contrast to the situation of *uncertainty,* in which the decision-maker is not able to attach probabilities to his alternative outcomes). For decades the notion of risky decision meant issues in which *objective* probabilities were known. More recently, however, there has come the recognition that decision-makers operate on the world as they perceive it, not as it "really" is, and this has led to the newer concept of *subjective probabilities.*

Two types of subjective probabilities have been identified, and there has been some dispute as to whether both can be appropriately placed under the same label. In the first—and most widely accepted— usage, subjective probability is simply an incomplete or inaccurate reflection of objective probabilities. The inexperienced poker player may have a vague idea that four-of-a-kind occur more often than a full house. The experienced poker player may have a more accurate or precise prediction, although still subjective, while the statistician (whether a poker player or not) would be able to quickly calculate the objective probabilities. Here "subjective probability" refers to man's perception of the frequency with which particular events occur.

The other version of "subjective probability" refers to man's feelings of *likelihood* of a unique event occurring. The institution of marriage, for example, rests on man's (and woman's!) ability to make such predictions accurately. And the institution of divorce reflects the fact that such abilities are not inevitable.

Now so long as the decision-maker believes that he knows the probabilities of possible outcomes associated with his alternatives, the decision process is considerably simplified, and indeed can usually be handled by appropriate statistical techniques. The difficulties, if any, lie in how the decision-maker arrives at his subjective probabilities, and this we shall consider shortly. Before that, however, we need to consider the conditions under which outcome preferences become ambiguous.

Clarification of Preferences

Give man *freedom* to choose between good, better, and best, and so long as his perceptions are accurate we can be rather confident that he will select the best. He will prefer good health to poor health and wealth to poverty. But man seldom has that much freedom. These are situations in which the outcomes are cast simply in terms of more or less of the same thing; and we call them *unidimensional* situations. But man seldom gets a chance to make decisions under these conditions.

> *Economists and statisticians measure preferences in terms of utilities; there is a body of knowledge that is referred to as* utility theory.   <

Most decisions involve at least two outcome dimensions, and even if man perceives the differences between good, better, and best, he probably also perceives that there are different "costs" attached to each. (This is Cell III in Fig. 9.1.) Our most frequent experiences of this fact, perhaps, occur in our *purchasing* decisions, in which even if we know the differences between good, better, and best, we must take into account what money we have available.

A monetary system greatly simplifies decision-making in modern societies, for it helps the decision-maker translate different things onto a single dimension for comparative purposes and helps reduce the choice to one of "either/or": either money or the item in question. But obviously not all decisions can be couched in these terms, and as more outcome dimensions are stirred into the mixture the decision process becomes increasingly difficult. Should you settle for Ruth's beauty or Olga's cooking—or Takia's personality? This kind of trilemma may explain some bachelors—and bigamists—and clearly there are costs to both of these solutions.

Marriage is one experience which most of us share and in which the multidimensionality of decision is readily apparent. Two other such experiences are (1) selection of a job and (2) selection of living quarters. Frequently, many of us experience a third such problem in political elections. The "independent" qualified to vote may refuse to go to the polls because he prefers one candidate's position on some issues but the opponent's position on others.

In each of these cases, decision involves not only simplification of cause/effect connections but also clarification of preferences, and for many of us this turns out to be a very painful or difficult process. We would expect, therefore, that some people would take as the most agreeable solution to this kind of problem the refusal to give it serious consideration. "Standing pat" appears to be one solution; here the individual says that the present situation (job, housing, etc.) is as desirable on balance as any is likely to be. Standing pat reserves to the individual the right to complain, but saves the agony of having to wrestle with his preference scale.

To the extent that the individual's activities can be psychologically compartmentalized, he may be able to avoid acknowledgment of competing preferences. And one way this may be accomplished is by sequentially considering different goals, a process analyzed by Richard Cyert and James March. When episodes can be dealt with separately, sequential attention may make it possible to escape goal conflict. This is difficult to do, however, because episodes usually gain their significance from the larger action sphere which contains the competing goals.

Another way out of the difficulty, perhaps, is to find still another dimension which tips the scale in the direction of one outcome against another. Conceivably this can lead to a totally new outcome. Unable to choose between beauty (Ruth), cooking (Olga) or personality (Takia), our suitor may propose to rich Doris.

Probably more frequent and more familiar, however, are other methods of clarifying our preferences, especially two:

(1) *Adjustment of cause/effect predictions.* Here the individual who is unable to sort out alternatives because the advantages of each offset the disadvantages of each may eventually revise his predictions. "Maybe the boss on that job won't be quite as disagreeable as I have been assuming." "Perhaps the commuting problem in that neighborhood won't be as easily solved as I thought." "Maybe Ruth's beauty is only skin deep—or wig deep."

To the extent that the decision-maker's expectations of cause/effect connections are uncertain, he may be able to slightly revise his estimates of likelihood or probability, and thus tip the scales in one direction or another.

(2) *Actual reranking of preferences.* This is a most difficult process, especially because preferences are not primarily reasoned, or revised by reasoning. Yet preference scales do get revised by people through what has been called "reality testing," or sometimes "experience." The child who insists that nothing would be better than a roller-coaster ride may revise that preference ranking drastically after one ride. But there is also evidence that, with experience, individuals learn to adjust their preference scales to what appears reasonable. The level of occupational aspirations, for example, tends to be adjusted to fit the objective probabilities, and children in different segments of the socioeconomic system have different educational aspirations.

In sum, we are saying that in the abstract, the processes of decision are simple, but that reality may present such degrees of complexity that the cognitive capacities of man are overwhelmed when he tries to make comprehensive decisions. Reasonableness and prudence therefore force man to simplify by establishing boundaries around his situations, thus reducing the inherent complexity to something approximating his cognitive abilities: his capacity to experience and to acquire information, his capacity to process information, and his capacity to sort information against his multiple preferences.

But until now we have considered decision only as a private process. It turns out in contemporary societies that decisions often have a social context; hence the processes of decision often become social processes. We turn now to those additional complications.

DECISION AS A SOCIAL PROCESS

It is the fact of social interdependence which transforms decision processes into social processes, and interdependence has a variety of effects which both complicate and simplify decision-making.

Bounded Rationality and Social Structure

Man often meets the necessity or the opportunity to make decisions in his capacity as an occupant of a role, which puts order and significance into the reality around him and thus reduces complexity. The role defines the occasions on which decisions are required or permitted, and the social structure identifies the others significant to the decision process. The social context often specifies or delimits the goals that are appropriate to a decision, and the beliefs about causation that are relevant. The role network contains the norms that are applicable to the decision process. Thus social structure, as well as psychological processes, places boundaries around aspects of reality, rendering decision situations more manageable.

This fact makes possible the emergence in modern urban societies of large-scale organizations for instrumental activities. These are complicated social structures which compartmentalize many of their activities into specialized positions, confining the attention of decision-makers to a segment of the overall goal, to a portion of the total resources, and to a particular sphere of competence. The authority of the decision-maker is thus defined. Decision-makers in these positions are expected to adhere to norms of specificity, universalism, and discipline, as well as achievement.

> *This basis for authority is distilled in the bureaucratic model, especially by Max Weber, who contrasts it with* traditional *and* charismatic

types of authority. The impact of bureaucratic structure on decision-making has been elaborated by Herbert Simon and others.   <

Social structure thus does delimit reality and establish boundaries for rationality; it simplifies decision-making enormously for open-system man. But social structure at the same time poses new problems for the decision-maker, because of his interdependence with others.

The Location of Cause/Effect Knowledge

The more we become specialists in one aspect of modern life, the more we become laymen in many other sectors. Other persons then possess the cause/effect understandings we seek in order to make decisions. Acquiring intelligence may proceed through private research, such as an evening at the library; frequently it occurs through word of mouth among friends or acquaintances; it may involve paid consultation, such as a visit to the doctor; or it may occur in bargaining negotiations between opponents, in which each gives up as little information as necessary in order to gain as much as possible. In any event, it requires interaction .

The Location of Other Resources

On occasion the decisions we want to make are not those we are able to carry out independently, and before we commit ourselves to the desirable alternative we must determine that the necessary resources are available from others; indeed we sometimes must acquire those resources before completing the commitment to an alternative. This problem occurs frequently enough so that in the economic realm it has an institutionalized solution called an *option*. For a price, the individual obtains the right to acquire the resource in question, but he is not required to do so. With an option, the decision-maker knows that that particular resource is available if the other elements in the situation fit together. In other instances, the need to acquire resources in order to make a preferred alternative feasible may lead to more lasting cooperative arrangements, such as partnerships or marriages.

When relevant information or other resources is hoarded by others, we would expect the individual who is frustrated to respond emotionally. The impersonal rules embedded in the bureaucratic hierarchy of authority serve to police the distribution of resources within large organizations and thus control emotional intrusions into decision-making.

The Impact of Consequences

In situations of interdependence, our decisions may have consequences not only for ourselves but equally or even more significantly for others. The man who decides to raise pigs on the lot next to your home may realize his preference to be wealthy, but his decision may lower the value of your home considerably. Many communities in modern societies therefore have established zoning regulations to control such possibilites. (We may note that as interdependence becomes wider and involves more people in networks of interdependence, contemporary societies respond by expanding and extending governmental devices.)

With the fly-by-night operation, the con artists, or the gyp joint, decisions may be made regardless of the harmful consequences for others; but in more stabilized relationships, one decision may be only one in a series. Pulling a fast one on the neighbor may invite retaliation, and a series of these exchanges may result in long-term feuds. Feuds do occur, but at least we might expect the decision-maker to try to take into consideration the consequences of his decisions for others, and their possible responses. With interdependence, these considerations add considerable complexity to decision processes.

The Evaluation of Decisions

In many of modern man's decisions, he acts as an agent making choices on behalf of others. Purchasing decisions, for example, often are made for the family or for the corporation or association. Choice of alternative jobs and locations, for the married individual, is clearly a choice for the family or, sometimes, by the family. Economic decision-making increasingly occurs within the complex organization, with the decision-maker as an employee. Doctors, lawyers, clerics and social workers are frequently placed in situations of making decisions on behalf of their clients.

Sponsors, employers, or clients thus are *evaluators* of the decisions made on their behalf, and to the extent that the decision-maker wants or needs to retain positive relationships with them, they are significant parts of the decision situation. Now the decision situation contains three major elements instead of two; to the decision-maker and the decision issue is added the decision evaluator. This especially adds complication because evaluators evaluate decision performance as they understand and interpret the situation, not necessarily as the decision-maker understands and interprets it.

Often the evaluator lacks the cause/effect understanding required to evaluate the decision process and outcomes on their *intrinsic* merits, and must fall back on *extrinsic* criteria; the layman may be forced to rely on judgments by other professionals or even less direct indications that the professional knows his business, such as the number of prizes won, papers published, or the source of the expert's educational credentials. The nature of his clientele may make a difference in the professional's decision; on some occasions clients demand fashionable drugs or treatments, even when the professional judgment indicates that less costly or strenuous actions are indicated.

> *There is growing literature on professional–client relations, especially in health and welfare contexts, which emphasizes the difficulties of decision and of lay evaluation.* <

Even when the evaluator is as well-qualified as his agent, or perhaps when he is even more experienced and prepared, he may lack some information that influenced the decision-maker. We can have complete faith in the boss's abilities but be uneasy as to whether he realized the kind of situation we faced, and under these conditions we might be expected to seek ways of calling our difficulties to his attention.

Diverging Consequences

Because of the presence of an evaluator in the decision situation, the decision-maker may perceive at least two sets of possible conflicting consequences: those consequences for the group or clientele for whom he acts as agent, and those consequences more directly related to him-self and his future states. Although there are cases of directly contra-dictory consequences, such as the rare bank teller who diverts your deposit to his own uses, for most of us the difficulties of diverging consequences are less black and white.

Since alternatives may differ in the time involved for their consequences to develop, the decision-maker may be faced with a choice between short-term benefits for his client or long-term benefits for his client. We cannot predict his choice in the abstract, but we can expect him to take into account the likelihood that the evaluating client has either a short- or a long-time horizon. The elected official choosing between short- and long-term effects for his constituency must also consider whether long-term achievements can be converted into re-electing votes in the short run. Where long-term results are not clearly different, we can expect selection of that alternative which has short-run advantages.

In the presence of an evaluator, there is the additional complicating possibility that some possible outcomes are more visible to the evaluator than others. Thus the choice may be between A, which is good for the client and will earn credit for the decision-maker, and B, which is still better for the client but less obvious to the client and hence less rewarding for the decision-maker.

Collective Decisions

With the widening ripples of interdependence that are characteristic of contemporary society, man frequently participates as one of several or many in reaching a collective decision. Commonly this occurs when either causation or joint preferences are at issue.

>   *Social psychologists have long been interested in the comparative performance of individuals and groups in solving problems and making decisions.*   <

When several interdependent individuals with common or similar outcome preferences are not certain about cause/effect connections, one solution is to call in a specialist for advice. But sometimes issues arise

for which there are no specialists or for which expert advice is contra-
dictory. Under these conditions the decision process usually involves
discussion until a *consensus* emerges, or, if large numbers are involved,
until a *majority* agrees.

>   *Political scientists especially have been interested in group decisions.*
Decision by consensus or majority vote is considered under labels of voting
behavior, political behavior, *or* judicial process.   <

Outcome preferences for the group can be ambiguous either because
individual members are uncertain, or (more likely) because members
propose different goals for the group. Whenever individuals with
dissimilar or opposing outcome preferences are nevertheless interdependent, they must somehow arrive at a jointly acceptable preference
ordering. Under these conditions, negotiation toward compromise is
an essential part of the decision process. Frequently this results in
multiple goals for the group and almost inevitably it involves competition. Competing goals are resolved sometimes by establishing priorities and sometimes by sequential attention.

Negotiating Transactions

When spheres of action of two or more persons overlap, their decisions
may be contingent on one another. Decisions made by the potential
buyer can have important consequences for the potential seller, and
vice versa. Each may wish the other to forego certain alternatives in
exchange for setting aside some of their own alternatives. The process
of searching for an alternative which is simultaneously acceptable to
both parties can be called a *transaction process,* and obviously it contains its own complications, for it poses questions of how much information to give up, in what order, and how quickly.

When bargaining or transaction processes occur not between interdependent individuals but between interdependent groups, further
complications are introduced. The bargaining process is easier to steer
if you have crystallized preferences and certainty regarding causation,
but these conditions are easier to attain and hold for the individual

than for the group. The opponent's tactic is frequently to divide and conquer.

Still more difficulty arises if the groups negotiating for decision are themselves agents of larger constituencies. Prominent examples are labor/management contract negotiations, international diplomatic relations, and legislative maneuvering in city, state, or national governments. Each of these units represents a much larger group and must consider the degree of solidarity of the power structure behind them.

THE REDUCTION OF VULNERABILITY

In considering decision as a private process, we focused on the reduction of complexity as a key problem. It remains an important problem when we consider decisions in social contexts, but the mechanisms for reducing uncertainty and establishing boundaries for rationality are necessarily different. When we are interdependent we are not free to arbitrarily use short-run versus long-run criteria or to employ our own definitions of what is a satisfactory alternative. The realities of interdependence expose us to vulnerabilities against which we must erect defenses.

Aspects of the social structure may act as defenses; perhaps the most widespread defense available is a system of authority. An authority system specifies that those people who are subject to it cooperate in exchanging information or knowledge of causation, and it specifies appeal channels in case they fail to do so. This mechanism is by no means foolproof, but on the other hand its effectiveness should not be underestimated. An authority system also specifies more or less clearly the hierarchy of preferences to be sought, thus reducing the cognitive complexities involved. Defensively, the authority system protects the decision-maker by establishing (more or less publicly) the boundaries of the individual's authority. By so limiting discretion, it reduces the variety of demands others may place on its agents.

Defense against vulnerability can be built by interpersonal maneuvering, such as discussed in Chapter 8, which results in others being obligated. These debts may be called upon when the individual is in a threatening decision situation. When interpersonal maneuvering is not sufficient to reduce a person's vulnerability, we would expect him to try to restructure role networks, either by renegotiating role expectations, or by manipulating the power/dependence relationships, as we discussed in Chapter 8.

RECAPITULATION

Modern societies with their emphasis on achievement hold out an idealized model of rational decision-making. The fact that decisions are made by open-system man in complicated environments makes the attainment of this standard virtually impossible, and leads man to reduce complexity and clarify preferences. Many decision episodes occur in social situations, and social structure both facilitates and constrains decision-making. Because of the discrepancy between the idealized version and the behavioral realities, emotions may intrude into decision processes. When decision-makers are faced with unsatisfactory decision situations, we expect attempts at interpersonal maneuvering, or renegotiating role expectations, or changing power/dependence relations. The ability and willingness to employ these tactics are related to personality, a matter which we shall consider further in Chapter 11.

RECOMMENDED BROWSING

John W. Atkinson, "Motivational Determinants of Risk-Taking Behavior," *The Psychological Review* **64** (November 1967), 359–372. An empirical study of how fear of failure affects aspirations and cause/effect judgments in decision-making.

Kurt W. Back, "Decisions Under Uncertainty: Rational, Irrational, and Non-Rational," *American Behavioral Scientist* **4** (February 1961), 14–19. An excellent discussion of diverse approaches to decision theory.

Reuben Hill, "Decision-Making and the Family Life Cycle," in Ethel Shanas and Gordon Streib, editors, *Social Structure and the Family: Generational Relations,* Englewood Cliffs, N.J.: Prentice-Hall, 1965, pages 113–139. Reports data revealing distinctive decision-making patterns among three generations.

Sir Frederick Bartlett, *Thinking*. New York: Basic Books, 1958. Examines strategy and tactics for thinking and deciding under different conditions.

Orville G. Brim, Jr., David C. Glass, David E. Lavin, and Norman Goodman, *Personality and Decision Process: Studies in the Social Psychology of Thinking.* Stanford, Cal.: Stanford University Press, 1962. A pioneering empirical study of the processes by which husbands and wives make decisions about the rearing of children.

Jerome S. Bruner, Jacqueline J. Goodnow, and George A. Austin, *A Study of Thinking.* New York: Wiley, 1956. A fascinating investigation of cognitive processes through the use of original experiments.

Richard M. Cyert and James G. March, *A Behavioral Theory of the Firm.* Englewood Cliffs, N.J.: Prentice-Hall, 1963. Sets forth a theory on the effects of organizational structure and conventional practice on the development of goals, the formation of expectations, and the execution of choices.

Ward Edwards, "The Theory of Decision-Making," *Psychological Bulletin* **51** (1954), 380–417; and "Behavioral Decision Theory," *Annual Review of Psychology, 1961,* Vol. 12, Palo Alto, California: *Annual Reviews,* 1961, 473–498. Comprehensive reviews covering the psychological and economic theories of riskless and risky decision-making, the theory of games, and the experiments relating to these theories.

Eliot Freidson, "Client Control and Medical Practice," *American Journal of Sociology* **65** (January 1960), 374–382. An insightful analysis of the social contexts in which physicians practice and the effects of these on their decisions.

William J. Gore, *Administrative Decision-Making: A Heuristic Model.* New York: Wiley, 1964. An elaborate analysis of the way in which managers and administrators confront highly uncertain and problematic situations.

George Katona, *Psychological Analysis of Economic Behavior.* New York: McGraw-Hill, 1951. The first work of its kind to integrate psychology into economic decisions.

Nathan Kogan and Michael Wallach, *Risk Taking: A Study in Cognition and Personality.* New York: Holt, Rinehart and Winston, 1964. A consideration of the psychology of taking risks in decision-making.

Charles Lindblom, "The Science of 'Muddling Through,'" *Public Administration Review* **19** (Spring 1959), 79–88. An attempt to characterize the processes by which decisions are made when issues are embedded in dynamic social contexts.

James G. March and Herbert A. Simon, *Organizations.* New York: Wiley, 1958. Includes a classic analysis of cognitive limits on rationality, satisficing, and bounded rationality.

Charles Perrow, "Organizational Prestige: Some Functions and Dysfunctions," *American Journal of Sociology* **66** (January 1961), 335–341. Highlights the importance of intrinsic versus extrinsic evaluations of organizations and the effects of these on decision-making.

David Rapaport (editor and translator), *Organization and Pathology of Thought*. New York: Columbia University Press, 1951. A collection of European research and theory from psychology, psychiatry, and psychoanalysis regarding thought processes.

Thomas J. Scheff, "Decision Rules, Types of Error, and Their Consequences in Medical Diagnosis," *Behavioral Science* **8** (April 1963), 97–107. An investigation of cognitive limits on rationality in the medical sciences.

Herbert A. Simon, *Administrative Behavior*, second edition. New York: Macmillan, 1957. Includes an extensive discussion of the significance of hierarchical structures of authority on decision-making.

Herbert A. Simon, *The New Science of Management Decision*. New York: Harper and Row, 1960. A readable but penetrating summary of contemporary work on decision-making.

Herbert A. Simon, "Theories of Decision-Making in Economics and Behavioral Science," *The American Economic Review* **49** (June 1959), 253–283. Classic confrontation of economic and behavioral science approaches to decision-making.

Richard C. Snyder, "A Decision-Making Approach to the Study of Political Phenomena," in Roland Young, editor, *Approaches to the Study of Politics*. Evanston, Ill.: Northwestern University Press, 1958. A behavioral science approach to political decision-making.

James D. Thompson and Arthur Tuden, "Strategies, Structures, and Processes of Organizational Decision," in James D. Thompson, *et al.*, *Comparative Studies in Administration*. Pittsburgh, Pa.: University of Pittsburgh Press, 1959. The handling of different types of issues in collective decisions.

Max Weber, *The Theory of Social and Economic Organization*. London: Wm. Hodge, 1947. Includes the classic statement of the rational-legal authority of bureaucracy and compares it to the charismatic and traditional types of authority.

CHAPTER 10

PERSONALITY IN EVERYDAY AFFAIRS

Now that we have considered some of the more important contexts of daily activity—the constraints and opportunities regularly afforded by participation in society—we need to think once more about personality. Earlier we indicated that the personality emerges as open-system man acquires content on four basic dimensions (goals, norms, and beliefs about reality and causation) and as these became organized around the self-conception. Thus the term "personality" refers to a person's uniqueness. But it also refers to fundamental qualities of the person, to an essential-ness which may not be known fully even to the individual himself.

Because the personality emerges through experience, through testing against varieties of episodes, the individual may be uncertain about how he will respond to unfamiliar conditions. The personality is a developing thing, and even though past experiences serve as an anchor for it, new experiences can reshape the personality—either incrementally and gradually or, when new experiences are jarring or traumatic, rather abruptly. Sudden tragedy or disaster may permanently alter the direction of development of the personality.

Granted that it is difficult to fully know one's own personality, it should not surprise us that it is virtually impossible to fully understand and appreciate the personalities even of those we "know" rather well and interact with frequently. By the same token we cannot expect to be thoroughly understood by very many others. Nevertheless these others are frequently indicating their evaluations of us, either explicitly or implicitly, and we would expect this fact to have consequences for our emotions.

EPISODES AND EMOTIONS

In our earlier discussion of one's self-concept, we indicated that it was formed in part from the evidence presented by the way others treat oneself. And to the extent that this is correct, there should not be great discrepancy between the private and the reflected versions of the self-concept. In the long run we believe this to be reasonably correct, but we think short-range fluctuations can be sources of moodiness in individuals in modern societies. (This seems to be a relatively neglected topic, and thus in this section we shall be forced to rely primarily on speculation.)

In a changing society, with evolving action spheres and new types of episodes arising for the individual, he may face two kinds of new information for his self-conception: (1) his private assessment of performance in new contexts, and (2) evaluations by others. We would expect either of these to be potential triggers for the emotions, and as they change we would expect changes in mood, especially because of potential discrepancies. Table 10.1 illustrates the possibilities.

TABLE 10.1

| | | Reflected self-conception | |
		Favorable	Unfavorable
Private self-conception	Favorable	I	II
	Unfavorable	III	IV

When the current private estimate of self and the self-conception presently reflected in the behavior of others toward the individual are both positive (Cell I), we would expect the mood to be favorable, ranging between self-satisfaction and euphoria, depending on the importance attached to current episodes. When the current private estimate is favorable but others indicate some lesser opinion (Cell II), we would expect the mood to range between frustration and anger, again depending on the importance attached. When, on the other hand, the private assessment is unfavorable despite positive reactions from others (Cell III), we would expect a certain ambivalence; the individual may experience satisfaction or relief at having "gotten off easy," but if he believes others have access to the same information he has, we would expect this to raise doubts about the sincerity or honesty of the others involved. Finally, when both the person and others are aware of inadequate performance (Cell IV), we would expect the mood to range from embarrassment to shame, again depending on the significance attached to the situation.

Now if the private self-conception is well anchored, having been tested through many experiences and bolstered in the frequent reflections from others, we would expect it to be somewhat insulated from the effects of temporary events. Protection for the older person's self-concept is also afforded by the tendency to avoid situations which experience has shown to be damaging to the self-conception. But with less experience to fall back on, the younger individual is likely to attach emphasis to contemporary reading of the self-conception, to be less able to avoid damaging situations, and to be subject therefore to rather volatile swings in mood: in the clouds today, the dumps tomorrow. We might note, also, that the anchoring of the self-concept in experience, which tends to afford emotional stability for the older person, with continued aging may result in an orientation to the past. When the individual cannot anticipate increased competence and achievement in the future, and cannot demonstrate optimum performance and worth in the present, he may optimize his self-conception by dwelling on and reliving past accomplishments.

If the individual can experience swings in emotional moods during interaction with others, he can also have an influence on the emotions of those he comes in contact with. He may express or indicate approval of the others, thus placing the *other* in Cell I or III. Or the individual, by expressing disapproval, may place the other party either in Cell II or IV, thus arousing frustration, anger, embarrassment, or shame. Experience in interacting with others should be an important variable in how the individual affects the emotional moods of others. The experienced individual is less likely (than the inexperienced) to be so concerned with his own maneuvering as to be unaware of difficulties the other may be encountering. The experienced individual may be quicker to foresee possibly frustrating or embarrassing situations shaping up for the other party, and thus may maneuver to head them off. Or the experienced party may tactfully be preoccupied or pretend not to observe the less-than-ideal behavior of the others, thus reducing the potential for embarrassment. But while experience may increase the potential for empathy and tact, it does not, of course, guarantee that the individual will be motivated to use them.

Another source of frustration in interpersonal relationships occurs when the individual knows that his situation or behavior appears to another—inaccurately—in an unfavorable light. Often the individual is caught between the urge to set the record straight and the possibility that attempts to explain will only make matters worse. Here, again, experience may help the individual learn to manage appearances as well as reality.

Perhaps a more pervasive source of frustration lies in the fact that most of our everyday episodes are structured in ways which do not permit full engagement of personalities. This seems to be true whether we are considering the folklike society or the more modern one, although the reasons for restrictions on the full play of personalities differ in the two cases.

Segmentation in Modern Societies

We have characterized modern urban societies as being highly specialized. Economic, political, religious, and educational activities tend to be carried out in specialized positions and organizations. Man's instrumental activities, then, tend to be governed by norms of specificity, but also norms of universalism, discipline, and a performance orientation. Roles defined in these terms do not require the full expression of the personality. In fact, they discourage the engagement of the total personality.

The relatively modern society, moreover, is usually in a state of rapid change. One consequence of this is that many individuals are not permanently locked into many structures. Occupational mobility, status changes with the life cycle, and geographic mobility all tend to increase the frequency of "turnover" of role partners. Each year may bring new associates and remove others, thus limiting the familiarity which can grow through prolonged interaction. This makes possible interdependent activities without the necessity of a firm base in friendship or kinship, and thus greatly increases the abilities of those in modern societies to cooperate. But the changing patterns of interaction, coupled with the segmentation of relationships, mean that few persons know the individual as an *integrated* personality.

Inhibiting Factors in Folk Societies

We characterized folk societies as small, homogeneous, and unchanging, with one basic network of relationships serving economic, political, religious, and educational needs. Although in modern societies disagreements can be restricted to one segment of life because relationships are segmented, in the folk setting differences of opinion may disrupt interaction on all other facets of life.

Such diffuse interdependence makes for a delicacy of relationships. Care must be exercised to observe the amenities associated with ascribed statuses, to deal with others in the particularistic ways they expect, and to avoid conflict or dissension. Rituals or stylized patterns of politeness, indirection, or avoidance usually are institutionalized to keep others psychologically at arm's length, thereby reducing the likelihood of disruptions at particularly vulnerable junctures. The result, of course, is that the individual is inhibited from completely revealing doubts, tensions, or private hopes. He is inhibited from expressing his uniqueness.

> *Cultural anthropologists have frequently reported the use of joking, avoidance patterns, and indirect communication as rituals for relieving the tensions inherent in diffuse folk relations.*   <

Thus in both the folk and modern urban societies, although for quite different reasons, the interpersonal relationships appropriate for everyday instrumental affairs constrain or inhibit the full expression of personality. They encourage only expression of a public version which is important but skin-deep. We would therefore expect the individual to seek some interpersonal relations strictly for their intrinsic qualities, uncluttered by instrumental requirements.

INTRINSIC INTERACTIONS

In both folk and modern urban societies, everyday affairs constrain and inhibit the full expression of the personality and hence full realization of the self-conception. Since we have assumed (Chapter 3) that man maneuvers to optimize his self-conception, we expect man to be uncomfortable with these constraints. In either type of society, then, we expect the individual to develop a few friendships which can serve to make possible the fuller expression of personality.

The Social Location of Close Friends

To get understanding and support, the individual in the folk society is likely to find his friends outside the inhibiting networks of roles in which his instrumental activities take place. Anthropological studies of almost-folk societies document the widespread recognition and legitimization of such roles as "best friend," "blood brothers," or "compadre" which permit the release and full expression of personality in the company of a few persons. In some societies these friendship ties are established in elaborate rituals or ceremonies and attain a quasi-legal status in the society. By avoiding the complications of being involved in the same instrumental networks, friends can feel freer to be themselves in each other's company. They can share anxieties, reveal private evaluations of the others they must cope with, confide aspirations, share secrets, criticize one another constructively, and commiserate openly. These are not things that can be done with others in diffuse instrumental networks. In the folk society, then, we would expect a major function of friendship to be permitting relaxation from the inhibiting context of daily life.

Friendship in the modern urban society need not be so far removed from daily instrumental affairs. Indeed it may develop when individuals involved in role-specific relations begin to share information about other aspects of themselves and their daily lives.   Generally speaking, we expect people who interact frequently with each other to develop awareness of new aspects of each other, and to feel friendly in one another's presence.   And since the work place often is a place for regular and frequent interaction, we would expect friendships to be generated in connection with work.   Indeed, this often is reflected in *informal organization* of the work place, and can make going to work an enjoyable experience even though the work itself is boring.   However, we would not expect friendship to develop at work if the individual's work station separates him from others, or if he is separated from others by distinctions in rank or authority.

>   *Patterns of interaction, friendship, and conflict in work are often grouped under the label* informal organization, *and studied especially by industrial sociologists and organizational or industrial psychologists. Informal organization as a topic was first identified by Elton Mayo and F. J. Roethlisberger.*   <

In the modern society, friendships may grow within the nuclear family. This appears to be a fairly modern and unusual development, for the diffuseness and instrumentality of family and kinship relations usually forces individuals to find intrinsic relations outside. The contemporary family, however, sends its members outside for most instrumental activities, which may make possible the development of intrinsic ties within the nuclear family. This seems especially likely when the family is geographically or socially mobile and thus removed from daily contact with outside friends.

Almost always, the friendships we have been discussing are between two individuals of the same sex. The equivalent close friendships across sexes would correspond to *love,* and there has been even less attention by behavioral scientists to love than to friendship. It seems clear from anthropological reports that the pattern of *romanticized love* so widely touted and advertised in modern urban civilization is *not* a universal phenomenon. But it is not settled whether or not heterosexual friendships develop in various folklike societies and function to encourage the fuller expression of personalities.

Quasi-Friendships

In addition to these deep and intrinsic friendship relations in contemporary society, emotional support may be provided by friendly interaction of a noninstrumental sort between persons brought into physical contact accidentally but regularly. Such quasi-friendships may form between men who own businesses on the same corner, or between women who regularly patronize the same service establishment, or between residents who share common facilities or utilities. In the relatively anonymous city, the neighborhood tavern may provide an excuse for such contacts, as may hobby clubs or voluntary associations. We regard these as *quasi*-friendships, for they usually do not include interaction in other settings and they tend to dissolve when the occasions end which brought the individuals together originally.

Informal work relationships probably start as quasi-friendships, and only in cases of prolonged and stable contact develop into close friendships. Generally we expect interaction to increase friendliness, and friendliness to lead to heightened interaction, in a gradually spiraling pattern. But if social or geographical mobility disrupt these relationships before full-fledged friendships have developed, we would expect the interaction to terminate when work relationships are broken.

Nevertheless, we believe quasi-friendships can provide some emotional support; even though the personality is not revealed to the same depth as in true friendship, quasi-friendships permit aspects of the personality to be aired that are not engaged in strictly instrumental relations. To the extent that such relationships grow up around common problems or shared situations, quasi-friendships make possible the sharing of anxieties, fears, hopes, and solutions. They enable the individual to be reassured that he is not alone with his problems; back in the home office, the salesman or policeman or teacher may be able to confide in colleagues the difficulties he is having with a client or prospect or adversary, and colleagues may reassure the individual that "failure" with such cases is not really failure, since the outcome was inevitable. Or colleagues may suggest a tactic which had worked for them in a similar situation. Or they may simply reassure the individual by fully understanding the difficulties of his current situation.

The Development of Close Friendship

In any society, intense friendships generally form at the time when the persons are both experiencing transitions in the development of their personalities. We would expect some close friendships to develop among those who are simultaneously experiencing the transition from childhood to adulthood. The emergence of romantic love as a basis for marriage in modern urban societies seems geared to this transition, with individuals being encouraged to shift allegiances from family and same-sex peer groups, and develop intense friendship across sex lines. In modern societies we would expect some friendships to form among those simultaneously receiving training for professional status. We would likewise expect that those simultaneously undergoing occupational retirement might form new friendships. At these and other critical junctures in the emergence of the self-conception, intimate friends may be significant in helping integrate new elements into the personality.

>   *Cultural anthropologists have studied the formation of friendships among those undergoing similar* rites of passage. *Transitions in the life cycle and* identity crises *have been examined by psychoanalysists specializing in* ego psychology.   <

Since these transitions in personality are linked to the life cycle, friends tend to be of similar ages, whereas quasi-friendships are not so likely to be age-uniform. Even in the modern urban society, in which family members may serve as close friends, this function tends not to cross the generational lines.

PERSONALITY DEFICIENCIES

There are at least two perspectives from which to describe personalities as deficient. One is from the point of view of the individual himself, who perceives himself to be at odds with his environment to the point of being unable to function adequately. The second is from the point of view of others in the person's environment, who judge him to be lacking in content they deem necessary.

Self-Perceived Deficiency

One variety of personality deficiency occurs when the individual has acquired extremely high aspirations but is unable to either meet them or reduce them to more realistic levels. In such cases we would expect the individual eventually to feel overwhelmed. Similarly, an individual may be unable, psychologically, to achieve bounded rationality, and become overwhelmed by what appears to be infinite complexity and uncertainty. In some societies, either of these conditions is likely to be evaluated as some form of mental illness.

On the other hand, personality deficiency may also occur through the loss of interest in goals. When pursuit of customary goals is no longer satisfying, life in achievement-oriented societies may appear meaningless to the individual involved. Some suicides appear to occur for this reason.

> *Suicide is a multidisciplinary and complex matter, but the pioneer exploration of this type of suicide was done by the French sociologist, Emile Durkheim.* <

The Labeling of Deficiency

We would expect some personalities to be so deficient that the resulting behavior would be considered deviant in any society. For the most part, however, whether behavior is labeled deviant depends on the definitions of the majority in the system. The same behavior might be considered in one society as eccentric, in another as criminal, in another as crazy, and in others as normal. But within the dominant norms of a particular society, whether the individual is labeled as deviant depends to a large extent on how exposed he is. Some who would be labeled by the society as juvenile delinquents might be protected from official discovery by indulgent parents and neighbors or by lenient officials. Others who would be labeled as mentally ill, if their behavior were fully observed, may escape the consequences of the label when family members shield them from interaction with the larger community. Others performing the same acts in the same society, but lacking such protection, may indeed be labeled as delinquent or as mentally ill, and treated accordingly.

> *The processes by which individuals come to be regarded as mentally ill, delinquent, or criminal have been studied by students of deviance in sociology, and the concept* labeling theory *is applied to these processes.*   <

In the achievement-oriented modern society, an obvious problem is to ensure that behavior in pursuit of goals is channeled into socially approved avenues. When the individual's goal dimension is stronger than the normative dimension, others are likely to regard him as dangerous. When the resulting behavior violates legal norms, it is regarded as crime, but short of this, norms of distributive justice and equity may be challenged, and the individual considered unethical or opportunistic.

> *The pioneering exploration of this problem of balancing goals and means, in the context of modern society, was offered by Robert K. Merton in his discussion of social structure and* anomie.   <

Deficiencies in personality may be temporary at specific stages of the life cycle, due to imbalanced socialization or to changes in the society. It is not unusual, in modern societies, for the young to acquire competence in the abstract, nonpersonal content of roles more rapidly than interpersonal skills and sensitivities, in which case they may insist on instrumental results without taking into account the consequences they may have for others, or the reactions of others to them. In changing societies, too, even the fully socialized individual may eventually become inadequate to new situations if they outpace his capacity or opportunity to learn.

Compensating for Deficiencies

We have already suggested that integrated and adequate personalities benefit from intrinsic interactions, which afford relief from the tensions and constraints of daily public transactions. Intrinsic interactions would seem even more significant when persons with personality deficiencies are involved. We would expect a high frequency of intrinsic interactions to compensate for those deficiencies to the point sometimes that the individual could continue to cope with his everyday affairs. Indirect evidence for this lies in the fact that the majority of psychiatric hospital patients were without friends prior to hospitalization.

Perhaps the most pervasive method of compensating for personality deficiencies is to withdraw from action spheres which repeatedly present overtaxing situations. In accordance with our suggestion that man maneuvers to optimize his self-concept, we would expect him to seek action spheres that enable him to appear and feel competent. Thus the individual who is weak on interpersonal skills may prefer occupational careers that emphasize dealing with materials, and minimize interpersonal transactions; the similarly deficient housewife may avoid issue-oriented role networks in community affairs, preferring those in which she is expected to adhere to ascribed and routinized norms. And the parents ill-equipped to deal with complex issues may avoid decisions on child-rearing by resorting to the rigid application of rules. On the other hand, our reasoning would lead us to expect that the person with well-developed interpersonal and decision skills would seek to avoid action spheres with dull and repetitive situations.

RECAPITULATION

The episodes of everyday life, by affording new and sometimes inconsistent signals as to the competence of the individual, may be responsible for short-run shifts in mood: from euphoria to extreme anger, from self-satisfaction to apprehension. These daily episodes also tend to suppress the full expression of the personality, either by restricting activities to unconnected segments of the total or by inhibiting the expression of uniqueness. For these reasons, most individuals in all types of societies develop friendships which are valued not for instrumental but for intrinsic qualities. These intrinsic relationships help refuel the personality by affording fuller expression of and feedback on personality. Where there are personality deficiencies, some of the consequences may be mitigated by these intrinsic relationships.

The aspect of personality publicly involved in everyday affairs is a crucial determiner of the manner in which—and the extent to which—the individual participates in his culture and society, and we turn to this matter in the next section of the book.

RECOMMENDED BROWSING

Elizabeth Bott, *Family and Social Network: Roles, Norms, and External Relationships in Ordinary Urban Families.* London: Tavistock, 1957. Contains evidence on friendship and family patterns in different types of urban families.

Albert K. Cohen, *Delinquent Boys: The Culture of the Gang.* New York: Free Press of Glencoe, 1955. A classic discussion of webs and chains of circumstances which result in the delinquent subculture.

Yehudi A. Cohen, "Patterns of Friendship," in Yehudi A. Cohen, editor, *Social Structure and Personality: A Casebook.* New York: Holt, Rinehart and Winston, 1961, 351–386. A survey of 65 societies, which distinguishes four types of friendship. The volume in which the article appears is a solid interdisciplinary reader on the general topic of personality.

Emile Durkheim, *Suicide.* Glencoe, Ill.: The Free Press, 1951. A classic study of the fit of personalities and societies and their relations to different types of suicide.

Erik H. Erikson, "Identity and the Life Cycle," *Psychological Issues* I (1959), No. 1. A theoretical statement of psychosocial development, with emphasis on identity crises.

Erving Goffman, "Embarrassment and Social Organization," *American Journal of Sociology* 62 (November 1956), 264–271. Analyzes the conditions under which embarrassment occurs and how it is handled.

William J. Goode, "The Protection of the Inept," *American Sociological Review* 32 (February 1967), 5–19. Explores patterns of protection of the less able in various societies, as well as protection of society from the inept.

William J. Goode, "The Theoretical Importance of Love," *American Sociological Review* 24 (April 1959), 38–47. A review of what is believed about love and its expression in various societies.

Alvin Gouldner, *Patterns of Industrial Bureaucracy.* New York: Free Press of Glencoe, 1954. This study of a mining and manufacturing organization includes useful evidence on the bases of primary groups in work structures.

David Gottlieb, "The Neighborhood Tavern and the Cocktail Lounge: A Study of Class Differences," *American Journal of Sociology* **62** (May 1957) 559–562. Contains insight into supportive relationships in an urban setting.

Peter B. Hammond, "The Functions of Indirection in Communication," in James D. Thompson *et al.*, editors, *Comparative Studies in Administration*. Pittsburgh, Pa.: University of Pittsburgh Press, 1959, pages 183–194. Explains the use of joking, ritualized avoidance, and reliance on intermediaries in diffuse, volatile relationships.

George C. Homans, *The Human Group*. New York: Harcourt, Brace, 1950. An important treatment of the conditions under which interaction leads to friendship and group solidarity.

Edward O. Laumann, *Prestige and Association in an Urban Community: an Analysis of an Urban Stratification System*. Indianapolis, Ind.: Bobbs-Merrill, 1966. Evaluation of the impact of occupational rank on intimate social interaction patterns.

Robert K. Merton, "Bureaucratic Structure and Personality," in Merton, *Social Theory and Social Structure*. New York: Free Press of Glencoe, 1949, pages 195–206. Well-known statement of the implications for the personality of roles governed by universalism, discipline, specificity, and achievement norms.

Robert K. Merton, "Social Structure and Anomie," in Merton, *Social Theory and Social Structure*. New York: Free Press of Glencoe, 1949, pages 131–160. A classic and controversial examination of the conditions under which individuals identify with their social system.

Theodore M. Newcomb, *The Acquaintance Process*. New York: Holt, Rinehart and Winston, 1961. A major study of the formation and development of non-instrumental relationships.

A. R. Radcliffe-Brown, "On Joking Relationships," and "A Further Note on Joking Relationships," in *Structure and Function in Primitive Society: Essays and Addresses*. Glencoe, Ill.: The Free Press, 1952, pages 90–116. One of the early statements of the importance of joking for society and social interaction.

Anne Roe, *Psychology of Occupations*. New York: Wiley, 1956. Contains empirical evidence on the relationship of personality and different occupational roles.

Morris Rosenberg, *Occupations and Values*. Glencoe, Ill.: The Free Press, 1957. A study of types of personalities and self-selection of occupational channels.

Thomas J. Scheff, *Being Mentally Ill: A Sociological Theory*. Chicago: Aldine, 1966. Thoughtful consideration of the situations and processes by which individuals come to be defined as mentally ill.

Edward H. Shils and Morris Janowitz, "Cohesion and Disintegration of the Wehrmacht in World War II," *Public Opinion Quarterly* **12** (Summer 1948), 280–315. Examination of the importance of primary interaction for the stability of an instrumental organization.

Georg Simmel, "The Sociology of Sociability," *American Journal of Sociology* **55** (November 1949), 254–261. An analysis of the forms in which noninstrumental interactions take place.

Neil J. Smelser and William T. Smelser, *Personality and Social Systems*. New York: Wiley, 1963. A useful collection of articles on interaction of personality and society.

Arnold Van Gennep, *The Rites of Passage*. Chicago: University of Chicago Press, 1960. A classic analysis of ceremonies accompanying an individual's life crises.

Max Weber, *The Protestant Ethic and the Spirit of Capitalism*. London: Allen and Unwin, 1930. An important but controversial statement of the impact of religion on the emergence of personality and on the significance of this for industrializing society.

CONTEMPORARY SOCIETY AND CHANGE

Not all humans are equally prepared to contribute to the modernizing society, nor do all have equal opportunity to participate in the results. We can, therefore, observe different adaptations to the contemporary society, and we need to explore the different patterns. But both men and societies change. The processes of modernization present families with changing action spheres and thereby elicit new behavior and new adaptations.

In the aggregate, the new responses constitute new patterns in the society. Thus we look for changes in society to change the behavior of men and women, and for the changes in the behavior of men and women to change society.

CHAPTER 11

PARTICIPATING IN CONTEMPORARY SOCIETY

Throughout this volume we have worked with concepts of folk society and modern urban society. It is time to reemphasize that these are pure types, and that no contemporary society conforms to either of these conceptual patterns. Every contemporary society is to some degree in the process of modernizing, but none, including the "more advanced," is a modern urban society. It is possible to rank societies on the degree to which they have moved toward modernization. But whatever that degree, no society is wholly consistent; some elements are further in the direction of modernization than others. Every contemporary society is therefore a *conglomerate* society composed in part of almost-folk components, and in part of relatively modern elements. When we speak of the degree of modernization or development, we are generally referring to the ratio of these components. "Underdeveloped," "rapidly developing," and "modernizing" nations of Latin America, Asia, and Africa are societies in which the almost-folk elements are considerable, but in which the modern urban components are increasing. The "advanced" nations of North America and Europe and the Orient have large relatively modern urban components, but have elements of the almost-folk as well.

Because contemporary societies are conglomerations, they contain recognizably different subcultures or cultures, and therefore different channels of preparation, different content to open-system man, and different styles and intensity of participation in the society.

DIFFERENTIAL PARTICIPATION

Participation in any society can be of two sorts: as contribution to and as beneficiary of the collective effort. There is a distinction between production and consumption in conglomerate societies, with many individuals being specialized producers and therefore generalized dependents and consumers. Production and consumption tend to take place in separate structures. The degree to which production is specialized and divorced from consumption is likely to be related to whether the family is in an almost-folk component or a relatively modern segment. In each of the institutionalized spheres of activity of conglomerate societies, there are variations in the goods and services available.

Variations in Goods and Services

Conglomerate society contains cultural components which make possible wide varieties of food, shelter, clothing, and furnishings. Such variety is associated with industrialization, which permits specialization in growing or manufacturing goods, and in preserving and transporting goods. How widely these results of modernization are distributed is a variable, but somewhere within conglomerate society knowledge and skills are lodged.

Some almost-folk societies have high-protein, high-energy diets, but this is an accident of local availability of protein-rich fish or animals. But modernized components of contemporary societies are released from the constraints of local foods. For these components, families can enjoy nonlocal and out-of-season foods, and because of stockpiling and techniques of preservation, families are not subject to cycles of feast and famine. Knowledge of biological and biochemical processes afford possibilities of maintaining balanced as well as energy-rich diets, and of maintaining or enriching nutritional values of food. The range and variety and the removal of constraints to local or temporal conditions permits widening choice of food items, menus, and preparations, and results in the development of the art of eating.

> *Although the topic is not highly developed, understanding of the distribution and use of goods and services, under the heading of* consumer behavior, *is being developed by academic students of marketing as well as by economists.* <

But these benefits of modernization are not uniformly available to all segments of the conglomerate society. Some rely heavily on home-grown foods, on repetitive menus, and frequently on high-starch diets. Whether the diet is nutritionally balanced is determined in part by seasonal cycles and by feast or famine conditions.

Shelter affords an equally wide range of possibilities, for some sectors of contemporary societies. Aside from variations in size and luxury, housing differs in facilities and functions. Somewhere within conglomerate society exist the knowledge and skills for escaping various limitations or uncertainties of the environment: animals, insects, cold, heat, storms. Such housing affords a variety of labor- and time-saving conveniences, including running water, plumbing, refrigeration, energy sources, and cooking equipment. Housing can be built in convenient locations, by replacing forests, filling in waterways, or erecting high-rise buildings. Even in congested urban settings, housing can afford privacy, the ability to be alone. Or it can facilitate recreation and entertaining of friends in private surroundings.

Obviously such housing is not uniformly distributed among all components of the society. Some must rely on construction using locally available materials and employing simple tools and engineering know-how. Urban tenements are found in all contemporary societies; these involve high-density living and lack of privacy.

The same sorts of statements can be made about clothing and home furnishings. In some parts of contemporary societies, there are wide arrays of materials, styles, and special-purpose designs, affording opportunities for choice and refinement of taste. There also are varieties of communication instruments, such as telephone, radio, television, all affording connections with communication networks of the wider society. Then again, these are not uniformly available throughout contemporary societies.

Within conglomerate society there is contained highly specialized and refined knowledge about physical and mental health. This includes equipment and surgical skills for repairing or replacing vital organs and limbs; chemical knowledge and medical know-how for the treating of diseases and chronic illnesses; a variety of professional skills, such as engineering, nursing, or sanitation, for the prevention of diseases through immunization and hygienic practices; and specialized attention to the causes of and therapies for mental illnesses. This wealth of knowledge and ability is made possible by extensive networks of interdependence which permit specialization in research and in the manufacturing of drugs, tools, and equipment which free the practitioner from traditional knowledge, locally grown herbs and locally produced instruments. This wealth of medical culture not only results in prolonged life, the reduction of infant mortality, and restored productivity of the ill and the injured, but also in cosmetic practices for altering individual appearances.

> *The organization and distribution of health services within a society is studied by* medical sociology, *which is a relatively new specialty. Students of the* sociology of professions *have also focused considerable attention on health.*   <

Societies vary in the degree to which health services are available throughout the population, but in a conglomerate society we would not expect to find uniform distribution of all of these services to all components.

Almost-folk societies contain some devices for deferring consumption of current production: for saving and investment. But conglomerate societies contain components with highly developed institutions for savings, investing, and the generation of credit. Whereas almost-folk societies provide for the building of credit by providing personal favors to a limited array of known persons, modernized components permit the amassing of credit on an impersonal, nonlocal basis through financial institutions. Whereas folklike societies cushion the impact of personal disasters through the norm of mutual aid, modernized components contain elaborate insurance institutions for the widespread and impersonal sharing of risk. Whereas folklike societies provide for the investment of energy in capital goods such as implements, draft animals, and transportation devices, conglomerate societies frequently contain devices for the accumulation and investment of surplus in complex cooperative endeavors that are beyond the family's capacity, such as those industrial or agricultural technologies operated by complex organizations. Such investments often are facilitated by the development of centralized markets for exchange, not only for corporate securities but also for land or commodities or other materials.

> *The financial behavior of individuals and families has been relatively neglected in the behavioral sciences. Some of the initial research has been done by James S. Dusenberry, George Katona, Richard Lambert.* <

Conglomerate societies contain—in some sectors, at least—a host of other services which in the folk society may exist only in rudimentary form if at all. In modernized sectors are found specialized and highly developed organizations and technologies for the generation and distribution of various forms of energy: steam, electric, gas, or atomic. Such sectors also contain varieties of devices for rapid transportation over long distances: roads and automobiles, aircraft, ships, and the necessary coordinating agencies. Such sectors contain intricate networks for communication: postal services, radio and television broadcasting stations, telephone systems, and newspapers, magazines and books. They provide collective defenses against natural calamities such as fires and floods, and man-made calamities such as crime and invasion. For social controls, there are elaborate agencies dedicated to the development and application of laws, the detection and apprehension of violators, the judgment of violations, and the punishment or rehabilitation of violators. And as these many services expand, agencies emerge for their planning and regulation.

> *In the social sciences there is a growing interest in the relationship of legal institutions and societies. They are studied under such headings as* sociology of law *and* penology. <

Conglomerate societies contain elaborate cultures and the products and services flowing from them, but these are not uniformly consumed in all sectors of contemporary societies. Because we might expect some relation between participation and contribution, we need to consider variations in contributions.

Variations in Contributions

The possibilities of contribution in contemporary society include specialized occupations and careers linked to national or international networks of interdependence which involve the assembly of resources and tools from many points and use of highly refined knowledge. Such occupations require the exercise of discretion and the regular incorporation of new knowledge, and involve planning so that all the specialized pieces and activities fit at appropriate points in time and space. With such organization and facilities for wide distribution, individual productivity can reflect economies of scale.

In the almost-folk components of the contemporary society, work tends to be embedded in small networks of interdependence for localized production and localized use. With small-scale production, each individual tends to make multiple contributions, to be a jack-of-all-trades, and necessary discretion tends to be governed by tradition and custom.

Conglomerate society not only contains the two kinds of components; to some extent, they overlap. This may enable individuals from the almost-folk component to make contributions in the modernized sector. Typically this involves a routinized occupation in which the necessary skills can be quickly learned, and discretion is at a minimum.

DIFFERENTIAL PREPARATION

We would have to expect, generally speaking, some correspondence between the degree to which a family is *prepared to contribute* to the collective effort and the degree to which it is *prepared to benefit* from that collective effort. Preparation to benefit from the society is learned, just as is preparation to contribute. Channels of development vary in their content, but within any one channel we would expect reasonable consistency in the experiences preparatory to production and consumption. The longer the channel and the more varied the experiences it provides, the greater the preparation to contribute and to benefit. Specialized channels which produce persons for highly specialized production in late-ceiling occupations usually also prepare that person to penetrate deeply into the several specialized institutions providing goods and services. Conversely, the channel which results in meager preparation for production is also likely to afford minimum knowledge about consumption.

(This is not to say, necessarily, that benefits will in fact correspond to contributions, for this is a most difficult thing to measure in complicated societies, and there are a number of important variables which may intervene between production and consumption. We shall return to this point shortly.)

In whichever segment of conglomerate society we look, we would expect to find the majority of families prepared both to contribute and to benefit from the results of that segment; but not to participate effectively in other segments. Within their own segments, the families most highly prepared to contribute are likely to be those most highly prepared to acquire benefits. Within folklike segments, we would expect to find families with varying degrees of preparation to employ a variety of skills in the production of goods and services for local consumption, and with varying degrees of preparation to live with the production available within the immediate environment. Within modernized segments, we would expect to find different degrees of specialization in preparation for contributing to extensive and impersonal networks, and different degrees of training to deal with many separate, specialized, and impersonal channels of consumption.

Conglomerate societies, consisting of both folklike and relatively modern components, inevitably involve some interaction among these coexisting parts, and this results in rechanneling experiences for some individuals and families. Typically it is individuals or families in the folklike segments which become rechanneled, learning to participate in more modernized segments. Generally the reverse is not true; those in relatively modernized segments are not brought into meaningful contact with folk segments and therefore do not learn how to participate in them.

Rechanneling in either direction is difficult, however, because it involves more than simply learning technical, occupational skills. Whereas the folk culture emphasizes custom and tradition and spontaneity and living for the short run, modern society requires families with ability to meet complexity through discipline, planning, decision, and extended time horizons. Rechanneling in the direction of modernization requires learning something about the wealth of content of the culture, and thus learning that institutions are differentiated and specialized. It involves learning that within each of these institutions there are alternatives. It involves learning which institutions to turn to, for a given problem, and which set of alternatives to approach. It involves learning the interpersonal skills needed for transacting in these institutions, or making contact with agents who can diagnose the situation and refer the individual to appropriate points of entree into specialized structures.

>   *The vast amount of learning which is necessary to be an effective consumer in modern society is beginning to be understood through the research of scholars such as David Caplovitz.*   <

The increasing specialization in production of modernizing society means that the family is increasingly dependent, but also that it requires greater learning in order to find its way through the varieties of goods and services available. Where this learning is incomplete, as it is likely to be during rechanneling, the family may consume ineffectively either because its members are unaware of the availability of something or because others exploit their naïveté. Here is fertile ground for loan sharks, medical quacks, dishonest police, legal shysters, religious charlatans, or unethical merchants. The individual whose developmental experiences began and unfolded within the modernized segment of society is likely to have absorbed the appropriate techniques for consuming, and thus to be less vulnerable to exploitation.

>   *The significance of both* lay *and* professional referral systems *has been shown particularly by medical sociologists.*   <

In conglomerate society, then, we would expect to find some families deeply penetrated by and penetrating into folklike segments, other families deeply engaged with modernized segments, and still others in marginal or transitional relation to the more modern components. If we look at the families in all segments from the point of view of modern urban society, however, we would expect to get a different result. If we could assume that those contributing the most to the modernized segment also reap the greatest benefits of that segment, then from the point of view of modern urban society we would expect a neat stratification system, with those prepared only for the folk society at the bottom, and the marginally prepared above them. This raises the question of stratification in conglomerate societies.

STRATIFICATION IN CONGLOMERATE SOCIETIES

Stratification systems, we said in Chapter 5, reflect rankings on the basic values of their societies. Since the modern urban society stresses achievement and the opportunity for the family, through its achievements, to move upward, stratification in the modern urban society takes the form of a class system. To the extent that a conglomerate society has a relatively large modernized component, then, we should find a well-developed class system even though there are pockets of folklike segments. The society in the early stages of modernization may not yet have evolved a recognizable class system. It may appear instead to have a large indigenous population plus a small cadre who have received modernizing education and who live in the modern urban style.

Blurring of the Upper Class

In those conglomerate societies with sizable modernized components, then, we find recognizable class systems, and there usually is enough interdependence and contact among the components that most families can be judged against that class system. But in conglomerate societies the achievement-based class rankings are inevitably distorted, because of mixed criteria for evaluation.

As the pure concept of class would suggest, those best prepared to contribute to the modern segment usually reap its benefits and consume widely, and show up in the upper class. But laymen as well as professional social scientists cannot directly measure contributions (see Chapter 4), so variables are used that are assumed to indirectly measure contributions: Level of education is taken to indicate preparation to contribute, occupation is assumed to indicate something about type and extent of contributions, and consumption is taken to reflect income received as a result of contributions. Still, some families are considered upper-class on the basis of consumption patterns that reflect wealth not achieved by those families but accrued through ascription from another era; families whose ancestors acquired control of resources which become important to the modernizing component may through inheritance gain the wealth to consume in an upper-class style. This kind of phenomenon often results in "reform" movements during modernization, with land redistribution, income and inheritance taxes, capital expropriation, and similar programs. Still other families whose consumption patterns gain them upper-class standing acquire their wealth through illegal activities or by exploiting the naïveté of families in transition from folklike segments. The possibility of gaining upper-class standing without making legitimate contributions to the pool of goods and services is enhanced by the fact that productive activities in modern society are separate from consumption activities, and it is possible for some families to exhibit an upper-class style of consumption to others who have no way to check this against actual productivity. And a few families may meet all the criteria that indirectly measure contributions, but still not be actually contributing as would be expected. Some older members of the labor force may have the education, occupation, and income that would place them in the upper class, but may be making only marginal contributions because their training is obsolete. They may continue in their positions by virtue of the protection others give them. To the extent that educational institutions and occupational recruitment practices are susceptible to ascriptive criteria, even younger members of the labor force may gain positions of considerable rank with corresponding income, but without making commensurate contributions.

Multiple Priorities in the Middle Classes

The middle classes of conglomerate societies generally contain families making specialized contributions to one of the several institutions in the modern sector. Although their productivity is contained in one institution—education, commerce, manufacturing, government, religion, medicine, or law—their consumption is generalized, so that it is possible to speak of a middle-class style of life. Evaluation of a family as middle class tends to emphasize consumption patterns because it is difficult to compare or equate occupational contributions made to different institutions. This fact makes possible disparate private rankings of families which do not have to be validated, and results in lack of crystallization of the several strata in the middle classes, but it is nevertheless possible to make gross distinctions between the lowest and highest strata within the middle classes.

Segmentation in the Lower Class

The pure concept of class as based on contribution and achievement assigns to the lower class those who make the least contribution, and often it is concluded therefore that families in the lower class are incompetent. Certainly in conglomerate societies we do find within the lower class persons incapacitated by physical inadequacy or mental incompetence, but not all who are considered lower class are in those categories. Some families are competent but their competence is directed toward folklike activities not in demand by modern components; these are members of a folk society engulfed in predominantly modern society. They are in but not of the conglomerate society. They may appear as nomadic groups, as isolated religious sects or cults, as hillbillies, or as bush tribes. These groups very well may and usually do have their own stratification systems based on folk values, and refuse to recognize rankings of the dominant system.

A third segment of the lower class in conglomerate society consists of those families at the interface of folklike and relatively modern components, who are forced to participate occasionally in modern society but do not identify with it. When faced with the need for medicine, clothing, or other services not adequately provided by the folk society, these families find temporary employment in occupations which from the modern point of view are unskilled. Usually they work only until the need is met, and often this means until the first paycheck. Because they are in alien surroundings this participation strains the personality, and the individual may return to the folk setting at the first opportunity. From the standpoint of the values of modern society, these people thus appear to be undependable and lacking in discipline.

Still another category within the lower class of conglomerate society are those families in transition, at the interface but in the process of identifying with the modern component and leaving the folk. Many of these families climb out of the lower class after they have had opportunities to learn modern content. On the other hand, there are families at the interface who do not climb or who have, in fact, occupied middle-class statuses previously, but whose productive skills have become obsolete with continued modernization of the society. These are the downwardly mobile of conglomerate society.

Thus the lower class in conglomerate society is anything but a homogeneous collection of incompetent and worthless families. It includes some whose preparation for modern society is as yet incomplete. And frequently it also contains able families which are prevented from acquiring the preparation necessary for modern society because of caste discrimination.

Out-Castes in Conglomerate Societies

In the pure modern society, there would be no castes because ascription would be meaningless. Although there is world-wide evidence indicating that, as nations modernize, caste-like discrimination is reduced, castes are by no means eliminated from even the most modernized societies. Often caste operates to prevent potentially talented persons from gaining the requisite preparation for participating fully. Caste may be the result of legal regulation, as in the case of *apartheid*; it may result from custom, wherein certain racial or ethnic or religious groups are physically segregated from those localities in which access to preparation for modern life might be available. This is most clearly seen in the cases of urban ghettos. This developmental emergence of the individual in the out-caste family which prevents him from preparation for the modern segment is likely to confine him to the lower class of conglomerate society.

> *The study of prejudice and discrimination has been emphasized within the sociology of* race *and* ethnic relations. *Prejudice in relation to personality has been examined in* clinical *and* social psychology.   <

With continued modernization, we would expect less rigidity in the caste system, with the result that some members of the caste learn some of the skills which are in demand in the modern sector. These families thus gain entree into the middle classes and acquire some of the goods and services characteristic of that life style. These goods and services, however, are likely to be somewhat less than others receive for similar contributions. This may appear in segregated residential patterns, political participation, access to schools, or medical care. On the production side, it may result in individuals being barred from certain kinds of occupational careers.

Vestiges of caste, in conglomerate societies, may ultimately appear in the upper class, particularly in the form of discrimination in leisure activities and recreation. Private clubs, for example, may continue to exclude those whose ancestors were members of a caste. We would expect to find clustered in the most modernized sectors—the urban centers—the victims of such discrimination, for by clustering together they can develop their own social outlets and their own experiences for protection of the personality.

(Although this discussion has focused on caste and stratification of families, we should remember that discrimination based on other ascribed statuses can fall directly on the individual, giving them fewer opportunities for preparation, unequal rewards for equivalent contributions, or unequal access to facilities for leisure activities. Women and older persons frequently are the victims of this.)

Conglomerate societies, which contain differentiated cultural components and a variety of classes, thus encompass a variety of life styles and life spaces. How families appraise these life styles and life spaces will determine their adaptation to the society they confront.

ADAPTATIONS TO CONTEMPORARY SOCIETIES

It should be clear by this time that which segment of a conglomerate society a particular family or individual participates in is not a random matter; channels of development are likely to deposit them in particular relation to their society. Generally speaking, we would expect those whose development has been within the more-modern component and who then participate in that component to feel reasonably comfortable with their fit to society. By the same token, we would generally expect those developed within the folk component who then participate in that component to also feel reasonably comfortable. But conglomerate societies are in the process of modernizing, and some individuals and families are faced with objective realities considerably different from what their developmental experiences have prepared them for.

On a world-wide basis, individuals and families even in folk sectors are attracted by goods and services generated by the more modernized segments. The technologies of modern segments are visibly more efficient in providing solutions to problems of housing and equipment, diet and food, health and medicine, and transportation. Whatever the byproducts and problems of modernization, these attractions seem ultimately to advance modern components into dominant position within contemporary societies, at the expense of folk components. For this reason, we are going to examine how families and individuals with different preparations and spheres of action adapt themselves to contemporary societies, *as seen from the point of view of the modernized sector.*

Forms of Adaptation

In considering the ways in which individuals and families orient themselves to modernization, we shall work basically from an analytic scheme first suggested by Robert K. Merton. (We shall make some adaptation, because Merton was not specifically considering the case of orientation toward the modern segment and away from the folk-like segment.) Essentially we shall be working with two variables: (1) the degree to which the desired life style is folk or modern (we shall speak of this as *life-style goal*), and (2) the degree to which the individual or family is prepared to participate in folk or modern components (we shall speak of this as *preparation to participate*). In both cases we would emphasize that these are matters of degree, but for purposes of discussion we shall think of them as dichotomous and consider the four extreme possibilities (see Fig. 11.1).

		Life-style goal	
		Modern urban	Folk
Preparation	*Modern*		
to	*urban*	Conformity	Reaction
participate	*Folk*		
		Innovation	Retreat

FIG. 11.1. *Predominant adaptation to contemporary societies.*

> *A considerable amount of research and theory on adaptations, par-*
ticularly on deviant behavior, has been spawned by Merton's classic essay
on social structure and anomie.   <

In the adaptation we have labeled *conformity,* achievement is prized,
empirically validated beliefs about causation and reality are preferred,
and the orientation is cosmopolitan. This is *not* a static adaptation,
but one oriented to change. Using this adaptation, we would expect to
find mainly individuals or families who are considered middle or upper
class, people who have achieved the desired life style or who are in
the process of achieving it through development of industrial, governmental, military, religious, or political careers. Their progress suggests
that their preparation is adequate. These are people who are winning
the game. Many of these have emerged from channels of development
quite consistent with their present position, but some have been rechanneled during development and may experience personality stress.
If some of their reference groups (family members or friends or members of the same minority group) remain in the folk segment, they may
feel guilty. One frequent result of this is sending help back; another
is political activity to alleviate the problems of folklike reference groups.
Still another possible response is to reduce the cognitive dissonance
by elimination of the reference groups, either by withdrawal of interest
or by active rejection.

> *In sociology this topic is considered under the heading of* occupa-
tional *or* social *channels of* mobility.   <

With the *reaction* adaptation, the individual is equipped with beliefs about causation and reality that are appropriate to the modernized
segment, but for some reason is more oriented to particularism, diffuse
relations, and ascribed statuses, and the orientation may well be local.
These people prefer the life style which they associate with an earlier,
less complicated society. Clusters of young reactors often develop
unique identities—as Bohemians, beatniks, or hippies. Generally we
would expect these individuals or families to be on an achievement
plateau or to be downwardly mobile, and not to be satisfied with the
life-space as they perceive it. They may be found in upper, middle,

or lower classes, but in any event they feel that their statuses are being threatened by a world that is modernizing more rapidly than they are. Included may be the wealthy who inherited their wealth and who are receiving less deference in modern society because they are not contributing. It may include members of the middle class who see such developments as automation as rendering them obsolete. It may also include members of the lower class who see possibilities for achievement disappearing as universalistic norms open doors to more able individuals who were formerly oppressed by caste status; the notorious Ku Klux Klan illustrates this.

In the adaptation labeled *innovation,* achievement is prized but the preparation for modern urban life styles is incomplete or the individual or family is prevented from obtaining the relevant preparation because of caste discrimination. But in either case they turn to atypical means of achievement. In the middle class, this may take the form of entering on a marginal career which gradually gains respectability; the development of psychiatry in the twentieth century is a good example. Another example of this type of adaptation in the middle class is the management of illegal activities such as traffic in contraband goods. The predominant innovative activity is probably located in the lower class, however. This may occur with the development of folklike art forms which are promoted in the modernized sector; innovating with jazz or primitive art are examples. Frequently the innovative adaptation involves crime. This may occur either where folk practices are considered by modern segments to be illegal—such as the case of making moonshine whiskey—or where there is deliberate searching for points within modern segments where deviance can be profitable: robbing stores, mugging or hustling strangers, selling contraband, or running gambling operations. It is not unusual for the person to learn skills for the second type while imprisoned for infractions of the first type.

An important phenomenon of the modernizing society is the migration of folk families into urban centers as they are forced off the land by new technologies or by war. The fact that they become located in urban centers may mean that they learn to adopt the aspirations of the modern life style, but it does not mean that they learn the content with which to pursue those ambitions. Some of these folk in the cities do gradually acquire preparation for the modern segment; this is more likely for the children than for adults. But if the migration is very large, we would expect concentration in neighborhoods of families from a common folk culture and the rapid transformation of that culture to permit existence in the landless urban context. An important occurrence in the process of modernization appears to be the generation of *nonrural folk cultures.*

>   *There is a controversial concept of a* culture of poverty, *first introduced by Oscar Lewis, which lacks precision and adequate testing but which suggests that there are basic similarities in the many localized cultures of the impoverished.*   <

Neighborhood concentration in the cities tends to encapsule the family, with the result that the experiences of the children in neighborhood schools often do not provide effective contact with modern preparation.

>   *Perhaps the best-documented study of the obstacles to modernization of the young through urban schools has been provided by James Coleman and his associates, done for the United States Department of Health, Education and Welfare.*   <

In the adaptation we have labeled *retreat,* the individual is oriented to and prepared for the folklike life style. When the individual or family is engulfed in a conglomerate society, we would expect them to prefer isolation, to withdraw or to retreat from modernizing threats. In some contemporary societies there may be geographic pockets which insulate these families from the modern segment fairly well; the main contact would be the occasional trade or temporary employment on the unskilled and dirty fringes of the modern sector in order to get cash for tax or similar purposes. Their desire to avoid contact with modern secular society is likely to be associated with a strong emphasis on the sacred, which permits the anticipation of rewards in another life. But this retreatist adaptation is not simply a rural phenomenon; it can also be found in urban centers, as illustrated by the alcoholics and drug addicts of Skid Row as well as by the self-segregated cults or religious sects. Although those with the retreatist adaptation may refuse to acknowledge the class system, from the point of view of that system they usually are lower class.

CHANGING ADAPTATIONS

We would expect man's adaptations to his society to be fairly permanent, and not to fluctuate in the short run. Yet there are at least two important reasons for expecting some individuals' adaptations to change in modernizing societies: (1) the built-in changes associated with life cycle may result in a shift in either identification with or ability to perform in the modern sector, and thus call for a revised adaptation, or (2) accumulated modernization may reduce the individual's usefulness to the system, and thus call for a different adaptation. For both these reasons, members of the older generations frequently find it difficult to hold on to the conforming adaptation, and resort instead to reaction or retreat.

Those individuals who can successfully maintain the conforming or retreatist adaptation probably are optimizing their self-conceptions. Generally we would expect them to be relatively satisfied to maneuver within the opportunities and constraints afforded by their spheres of action. Others, however, may find their spheres of action confining and yielding something less than satisfactory self-conceptions. We assume that individuals maneuver to optimize their self-conceptions, and under these circumstances, we would expect them to seek changes in those parts of the environment that produce unsatisfactory action spheres. We turn to this topic in the next chapter.

RECAPITULATION

Contemporary societies are conglomerations of folk and modernized segments containing widely different patterns of participation. Because of the operation of channels of development, some families are prepared both to contribute to and consume in the modern sector; others are prepared for the folk sector; and some make the transitions.

From the standpoint of the modern segment, there appears to be a single stratification system, with those most prepared to participate in that segment at the top, and those least prepared to participate at the bottom. The class system in contemporary societies reflects this, but is blurred by vestiges of ascribed statuses, and sometimes caste. In addition some families are oriented away from the modern class system. Conglomerate societies, then, yield four predominant styles of adaptation to modernization: conformity, innovation, reaction, and retreat. These adaptations yield varying degrees of satisfaction for the self-conception, with the result that some may seek changes, not in themselves but in their society, to improve their action spheres.

RECOMMENDED BROWSING

Edward C. Banfield, *The Moral Basis of a Backward Society*. New York: The Free Press, 1958. Study of an Italian village unable to emerge from an older culture to participate fully in the modern society.

T. B. Bottomore, *Classes in Modern Society*. New York: Pantheon Books, 1966. Examination of the impact of industry on stratification in contemporary societies.

David Caplovitz, *The Poor Pay More*. New York: The Free Press of Glencoe, 1963. Empirical study of patterns of consumption of goods and services within the lower class in New York City.

James S. Coleman and others, *Equality of Educational Opportunity*. Washington, D.C.: U.S. Government Printing Office, 1966. A major research report showing significance of the home, neighborhood, and peer environment on the child's experiences of school.

James D. Dusenberry, *Income, Savings, and the Theory of Consumer Behavior*. Cambridge, Mass.: Harvard University Press, 1949. A pioneering book in the development of research into consumer behavior.

Nelson N. Foote (editor), *Household Decision-Making*. New York: New York University Press, 1961. This book, Volume IV in a series of books on consumer behavior, emphasizes decision processes of contemporary families, especially with regard to economic and financial matters.

Eliot Freidson, "Client Control and Medical Practice," *American Journal of Sociology* 65 (January 1960), 374–382. An important exploration of the processes by which laymen make contact with modern medicine.

Herbert J. Gans, *The Urban Villagers: Group and Class in the Life of Italian-Americans*. New York: The Free Press, 1962. An insightful study of the life styles and life spaces of an ethnic group in the city slum.

Barney G. Glaser (editor), Part IV: "Managing Demotion," in *Organization Careers: A Sourcebook for Theory*. Chicago: Aldine, 1968. An excellent collection of articles on demotion in organizations, and how individuals adjust to it.

Erving Goffman, "On Cooling the Mark Out: Some Aspects of Adaptation to Failure," *Psychiatry* **15** (November 1952), 451–463. An insightful analysis of the vulnerability of the naïve to being victimized.

Michael Harrington, *The Other America: Poverty in the United States*. New York: Macmillan, 1963. A significant portrayal of conditions of life for various groups we have characterized as retreatists.

P. K. Hatt, "Occupation and Social Stratification," *American Journal of Sociology* **55** (May 1950), 533–543. A provocative article suggesting that it may be unrealistic to think of the occupational structure as a single continuum; rather it may be more feasible to compare occupations within particular institutions.

August B. Hollingshead and Frederick C. Redlich, *Social Class and Mental Illness*. New York: Wiley, 1958. An early important study of the incidence of mental illness within various social classes and of the class-related variations in treatment of the mentally ill.

George Katona, *Private Pensions and Individual Saving*. Ann Arbor, Mich.: Institute for Social Research of the University of Michigan, 1965. An empirical study of factors related to private saving in the United States.

Richard D. Lambert, "The Social and Psychological Determinants of Savings and Investments in Developing Societies," in Bert F. Hoselitz and Wilbert E. Moore (editors), *Industrialization and Society*. The Hague: UNESCO: Mouton, 1963. An examination of the extent to which attitudes and values of the cultures determine the amount, nature, and use of savings.

Gerhard Lenski, *Power and Privilege: A Theory of Social Stratification*. New York: McGraw-Hill, 1966. Considers the multiple bases of stratification in what we have termed conglomerate societies.

Oscar Lewis, *Five Families*. New York: Basic Books, 1959. A famous study which produced the concept of the "culture of poverty."

Eliott Liebow, *Tally's Corner*. Boston: Little, Brown, 1967. An extraordinarily illuminating study of an important type of Negro ghetto-dweller.

Robert K. Merton, "Social Structure and Anomie," in Merton, *Social Theory and Social Structure* (revised edition). Glencoe, Ill.: The Free Press, 1957. A classic formulation of possible adaptations to societies, depending on combinations of goals and means, which has led to a proliferation of research projects on the topic.

Wilbert E. Moore and Arnold S. Feldman (editors), *Labor Commitment and Social Change in Developing Areas.* New York: Social Science Research Council, 1960. An important collection of papers on the world-wide question of motivation of people to learn and perform occupational tasks in modernizing sectors.

Manning Nash, *Machine Age Maya.* Glencoe, Ill.: The Free Press, 1958. A stimulating study of the impact of industrialization on a Guatemalan community.

Arthur B. Shostak and William Gomberg (editors), *Blue-Collar World: Studies of the American Worker.* Englewood Cliffs, N.J.: Prentice-Hall, 1964. A significant collection of articles covering the range of participation in contemporary society by members of the middle and lower classes.

George E. Simpson and J. Milton Yinger, *Racial and Cultural Minorities* (third edition). New York: Harper, 1965. A good overview of discrimination and relations among various minority groups.

William I. Thomas and Florian Znaniecki, *The Polish Peasant in Europe and America.* Boston: Richard G. Badger, 1920. A landmark volume examining the transition from folk to modernizing society.

Jack E. Weller, *Yesterday's People: Life in Contemporary Appalachia.* Lexington, Ky.: University of Kentucky Press, 1966. An objective analysis of a folk living on the fringes of modern urban society.

Harold L. Wilensky, "The Uneven Distribution of Leisure: The Impact of Economic Growth on 'Free Time,'" *Social Problems* **IX,** (Summer 1961), 32–56. Examination of the impact of modernization on the lives of those in different parts of the society.

Harold L. Wilensky and Charles N. Lebeaux, *Industrial Society and Social Welfare* (paperback edition). New York: The Free Press, 1965. An examination of the consequences of modernization which give rise to welfare problems and programs.

CHAPTER 12

CHANGING THE CONTEMPORARY SOCIETY

THE NEED FOR ADJUSTMENTS

Because modernization involves widening networks of interdependence, the processes of adaptation—the activities of solving life problems—have consequences for others, and by the same token, the adaptations of others have consequences for you. Compromise and adjustment are necessary in any society. The networks of interdependence in the folk society are such that these adjustments can be negotiated within the local group, but with modernization, interdependence swells to include unknown persons and cause-and-effect relationships which are difficult to trace. Conglomerate societies, then, must have social structures and processes to produce compromise decisions when social units are involved in extended and impersonal but nevertheless real interdependencies. As the society moves toward the modern urban type, markets and political processes inevitably emerge.

Consequences of Adaptations

The activities associated with the adaptations sketched in the preceding chapter have, in the aggregate, consequences for the shape of the system. The family's private solutions to its problems, when combined with similar solutions of other families in similar circumstances, may describe a trend. The conformist family pursuing the modern style of life through occupational mobility may have no interest in promoting urbanization but, by moving to the urban center contributes to it. The innovative family which diligently promotes a recreational activity may spawn a new industry and thus contribute to occupational specialization.

The significant social, economic, and political trends associated with modernization can be seen as resulting from the aggregation of private solutions to major family problems. The adaptations of the majority of families eventually account for urban centers and their problems: sanitation and pollution, housing, traffic and transportation, crime, welfare programs, and overload of public educational facilities. Private adaptations to modernization tend to change the structure of the family; as children become economic liabilities rather than assets, we expect family size to decrease, and as the nuclear family takes on increased significance with mobility, family responsibilities for the older generation tend to be shifted to the society. With continued specialization of technologies and proliferation of knowledge, the private demands of families result in public demand for extension of universal education to higher levels. As families seek to contribute more fully in modern society, some get enmeshed in networks for importing resources or exporting goods and services, and in the aggregate this crossing of territorial boundaries joins regions, states, or nations into interdependence. Because the myriads of private decisions made by families and individuals ultimately change the structure of society and thus spheres of action for many, modernization requires the development of political processes for compromise.

> *Karl Deutsch has pioneered in the measurement of inter-nation communication and interdependence. Within-society interdependence is studied by* human ecologists.   <

POLITICAL PROCESSES

With expanding networks of interdependence come expanding networks of power, for as we have said power can be viewed as the obverse of dependence. In the folklike society, interdependence is largely contained within the boundaries of the extended kinship system, the tribe, or village, and allegiance and identification are confined to the same unit. As interdependence spills across the boundaries of those local units, there arises the need for structures which can manage the broader network of interdependence and power. This in turn calls for the shifting of allegiances to larger, less personal collectivities. Modernization is a process continually calling for widening allegiances as interdependence expands. It seems inevitable, then, that at least three devices emerge for the regulation of interdependence and power, and that these will arise regardless of the constitutional form of government. One of these is the formalized legislative process; a second is a recognized judicial system, and the third is less formal: a system of interest groups to exercise countervailing power.

The Legislative Process

The modernizing society, we have said, generates social differentiation, with categories or collections of people sharing some circumstances and thereby being set apart from other categories or collections facing different circumstances. But in the modernizing society, cause/effect relationships criss-cross social categories, for members share territory and services and make competing claims on common resources. Inevitably, then, there arises some legislative structure. By this term we refer to a decision-making body composed of representatives of various constituencies, with each member bringing to bear the interests of some constituency, some collection of people who share some circumstances. Just how representative this body is, is a major variable. So too is the question of the bases on which constituencies are identified: religion, territory, economic class, ethnic origin, or other bases.

In the early stages of modernization the legislative structure may not be widely representative. To the extent that significant interests are under-represented, the legitimacy of the legislative body would seem questionable. Open-system man does not inherit genetically the ability to relate to a representative system; placing his trust and allegiance in it requires learning. Opportunities both to learn of the needs for legislative processes and to learn how to participate in them are not uniformly available throughout a society. We have to expect that some will perceive more quickly than others that their interests are affected by widening ripples of cause and effect, and that some will learn more quickly than others how to be effective through legislative

channels. At this stage of transition, then, we would expect a polarization of orientations, with some vigorously advocating development of
the legislative process and others vigorously resisting, urging return
to simpler tribal or provincial arrangements.

We would expect, then, in the early stages of transition a period
in which not only is learning incomplete but in which the legislative
body is relatively unstable and the legislative process halting. Especially during such a period, *coup d'états* and palace revolutions seem
rather likely. In later stages, legislative structures may become more
reliable and more representative, and therefore more legitimate, thus
making palace revolutions less likely.

There are a great many possibilities for sorting families into constituencies: tribal, ethnic, racial, linguistic, territorial, religious, urban/
rural, or other criteria significant to the population. In the early stages
of modernization, we would expect constituencies along only a few
very recognizable and ascribed lines. With growing modernization,
action spheres become less controlled by ascribed statuses, more
differentiated and segmented into specialized institutions, with the
result that the individual and family develop multiple interests. The
modernizing society becomes a *pluralistic* society, and it becomes increasingly difficult to assign a family to a single constitiuency.

> Political development *is a rapidly growing specialty in political
science. The understanding of* political socialization *is being developed by
political sociologists and by the political behavior specialists within the
field of political science.* <

The segmentation of the action sphere means that the individual
and family are subject to competing interests and cross-pressures.
Learning that the events that impinge on the family can no longer be
handled adequately through a simple, ascribed, bloc system may be
extremely painful. There may be a period in the transition in which
there is a lag in the transfer of allegiance and trust to more complicated
and flexible coalitions, some continuing to advocate loyalties to old
collectivities. Eventually, coalitions emerge in the form of either a
limited number of parties, each of which embraces a multiplicity of

issues, or of a proliferation of parties, each identified with a dominant issue. When there are only a few parties, coalitions take place within them; when there are multiple parties, coalitions emerge between them.

>   *These matters are extensively studied by political scientists who specialize in the* legislative process.   <

The emergence of constituencies and their representation appears to be an inevitable process associated with modernization, despite extreme variations in the nature of the constituencies, the manner in which representatives are selected, the procedures governing the legislative process, and the relationship of the legislative structure to the chief executive.

With segmentation of action spheres, families are increasingly interdependent with others in a variety of social structures, and the formal legislative process cannot respond rapidly enough or in sufficient detail to yield the necessary adjustments. Interest groups inevitably emerge in pluralistic societies.

Interest Groups

When the legislative machinery is geared to complicated coalitions dealing with immediate and multiple issues, it is also necessary that there be channels by which the concerns of individuals and families can be mobilized. Specialized interest groups afford channels for the expression of such concerns by acting as pressure groups lobbying for or against legislation.

The significance of interest groups in a modernizing society is by no means confined to the legislative process; they act in various other capacities. In situations in which the individual or the family can be affected by actions of others he does not know, through cause-and-effect connections he does not know, the interest group can act as a funnel to report and interpret developments of special relevance. Through the interest group, the individual or family may learn the identities of others with similar interests. They may also learn the identities of those whose actions are having consequences for them.

On the basis of this knowledge, the interest group may act as a counter-vailing power. By bringing to the attention of others the fact that their actions are having detrimental consequences for members of the interest group, the interest group may be able to win modifications of those activities on behalf of its members.

> *Attention to interest-group phenomena is found in a variety of fields, including* political behavior, sociology of collective behavior, labor/management relations, *and* public opinion. <

As family and individual action spheres become increasingly segmented, it is likely that their varied interests lead them to become members of multiple interest groups. Even though the individual and family may participate in the several institutional sectors of their society in a segmented fashion, those sectors ultimately are interconnected, and the individual and family which participate in a variety of interest groups may find some of these taking conflicting stands on issues. This can result in dissonance and force the individual or family to reassess priorities. This problem may be extremely difficult if the individual's identification with the interest groups has been long-standing. There are, however, in modernized societies, a variety of *ad hoc* interest groups which may claim only temporary attention.

In general, we would expect those who are most deeply engaged in the modernized component to be most active in interest groups. Those conformists most involved in the modern segment have diverse action spheres which make them more likely to be identified with a wide variety of interest groups. Those individuals or families at the interface between the modern and more traditional sectors—the innovators and reactors—are likely to be involved in fewer interest groups. We would expect their involvement to be intense and the interest groups to which they belong to be those directly involved in issues related to interface tensions.

Judicial System

With interdependence, the necessary compromises may require the presence of disinterested third parties who can judge the relative merits of competing claims, invoke relevant criteria, and settle disputes. Among societies there are a number of forms the judicial system may take, with some employing a formalized adversary system and others not; some with multiple justices, others with just one; some with appointed judges, others electing them; and various uses of juries. Without assuming that one form is better than others, we can note the inevitable emergence of some judicial system as evidence of the need in contemporary societies for the application of general norms to specific cases, and the facilitation of compromise.

Broadening Allegiances

At some point in the modernization process, networks of interdependence appear generally coterminous with the society's boundaries, and legislative and judicial processes grow to handle the emerging power. At this stage we would expect allegiance and loyalty to attach to the nation-state, and nationalism to be the dominant ideology. Although nationalism may recur from time to time as the society appears to be internally or externally threatened, we would expect it to be particularly intensive when it first appears, for it involves a conversion from a former loyalty to a new ideology and the conversion process intensifies involvement.

Just as modernization leads to interdependence that is coterminous with national boundaries, it also contains the seeds for extension of interdependence across national boundaries. Powerful national leaders may attempt to keep the nation self-sufficient and thus contain interdependence within its boundaries, but this is artificial and inevitably gives way to forces of modernization. To the extent that dependence crosses national boundaries, power does, and we would expect the emergence of political structures and processes to encompass the interdependence. Thus with modernization there appears a wide variety of international arrangements, illustrated by treaties; international agencies to control such things as currencies, or tariffs, or public health; economic communities such as the European Common Market; political communities such as the United Nations; or national amalgamations such as the United States of America, the Union of Soviet

Socialist Republics or Malaysia. Interest groups which reflect cross-boundary interdependence may encourage and help legitimate the development of inter-nation allegiances and identities.

> *These topics claim much attention among political scientists under such labels as* political integration *and* nation-building. *Among the prominent researchers in this field is Karl W. Deutsch.*   <

DIFFUSION OF RESPONSIBILITIES

With the long-distance, impersonal interdependence associated with modernization, responsibilities also appear in more complicated, in-direct, and remote forms. Obligations are not met simply in interper-sonal, face-to-face networks. The complicated issues calling for sus-tained collective action to meet obligations are not met by *ad hoc* or spontaneous activities. In the almost-folk society the family's respon-sibilities were toward its own members or, at most, toward the village or tribe; responsibilities were particularistic and local. With modern-ization responsibilities fan out in multiple institutional channels to include support for unknown others, and this support takes forms be-yond the capacity of individuals or families to make decisions, to plan, or to amass and commit resources.

Resource Redistribution

Participation in the results of modern urban society calls for the avail-ability of goods and services made possible only through economies of scale and hence beyond the capacity of the family or local group to generate. Participation in the educational institution requires the availability of specialized instructors, equipment, and libraries, no longer privately available within the most resourceful family or village. Modern education is impossible without economies of scale, and there-fore agencies emerge to provide common educational facilities. Partici-pation in the medical institution requires the availability of specialized personnel, medicines, and facilities which require organization and scale beyond the capacity of any family. Geographic participation in modern society requires travel facilities such as sea- and airports, streets and highways and traffic controls, weather-reporting services, and vehicles generally beyond the productive capacities of private families.

In these and other institutions of modern societies, participation involves not only the use of common goods and services but also contribution toward their establishment by the pooling of families' resources. Specific use of a particular family's contribution to the pool is beyond the discretion of that family. Generally, then, we would expect those whose resources are being tapped for common facilities to wish to exercise some control over policies governing use of those resources. Frequently governmental agencies are created through political processes to monitor, regulate, or operate the common facilities. Thus as interdependence grows and political processes develop, so also do governmental or quasi-governmental administrative agencies.

In addition to redistributing resources into common facilities, modernizing societies also rechannel resources from some families to others. Because the action spheres of families are being changed by events and the actions of unknown others at long distances, families are unable to fully anticipate and prepare for contingencies. In the folklike society families can rely on stable relationships involving direct reciprocity with known others. The local group contains all the knowledge and resources available to deal with unanticipated events— plus obligations of mutual aid. In the modernized society, even the obligation of mutual aid may be insufficient because the source of the family's problem as well as the knowledge and resources for its solution may be lodged in specialized and remote structures.

International currency instability, for example, may result in economic recession which causes unemployment within particular families. World travelers may return with a disease which causes an epidemic, incapacitating an innocent family. Technical inventions, such as the mechanical cotton picker, may render certain families economically obsolete, equipped only with skills no longer needed. Few modern families have the resources to cope with contingencies alone; therefore agencies arise for the impersonal redistribution of resources among families. Sometimes private interest groups take on this kind of responsibility, but with increasing modernization we would expect increasing governmental involvement in response to legislated programs.

> *Economists have been active in conceiving of and measuring the results of modern societies: national income, accounting, and gross national product. Various social sciences are interested in income redistribution.* <

Income redistribution seems to appear in response to three major problems in conglomerate societies. With pressures for prolonged and universal education to prepare individuals for modern society, the productive part of the society must subsidize the young for longer periods. The results of current production must be diverted from current consumption to ensure future production. On the other hand, with the continued technological change and lenghthened life expectancies associated with modernization, sizable portions of the population consume long after they have stopped producing. With families subject to contingencies beyond their capacity, responsibility for intergenerational transfers cannot reside entirely within a particular family. Responsibility is diffused.

The productive portion of conglomerate society may also divert a portion of its resources to support families who are unable to contribute, although in the contributing generation. Some of these may be families temporarily unemployed by economic or technological dislocation; others may become more or less permanently incapacitated early in their work careers; other families may be handicapped by death or disability of the major earner. The conglomerate society may also include families whose preparation for modern society is inadequate and who cannot survive in folk pockets. Because kinship and ascribed obligations are insufficient to protect families under these circumstances, modernizing societies diffuse responsibility and generate organizations to redistribute resources to them.

Private associations, such as insurance associations, churches and private charities, may carry out the redistribution of resources. But as interdependence expands and responsibility diffuses further, redistribution agencies are needed that can extend services to reach the boundaries of interdependence. It appears inevitable, then, that some policies for income redistribution become established through political processes and are carried out through governmental administrative agencies.

Diffusion of responsibility to impersonal agencies does not mean that the family is without obligations. For several decades, behavioral scientists and others suggested that the family was in the process of withering away as its responsibilities were being transferred to various public and private specialized agencies. It was felt that, at most, the family's function in modern society might be procreation and initial socialization until the formal educational system could take over. But evidence from the most modernized nations increasingly shows that view to be false. What appears to be developing, at least among the lower and middle classes, is a pattern of diffused responsibility supplemented by intergenerational responsibilities within the family. The emergence of the nuclear family is accompanied by separate residence for the older generation, but there remain practices of financial help and advice, which supplement the support available through public and private agencies.

Opportunity Equalization

With modernization, we would expect the norm of *distributive justice* to demand equal opportunities in line with emphasis on achievement and universalism. In the modernizing transition, machinery is developed to implement this version of the distributive-justice norm, and the judicial system may be taxed to reconcile the norm with reality. As there are no pure modern urban societies, there are no societies with full equalization of opportunities; but with modernization, demands increase for governments to work toward that norm. Even greater and more universally available educational, legal, housing and medical opportunities are sought for members of the society. In addition to measures for equal access to these facilities—and hence equal opportunity to prepare to participate in modern society—demands are made for measures to compensate for earlier differential opportunities. When these are due to inherited wealth, measures such as inheritance taxes, land reform, or the progressive income tax are enacted. When these are due to caste-imposed inequalities, measures are enacted to extend civil rights and to provide additional preparation in compensation for earlier deprivations. When folk elements migrate from the rural to the urban areas, programs may be developed to offset their relative inability to contribute by subsidizing housing and other facilities, and to provide compensatory education.

LEARNING FOR CHANGE

Abilities to participate effectively in political processes and to understand diffuse responsibilities are learned. The folk society honors tradition and abhors change and therefore its members are not taught how to bring it about; in the early stages of modernization the techniques of planning and implementing change are not well understood by many. These techniques have to be constructed during the process of change itself, because the folk society, during socialization, does not instruct its members in change techniques. With modernization, still more complicated techniques have to be developed to cope with the growing interdependence, just as new loyalties have to be learned. In the transitional society, we might expect the individual to be socialized in change techniques, but at best, each generation can only prepare the next for what it anticipates; hence each new generation must produce new capacities for change.

In conglomerate societies, preparation to participate in the change process is not uniformly distributed. Learning the need for compromise and for new allegiance is not achieved by all at the same time. Techniques for participation in interest groups and for relating to the legislative process are more thoroughly learned by some than by others. Some families are more attuned to—and prepared to adapt to—new policies and programs generated by the political process and the diffusion of responsibility. We would expect that those most deeply engaged in the various institutions of modernizing society would also be those best located and qualified to participate in change processes and to recognize new realities. Those individuals and families with superficial exposure to the educational institution, those who are not situated at the centers of economic interdependence, and those on the periphery of information networks would be less likely to be sensitive to and prepared for change processes. Because of differential distribution of awareness and preparation, transitional stages in modernization produce critical issues which from time to time may produce turmoil and divide the society, and test its cohesiveness.

The cohesiveness of a conglomerate society during a transitional stage may depend to a large extent on the abilities of those in power centers to anticipate the issues and modify resource commitments appropriately. This brings us to a discussion of power structures.

POWER STRUCTURES

The complicated sets of activities which constitute modern technologies call for planning and coordination of the use of collected resources, which can only be accomplished by complex organizations. The provision of services and the regulation of exchange among large numbers of persons distributed over large territories requires administrative capacities not available to small units. The protection of families from threat of war or disease under conditions of geographic mobility and extensive transportation systems can be provided only by administrative agencies deployed over large territories, but centrally coordinated.

> *The study of* complex organizations *has been undertaken in various fields, but especially in sociology and political science, often under the label of* bureaucracy. *Among the major scholars in this field are Max Weber, Chester Barnard, James March, and Herbert Simon.*   <

For such reasons resources in modernizing societies are lodged in complex organizations in which decisions about their use can have widespread effects. To the extent that action spheres of individuals and families are affected by decisions made in complex organizations, those individuals and families are dependent—and the organizations have power. Those in positions calling for decisions about the commitment of organized resources are therefore in positions of power. The emergence of power persons is inevitable as societies modernize, precisely because their positions are in organizations with consequences for many; this is true regardless of personalities, motives, or political ideologies.

But just as complex organizations have consequences for many individuals and families, they have consequences for one another. Organizations which supply materials or services for other organizations are dependent on the decisions of those customers, just as those who need materials or services are dependent on suppliers. Organizations cannot proceed merrily on their own, without considering the actions of competitors. Productive organizations needing expert knowledge and skills are dependent on educational organizations to equip the labor force. And just as individuals and families in modernizing societies are dependent on common facilities and the organizations which provide them, so are other complex organizations. Inevitably, in modernizing societies, legislative and judicial processes evolve to control or regulate inter-organizational dependencies and actions. Inevitably also, within the boundaries established by legislative and judicial processes (and sometimes outside those boundaries), decisions and compromises among organizations are required to handle on-going chains of cause and effect.

The interdependence associated with modernization links—for purposes of cooperation—organizations which are located in separate institutional sectors of society. Thus organizations are subject to multiple pressures to compromise. Adjustments to facilitate a cooperative endeavor across institutions may strain an organization's relations with other organizations within the institution. The development of commercial aviation, for example, involves the local construction of airport facilities, the manufacturing of aircraft, the training of specialized personnel, the commitment of financial resources, the informing of the public of the services, and the provision of navigational and related services. At a minimum, commercial aviation involves the cooperation of industrial, educational, financial, governmental, and news-media institutions. A major reorientation of an academic discipline—such as the modernization of mathematics—involves curriculum revision, retraining of teachers, production and distribution of revised text materials, financial resources, and persuasion of the public, as well as the realignment of the several levels of the educational system. Mobilization for war involves the coordinated adjustments of agricultural, industrial, educational, transport, religious, and family institutions, as well as the military.

With interdependence woven among organizations and between institutions, identification of problems and their sources and the generation of solutions and consensus are time-consuming. Those persons whose duty it is to direct the formal channels for political compromise frequently are not able alone to anticipate problems or manage solutions rapidly. For efficient action, organizations frequently must obtain resource commitments from other organizations without the delays inherent in the legislative processes, or must seek legislative or judicial commitments to facilitate cooperation. For all these reasons, inter-organizational and inter-institutional coordination must and does occur.

Because inter-organizational dependence generally becomes patterned, those in positions of power within organizations also become enmeshed in what social scientists call *the power structure.* This topic is highly controversial among social scientists, for a variety of reasons.

> *Both political scientists and sociologists are involved in the analysis of power structures. Among major contributors have been Robert Dahl, Floyd Hunter, C. Wright Mills, and Arnold Rose. A crucial figure in the emergence of power as a social science topic was Karl Marx.* <

There are disputes over how to conceive of and measure power structures, and therefore over the empirical realities of power. There is disagreement about the relative importance of economic dependence in accounting for power structures, with some taking an economic-dominance position and others insisting on a more pluralistic base. Some social scientists have maintained that power structures involve conspiracies, but others insist that motivations are more complex. We are not able to set forth a final resolution to these issues, but we suggest that when pluralism emerges in modernizing societies, economics is not the sole determinant of power, however crucial it is; we would expect the role of economics to vary during transition. Likewise, we believe motivation is a variable; conspiracies are possible, but to assume that they are inevitable is unwarranted. Regardless of motives or ideologies, power structures have to emerge along with the development of complex organizations in complex networks of interdependence.

Functions of Power Structures

Members of power structures are powerful because they are in positions to coordinate and commit resources involving the viability of the society. The society with specialized and interdependent elements may be threatened either externally or internally. External threats may be outright attacks, but more often come in the form of international changes which challenge the adaptive capacities of the society. Internal threats come from the lack of fit among the component parts of the society.

The specific requirements for viability vary with stages in the modernization process. At one point, internal viability may hinge on solving issues at the interface of folk and modern components; at another time, the dominant issue may be integrating former caste groups within the mainstream; at still another time, the overriding issue may be at the rural/urban interface. With increasing modernization, however, viability questions are likely to be more subtle and complicated, involving the simultaneous modification of several institutions so that the resulting action spheres of individuals and families are viable. The kinds of multi-institutional modifications that we suggested are associated with urbanization, for example, may ultimately be forged through legislative, judicial, and interest-group processes. But, to be successful, such modifications will require the early identification of growing problems, and the generation of solutions by those in positions to be aware of the complicated networks of cause and effect. Because members of the power structure are situated at inter-institutional junctures, they have both interest in and unusual opportunities to become alerted to the extended significance of activities of their organizations.

As interdependence spans national boundaries, some members of the power structure may become alerted to international developments which could pose problems for the viability of the society. Such developments might involve, for example, the stability of currencies, tariffs, common market coalitions, the build-up of international arms, or political realignments. These events may seem remote to many members of the society, but nevertheless may ultimately have profound significance for all members. They can lead to labor dislocation, world depression, currency inflation, or world war.

Because power-structure positions are deeply involved in expansive interdependence at national or international levels, persons in power are uniquely situated to anticipate consequences of current developments, to foresee emerging problems, to generate the search for possible solutions, to alert those involved in political processes, to urge that these issues be placed on the political agenda, and to modify the commitment of resources at their own disposal. When the power structure is functioning effectively, it would, for example, foresee migration trends pulling folk-prepared families into urban centers, and some of the myriad problems associated with this transition. If it is working effectively then, the society may have sufficient warning to prepare such measures as reorientation of educational systems, redistribution of income, revision of employment and training procedures, the extension of legal services to impoverished areas, new transportation services, and new housing.

The Dynamics of Power Structures

It is pretty clear that in modernized societies, the power structure is relatively amorphous, that it operates primarily through informal mechanisms, and that many of its members may never have met each other. This is not to deny the possibility of conspiracies, or formal coalitions among some members, or even that such clusters are in conflict with one another. The power structure is not a coordinated set of postions around a common goal; it reflects a multiplicity of interests in a pluralistic society. It changes shape depending on the issues, operating locally for local issues, tied loosely at the international level for expanding issues. But because local resources are tied into national networks, the task of resolving power issues usually gravitates to the national level.

Although members of the national power structure do not meet as a whole nor act in concert, clusters do interact directly around concentrated interdependence; and because some members of that cluster may also be members of another one, there is the possibility of information flow and compromise. Even if powerful persons are not directly or indirectly tied through such clusters, they may be aware of one another's existence and concerns and able to make contact should new issues call for new clusters. This awareness is usually fostered by cosmopolitan orientations which expose them to similar communications media, cause their headquarters to be in major metropolitan centers, put them on some of the same guest lists, register them at some of the same resorts, and propel them into some of the same voluntary associations. For such reasons, members of the power structure can sometimes take parallel or compatible actions without acting in concert or as conspirators. But in spite of such informal networks, power structures may fail to effectively serve the functions for society that we have suggested above.

VULNERABILITIES OF SOCIETIES

The power structure is necessary but not sufficient to effectively shape the society for modernization. It is necessary because decisions to commit and re-commit amassed resources must be made and formal political processes are not usually adequate. It is not sufficient for a variety of reasons. Leadership for modernization requires an effective power structure, but also its articulation with other important elements of the society; hence the society is vulnerable to either fragmented power or lack of articulation.

Fragmentation of power and therefore ineffectiveness may arise because of internal dissension, which may reflect either a unique and volatile combination of personalities or the absence of shared societal values. In conglomerate societies, some power is likely to be held by those who are not primarily oriented to modernization, achievement, and universalism, and who instead resist diffusion of responsibility and therefore identification with larger collectivities. These elements would be looking to promote their own, or local or regional interests rather than societal interests. Under some conditions during transition, then, power structures may become arenas for all-out competition or for live-and-let-live cooperation, rather than societal leadership. On the other hand, the power structure may be oriented to societal needs, but be fragmented because of disagreement over modernization goals. The composition and internal dynamics of power structures, then, are crucial questions for the modernizing society.

On the other hand, the power structure may be cohesive and oriented to societal values, but provide ineffective leadership because of blind spots in the decision process. Power resides in resource centers, and we would expect those responsible to be alert to cause-and-effect changes involving those resources, but we cannot assume the cause-and-effect knowledge of powerful persons to be complete. Some ramifications of complicated interdependence are called to the attention of powerful decision makers by feedback from other powerful persons whose resources are affected; this is the feature which underlies power structure compromises. To the extent that ramifications are diffuse or extend to those not represented in the power structure, decision makers may be insensitive or unaware of some of the consequences of their actions. There may be no power center to protest the use or exhaustion of natural resources until considerable damage has already occurred. Pollution of water resources or of the air may occur over extended time periods and before power is effectively mobilized to react. Many decisions on geographic commitment of resources may be made independently, and in the aggregate bring about urban problems before countervailing power centers emerge.

Some of the ramifications of actions which do not produce immediate feedback may be understood by experts or scholars not at the power centers. Economists, for example, can anticipate some of the consequences, in the aggregate, of parallel investment decisions of the powerful, where countervailing power does not exist. Physical scientists may anticipate future problems stemming from current concentration on applied research and neglect of basic research, for which there is no power-structure feedback. Some developments may not be due to decisions of the power structure, but may have consequences for their actions in the future; world population developments are an example. Here again, the consequences of these developments are more likely to be anticipated by the expert or scholar than by members of the power structure. One index of modernization is the identification and expansion of higher learning as a separate institution, adding research and development to its traditional function of transmitting the cultural heritage. Another crucial question for modernization, therefore, is whether there is an effective liaison between the power structure and those scholarly centers which specialize in refining and extending cause-and-effect understanding.

Even if there is an informed and coherent power structure, it can exercise leadership only if it maintains legitimacy within the society, only if individual and family action spheres remain relatively satisfactory. When individuals and families feel unable to achieve their goals and powerless to improve their action spheres, we would expect them to lose identity with the society and to feel *alienated*. This concept has a variety of connotations: powerlessness, rootlessness, normlessness, and social isolation. However we refine the notion, however, its general significance is that the individual feels to some extent apart from—uncommitted to—the established order. We would not expect the alienated individual to recognize established leadership, for example. In general, we can say that leadership which is not seen as providing viable action spheres is not viewed as legitimate.

>   *The concept of* alienation, *introduced by Karl Marx, has been given broader meaning; several different varieties of it have been identified through intensive study by political scientists and sociologists.*   <

We would not expect to find alienation among those with a conformity adaptation, since they are progressing within the existing system. Among those with innovative, reactive, and retreatist adaptations, however, we would expect some alienation. Whether persons in these categories are alienated is likely to depend on whether they see means of improving their presently unsatisfactory spheres of action and thus their situations in the future. A crucial factor in determining which individuals and families are alienated is the perceived ability to participate in political processes. Thus where the individual perceives that interest groups are absent or ineffective, or where elements of the society are not represented in the legislative process, or political parties are unresponsive, we would expect the innovators, reactors, and retreatists to feel alienated.

It appears inevitable that some members of conglomerate societies would feel alienated. But if the leadership is unable to maintain societal balance in transitions, and if action spheres of those with conformist adaptations are eroded, we would expect them to turn from that adaptation. Those who prize their skills, but see them becoming less useful with modernization, are likely to shift to the reactive adaptation, seeking former conditions more appropriate to their skills. Those conformists who perceive in modernization new goals that are attractive but beyond their capacities are more likely to switch to the innovative adaptation. At crucial stages in transition, if leadership is ineffective, the society will tend toward polarization along innovative and reactive lines. It seems quite possible under these conditions for the political processes to be stalemated or paralyzed, for numerous families and individuals to become alienated, and for the legitimacy of the power structure to be undermined. A crucial question for modernization is whether the leadership of the society can maintain the viability of the system and retain its own legitimacy.

If not, the society is ripe for new leadership.

EMERGENCE OF COMPETING ELITES

With polarization pulling families from the conformist adaptation, innovators and reactors seek new spokesmen who can articulate grievances, visualize new states of affairs, and compete with those presently in power. The types of leaders sought by those who are alienated tend to be different from the leaders sought by those who are not. The unalienated search for leaders who are more competent on modern criteria than are members of the present power structure—better educated, more energetic, and more politically aware. The alienated, who may be experiencing more general despair, are more likely to be attracted by relatively uncomplicated folk heroes: sports stars, popular religious leaders, well-known entertainers, military heroes, or others with charisma.

Competing elites may also emerge as generations are replaced. Not only does the dying-out of one generation gradually diminish the power of some members of the power structure, but also the entry of a new generation provides the base for new members of the power structure. The power structure of contemporary society may be transformed within a matter of a few years through attrition, without there necessarily having been turmoil or violence. When the new generation is proportionately large, there may be more difficulties in the transferral of power because the challenging elites represent a more drastic change. Although the socialization process does transmit some political orientations from one generation to another, a young generation may become convinced that generational differences call for different solutions. When new peer groups are large, and concentrated, and held together through extended periods of education, the peer group may become the predominant referent. With educational content that is more modern than that of the preceding generation, and with fewer commitments and investments, the young may perceive that their generation faces unique opportunities and constraints, and therefore adopt new values or rearrange the priorities of old values. Under these conditions, leadership of the new generation may arise to demand revamping of the power structure.

Whether the challenges of new elites stem from polarization in the society or from generational differences, two consequences seem possible. If the existing power structure is sufficiently flexible and sensitive to the challenges, the competing elites may be co-opted, thus broadening the base for power and reflecting the enlarged network of interdependence. When compromise of this type is not possible, the likely outcome is rebellion. When polarization and generational differences appear simultaneously, the system is particularly vulnerable to rebellion.

RECAPITULATION

With the expanding interdependence accompanying modernization come the diffusion of responsibilities and extended networks of power. As means to achieving compromises, families must develop new allegiances and learn to participate in new political processes involving legislative and judicial functions and interest groups. Modernization lodges resources in complex organizations, and their interdependence requires compromise and therefore power structures. Power structures may protect the viability of the society by adjusting resource allocations simultaneously to the demands of modernization and to the needs of family action spheres. For the power structure to be effective in these capacities, it must be cohesive and oriented to societal values and it must maintain liaison with centers of scholarship and political institutions. If the power structure is ineffective, the society may move toward polarization, or generational gaps develop and new elites emerge to compete for leadership.

RECOMMENDED BROWSING

Robert R. Alford, *Party and Society: The Anglo-American Democracies.* Chicago: Rand McNally, 1963. An important examination of political parties and social structure in societies having pluralistic political systems.

Gabriel A. Almond and James S. Coleman (editors), *The Politics of Developing Areas.* Princeton, N.J.: Princeton University Press, 1960. An important collection of papers by specialists on political development of several continents.

Gabriel Almond and Sidney Verba, *The Civic Culture: Political Attitudes and Democracy in Five Nations.* Princeton, N.J.: Princeton University Press, 1963. Empirical study of "political culture" in five modernizing nations in search of the attitudes supportive of stable democratic processes.

Bernard Barber, *Social Stratification: A Comparative Analysis of Structure and Process.* New York: Harcourt, Brace and World, 1957. A useful overview of the reasons for and consequences of stratification systems, and how they change, in various nations.

Chester I. Barnard, *The Functions of the Executive.* Cambridge, Mass.: Harvard University Press, 1938. A classic analysis of organizations as systems of cooperative effort.

Peter M. Blau and Otis Dudley Duncan, *The American Occupational Structure.* New York: Wiley, 1967. An examination of occupations and stratification in the United States.

Robert Blauner, *Alienation and Freedom: The Factory Worker and His Industry.* Chicago: University of Chicago Press, 1964. Compares variations in alienation in response to different technologies.

James S. Coleman, *Community Conflict.* New York: The Free Press of Glencoe, 1957. A classic presentation of the processes by which communities become polarized in the course of meeting issues.

Phillips Cutright, "Income Re-Distribution: A Cross-National Analysis," *Social Forces* **46** (December 1967), 180–190. Analysis of egalitarian pressures in 40 political systems, and resulting measures for redistribution of income.

Robert A. Dahl, *Who Governs?* New Haven, Conn.: Yale University Press, 1961. An important analysis of a pluralistic political system.

Karl W. Deutsch, *Nationalism and Social Communication: An Inquiry into the Foundations of Nationality.* Cambridge, Mass.: M.I.T. Press, 1966. An important consideration of social interdependence and political association.

Karl W. Deutsch, *The Nerves of Government: Models of Political Communication and Control.* New York: Free Press of Glencoe, 1963. Theoretical statement viewing government as a process for steering society.

Sigmund Diamond, "From Organization to Society: Virginia in the Seventeenth Century." *American Journal of Sociology* **63** (March 1958), 457–475. Analysis of the dynamic forces which transformed a commercial organization into a society.

S. N. Eisenstadt, *From Generation to Generation.* New York: The Free Press, 1956. Examines the significance of age groupings in a wide variety of societies, and their role in social change and stability.

S. N. Eisenstadt, *Modernization: Protest and Change.* Englewood Cliffs, N.J.: Prentice-Hall, 1966. Examination of modernizing societies, with emphasis on the development of institutional structures for absorbing social change.

William A. Gamson, *Power and Discontent.* Homewood, Ill.: Dorsey Press, 1968. Compares two major perspectives on power and unrest, and focuses on concept of *political trust.*

Harold Guetzkow, *Multiple Loyalties: Theoretical Approach to a Problem in International Organization.* Princeton, N.J.: Center for Research on World Political Institutions, 1955. Theoretical examination of the question of identification with and allegiance to widening collectivities.

Samuel P. Huntington, *Political Order in Changing Societies.* New Haven, Conn.: Yale University Press, 1968. Analysis of problems of political stability in societies undergoing rapid social and economic change.

Herbert H. Hyman, *Political Socialization: A Study in the Psychology of Political Behavior.* New York: The Free Press, 1959. A small volume summarizing the literature on political behavior as a product of learning.

Malcolm E. Jewel and Samuel C. Patterson, *The Legislative Process in the United States.* New York: Random House, 1966. A useful examination based on the national and four state legislative bodies.

William Kornhauser, *The Politics of Mass Society.* Glencoe: The Free Press, 1959. Includes discussion of estrangement of some from political processes of government.

Juanita M. Kreps, "The Economics of Intergenerational Relationships," in Ethel Shanas and Gordeon F. Streib (editors), *Social Structure and the Family: Generational Relations.* Englewood Cliffs, N.J.: Prentice-Hall, 1965. Analyzes the tendency of young adults and the aged to acquire claims against the national product of any given year without contributing to that year's product.

Robert E. Lane, *Political Life: Why People Get Involved in Politics.* New York: Free Press of Glencoe, 1959. An overview of what is known about political participation in the United States.

Joseph La Polambara (editor), *Bureaucracy and Political Development.* Princeton, N.J.: Princeton University Press, 1963. A useful collection of reports on the role of public organizations in modernizing societies.

Gerhardt Lenski, *Power and Privilege: A Theory of Stratification.* New York: McGraw-Hill, 1966. Considers various cases for the distribution of wealth and income within societies.

Daniel Lerner, *The Passing of Traditional Society.* New York: The Free Press, 1958. An empirical study of reactions to experiences in a variety of transitional societies.

Seymour Martin Lipset, *The First New Nation.* New York: Basic Books, 1963. An analysis of the emergence of the United States as a nation.

Eugene Litwak, "Extended Kin Relations in an Industrial Democratic Society," in Ethel Shanas and Gordon F. Streib (editors), *Social Structure and the Family: Generational Relations.* Englewood Cliffs, N.J.: Prentice-Hall, 1965. Presents a view of functions shared between families and bureaucratic organizations in modern societies.

Norton Long, "The Local Community as an Ecology of Games," *American Journal of Sociology* **64** (November 1958), 251–261. An insightful view of the aggregate social structure flowing from responses of individuals to their own spheres of action.

John Lofland and Rodney Stark, "Becoming a World-Saver: A Theory of Conversion to a Deviant Perspective," *American Sociological Review* **30** (December 1965), 862–875. Analysis of a process involved in giving up one adaptation to society and taking on another, in the context of an obscure religious cult.

James G. March and Herbert A. Simon, *Organizations.* New York: John Wiley, 1958. Important development of the inducements/contributions theory of complex organizations.

C. Wright Mills, *The Power Elite.* New York: Oxford University Press, 1956. Forceful statement of the controversial view that the American power structure is a rather small, cohesive, and deliberate group. For another view see Arnold Rose, below.

Talcott Parsons, *Societies: Evolutionary and Comparative Perspectives.* Englewood Cliffs, N.J.: Prentice-Hall, 1966. A small volume which succinctly presents the views of a major figure in sociology.

Arnold Rose, *The Power Structure: Political Process in American Society.* New York: Oxford University Press, 1967. An important examination of the roles of various elite groups in decisions at the national level. An approach to power structures considerably different from that of C. Wright Mills (above).

Melvin Seeman, "On the Meaning of Alienation," *American Sociological Review* **24** (December 1959), 783–791. A review and clarification of the various versions of alienation.

Neil J. Smelser, *Theory of Collective Behavior.* New York: Free Press of Glencoe, 1963. Identifies various forms of collective behavior, based on generalized beliefs, and seeks to determine the conditions under which they arise.

James D. Thompson, *Organizations in Action.* New York: McGraw-Hill, 1967. Analysis of bases for structure and power in the uses of organizations.

David B. Truman, *The Governmental Process: Political Interests and Public Opinion.* New York: Knopf, 1960. Re-issue of a pioneering analysis of political phenomena from the group perspective.

Ralph H. Turner and Lewis M. Killian, *Collective Behavior.* Englewood Cliffs, N.J.: Prentice-Hall, 1957. A collection of essays on collective behavior and society.

S. Sidney Ulmer (editor), *Introductory Readings in Political Behavior.* Chicago: Rand McNally, 1961. A useful collection of papers on the major topics of political behavior.

Arthur J. Vidich and Joseph Bensman, *Small Town in Mass Society.* Princeton, N.J.: Princeton University Press, 1958. Portrait of an American small town striving to maintain its identity in an urbanizing society.

John C. Wahlke, Heinz Eulau, William Buchanan, and LeRoy C. Ferguson, *The Legislative System: Explorations in Legislative Behavior.* New York: John Wiley, 1962. Empirical comparison of four state legislatures in the United States.

John C. Wahlke and Heinz Eulau, *Legislative Behavior: A Reader in Theory and Research.* New York: Free Press of Glencoe, 1959. An overview of the legislative process in the United States.

Max Weber, *The Theory of Social and Economic Organization,* translated by A. N. Henderson and Talcott Parsons and edited by Talcott Parsons. New York: Free Press of Glencoe, 1947. Classic statement of the significance of bureaucracies in the pursuit of rationality.

Harold L. Wilensky and Charles N. Lebeaux, *Industrial Society and Social Welfare* (paperback edition). New York: Free Press of Glencoe, 1965. Examination of the social problems which emerge with industrialization, and of the extension of social welfare services to meet them.

Maurice Zeitlin, "Political Generations in the Cuban Working Class," *American Journal of Sociology* **71** (March 1966), 493–508. Empirical study of the different generational interpretations of the same abrupt political and social transitions.

MAN, SOCIETY, AND THE FUTURE

Behavior is a function of the interaction between person and environment. This is the proposition which has guided this book. On its face, it is a simple truism. But when we begin to put together a relatively complex model of man and relatively rich and dynamic conceptions of environment, we can start to appreciate the diversity as well as the patterns of behavior.

There are models of man and of environment, other than those we have used, which have utility for some purposes. But for understanding purposive man—for thinking about men and women engaged in the daily activities associated with major life transactions—we believe that the open-system model of man is the most appropriate one currently available, and that the view of environment which centers on culture and social structure gives more leverage than others. The relevant test of a model or concept is its utility in understanding particular phenomena, and we hope that this book has indicated that the behavioral sciences are generating understandings of human behavior, using these kinds of models.

Because our focus has been on purposive man, we have assumed that man maneuvers in his environment to optimize his self-conception. Such maneuvering involves his perception of his environment as it impinges on him—his cognitive map of his action sphere—and this reflects both his personality and the realities of his environment. For some aspects of behavior, such as types of interpersonal maneuvering, information about personality may be extremely important in relation to information about the environment, while for such other aspects of behavior as career strategies, information about the environment may tell us considerably more than data about the personality. This does not negate our basic proposition; rather it indicates that it is the *interaction* of person and environment which is crucial.

With modernization, the social environment becomes increasingly significant, while the physical environment becomes less problematic. With modernization, less of man's energy is directly devoted to coping with the physical environment, and more of his attention is involved in interdependence with other persons. With modernization, then, man's action spheres are significantly shaped not only by those persons he sees and knows, but also by the aggregate activities of those families and individuals which constitute society. To understand "micro" behavior of the individual or family, we need to be able to account for the impact on his action sphere of "macro" phenomena. To the extent that this is true, knowledge of what is happening to societies at the macro level should give us some clues about behavior to be expected at the micro level. We shall try to illustrate this by working with some current societal trends to speculate about future action spheres and future behavior.

CONTEMPORARY SOCIAL TRENDS

Population growth undoubtedly is going to be a prominent feature, world-wide, of the next decades, and is linked to a number of other trends. The race between population and growth of food production is one important question. A bulge in the youth component of most societies appears inevitable, as does the proportion of the world's population living in urban centers. Mass communication and geographic mobility, enhanced by mass transport, seem certain to increase. With increased demands for goods and services, achievement seems certain to be emphasized and ascription weakened; caste, racial, and ethnic barriers to participation in modern society will be under attack. With broadening interdependence, increased demands will be placed on educational systems to provide broader understandings of complexity. This seems certain to aggravate, in the next decades, the strains at the interfaces between folklike elements and more modern components in and among nations. A likely product of these various developments is political instability, ranging from civil wars, to social unrest, to major political realignments.

What influences are these trends, taken collectively, likely to have on the shape of the action spheres of individuals and families? Our own arguments in this book preclude saying that we can predict exactly what these are going to be, but speaking generally, we can suggest some characteristics of action spheres which many families will experience. Societal change and the expectation of it will result in a strong element of contingency in most action spheres; awareness of transition will permeate planning for family and occupational careers and political participation. Societal change plus the large youth component and extended periods of educational preparation probably will result in peer groups becoming more important referents in the identification and solution of problems, with increased generational differences. With population density and functional interdependence, collectivities will loom larger in importance; individuals and families will perceive their destinies as intertwined with the future of others.

We would expect those characteristics of action spheres, generally speaking, to increase on a world-wide scale, because the trends which produce such characteristics are world-wide trends. There are other developments in progress, however, which will tend to have different effects on action spheres because nations are at different stages of modernization and are moving at different speeds. It should make a difference in action spheres to be oriented to modern urban values but to be engulfed by folk-oriented others, versus holding the modern orientation in a predominantly modern society; with the former, for example, the cosmopolitan orientation is more likely to cross international boundaries. It should make a difference in action spheres to develop in an affluent society rather than in a poor one, especially when the gap between the have and have-not nations appears to be widening. The person with the modern orientation in a poor society is likely to find his action sphere quite frustrating, and is likely to be tempted to join the flow of personnel to affluent societies, a move which has been termed the "brain drain." It should make an impact on the action sphere to develop in a politically unstable society or one engulfed in inter-nation conflicts, in which border skirmishes, or wars, or threats of wars are constant contingencies.

In summary, we anticipate that action spheres will increasingly be characterized by multiple contingencies and by orientation to collectivities, especially peer groups. We would also expect perceptions of action spheres increasingly to reflect awareness of societal instability and the problems associated with the transition, especially strains at the interface of folk and modern urban components, and discrepancies between the affluent and the impoverished.

To the extent that the action spheres of individuals and families reflect these characteristics in common, we might anticipate similarities in responses, and although we cannot predict every solution to action-sphere problems, there should be some net effects of the aggregate actions. Thus the collected responses of families and individuals at the micro level of analysis should have discernible consequences for society at the macro level of analysis. As families seek more flexible preparations for their children in uncertain futures, we can anticipate spreading demand not only for more education but for the kinds of knowledge which facilitate future adaptations. With the compromises necessitated by widening interdependence, we expect demands for more efficient grievance procedures, together with more responsive representation in political processes. With increasing awareness of differential advantages, together with interdependence, we can predict increasing emphasis on the norm of equity and demand for more effective programs for income redistribution. For all these reasons, we think there will come a continued shift of identification and allegiance to larger collectivities. The general trend in support for political leadership, we believe, is away from judgment on the basis of ascription and through a transitional stage of judgment on the basis of specific issues, but eventually in the direction of judgment on the basis of personal qualities indicating style of addressing an array of complex present and future problems.

The macro trends suggested above are not likely to unfold smoothly and uniformly. Frictions of transition are going to be universal, so that at particular periods of time reverse developments may be observable; reaction adaptations in the aggregate may prevail temporarily. Here and there, local developments may overshadow the underlying trends; the aggregate of innovative adaptations may divert the overall process. Temporary crisis may cloud longer developments. With transition, specific local issues may dominate the political picture from time to time. Nevertheless, we believe the general trends suggested above will prevail ultimately because they result from the aggregation of responses of those conforming to realities of modernization.

A SHIFTING ETHOS?

If there has been a major theme underlying modernization, we think it can be identified as *mastery of the physical environment.* Our epoch has been variously characterized as the age of the industrial revolution, the scientific age, or the atomic age. Whatever the label, it seems clear that for centuries there has been a continuity of attention to increased productivity and efficiency with regard to the physical world. Although this has gained its greatest momentum in the last century and has been most striking in the nations of the western world, demands for higher standards of living, expressed in terms of the physical environment, are everywhere evident. In response to this ethos and the demands it generates, the world has witnessed revolutions in agricultural and food-production processes, industrial productivity, power generation, transportation, and medicine. Unquestionably these have afforded those families participating in modernization relative freedom from the constraints of the local physical environment. Whatever the costs in human or social terms, mastery of the physical environment has resulted in higher standards of living, and it seems certain that a larger share of the world's population will be demanding and participating in the fruits of modernization.

Not everyone involved or benefiting from modernization is committed to the theme of environmental mastery, and indeed, some do reject the associated materialism. Still, mastery of the physical environment has been the baseline against which accomplishments or deprivations of families or nations are judged. Stratification in terms of classes reflects this concern for achieving mastery. With more and more nations joining the modernization movement, mastery of the physical environment seems destined to preoccupy attention for some decades.

Yet there may be a glimmer of a new ethos. We need not imply that the physical environment is fully mastered to suggest that the fears and threats to survival experienced by earlier generations are no longer meaningful to present generations most engaged in modern life. The fruits of modernization have yet to be widely distributed, but for the affluent the mysteries of how to master the physical environment have been largely dispelled. For them, the quest for mastery of the physical environment may be losing its challenge. We think we see a new challenge and new ethos on the horizon: *pursuit of social justice*. A new ethos does not evolve in a clearly defined form, and the energies of some of those alienated from the old ethos will be devoted to formulating and debating various versions and supporting arguments. We expect that at least one important ingredient of the new ethos will be redistribution of the results of ability to master the physical environment.

Whether the specific ingredients for the social-justice ethos will be created by philosophers, poets, writers, artists, or others we cannot predict, but there are signs of unrest among some of the younger generation which may indicate disenchantment with the old ethos and search for a new one. Perhaps the most compelling sign of unrest is the current political instability, not only in the poorer nations but also in the affluent, and not only in the relatively deprived sectors of the affluent societies, but in their most affluent sectors. Perhaps this can be interpreted as evidence that the young are seeking self-conceptions out of new molds, seeking personal meaning on a new dimension. Just as Maslow hypothesizes a hierarchy of values for the personality, with social values emerging as physical needs are satisfied, perhaps the ethos of social justice emerges as mastery of the physical environment is achieved.

It is often difficult to interpret the significance of present events, but some behavior of the most active among the younger generation can be interpreted as being challenges to the values and elites based on old ethos. To the extent that this rejection diffuses among the younger generation, generational strain will be aggravated. If the younger generation does reject the ethos of environmental mastery, it will also be rejecting the present bases for stratification, substituting a different set of values by which to judge contribution, and therefore attacking the core values by which other generations have defined their self-conceptions. Whether they were high or low on the socioeconomic scale, the miner, the farmer, the factory hand, the plumber, the teacher or the truck driver could all claim that their efforts contributed to mastery of the environment, and were therefore valuable. A view that questions the basic ethos questions their value.

We have been speculating as if mastery of the environment were virtually accomplished, but we should recognize the very real possibility that population growth may exhaust the world's capacity to master the environment. A likely possibility, therefore, is that the two ethics will have to be synthesized, and this, too, will be stressful.

Whether these particular expectations are borne out, it seems clear that modernization will continue to produce macro changes with important consequences at the micro level, and that individual and family responses will, in the aggregate, feed social change back into the larger society.

BEHAVIORAL SCIENCES: RELEVANCE FOR WHAT?

We believe that the behavioral sciences have been accumulating understanding at a rather rapid pace in the twentieth century, and we hope that this book has demonstrated that the behavioral sciences have contemporary relevance. But man's environment has been likewise changing rapidly. Phenomena that are well studied, documented, and explained in one decade may not be of major concern in the next. And herein lies a critical dilemma, not only for professional behavioral scientists, but also for lay consumers of the behavioral sciences.

As behavioral sciences have developed their capacities, social problems have loomed larger and the pressures have grown for behavioral scientists to search for solutions to current and pressing problems, to be "relevant." Clearly, if a science expects continued support from the host society, it is incumbent on that science to demonstrate its utility, but if scientists focus only on today's problems, they may reduce the capacity of the science to be relevant tomorrow. The utility of science at any time is ultimately based on its accumulated knowledge, so its utility for the future depends on continued attention to the accumulation of theoretically significant understanding.   A parallel argument can be made for the layman's approach to the behavioral sciences. To be sure, he should expect the behavioral sciences to have applied significance today, but only if he is acquainted with the accumulated basic knowledge of the behavioral sciences will he be equipped to focus intelligently on the social phenomena of the future.

INDEXES

NAME INDEX

257

SUBJECT INDEX

ABCDE79876543210